ROGUES
and
Rebels

ROGUES
and
Rebels

UNFORGETTABLE CHARACTERS
FROM CANADA'S WEST

Brian Brennan

University of Regina Press

Printed and bound in Canada at Webcom.
Cover design: Duncan Campbell, University of Regina Press.
Text design: John van der Woude Designs.
Copy editor: Meaghan Craven
Proofreader: Courtney Bates-Hardy
Cover photo: Police photos of Jack Krafchenko, 1914. (Archives of Manitoba, N21204).

Library and Archives Canada Cataloguing in Publication

Brennan, Brian, 1943-, author
Rogues and rebels : unforgettable characters from Canada's West / Brian Brennan.

Includes bibliographical references and index.
Issued in print and electronic formats.
ISBN 978-0-88977-398-1 (paperback).—ISBN 978-0-88977-400-1 (html).—
ISBN 978-0-88977-399-8 (pdf)

1. Rogues and vagabonds--Canada, Western—Biography. 2. Rogues and vagabonds—Canada, Western—History. 3. Canada, Western—Biography. 4. Canada, Western,—History. I. Title.

FC3208.B68 2015   971.2   C2015-903836-7   C2015-903837-5

10   9   8   7   6   5   4   3   2   1

University of Regina Press, University of Regina
Regina, Saskatchewan, Canada, S4S 0A2
tel: (306) 585-4758 fax: (306) 585-4699
web: www.uofrpress.ca

We acknowledge the financial support of the Government of Canada through the Canada Book Fund for our publishing activities. We acknowledge the support of the Canada Council for the Arts for our publishing program. This publication was made possible through Creative Saskatchewan's Creative Industries Production Grant Program.

To Charlene Dobmeier, who first encouraged me to write about western Canada's rogues, rebels, scoundrels, and scallywags.

Contents

Preface

So who are the rogues and who are the rebels? I leave that for you, the reader, to decide. How about Edward Arthur Wilson, the cult leader who is believed to have left behind $400,000 in gold coins when he fled from Vancouver Island police in 1933? Was he a rogue, I hear you ask? I respond with the immortal words of Francis Urquhart, the central character in the British version of the popular television series, *House of Cards*: "You might very well think that. I couldn't possibly comment."

Wilson, a.k.a. Brother XII, is one of the many colourful characters I came across while researching this sequel to *Scoundrels and Scallywags*, a book of short biographies I authored in 2002. I didn't want to repeat myself immediately, so I spent the next few years producing full-length biographies (including my own) before returning to a literary form—brief narrative—that's still very close to my heart. I began my writing career as a journalist, and biographical profiles have always been among my favourite assignments.

This love of the brief literary form may also have something to do with the fact that I'm Irish. Although I've identified myself as a Canadian citizen for more than forty years, I was born and raised in Dublin and still keep a current Irish passport in my desk drawer for sentimental reasons. The Irish are particularly fond of short forms. Because Irish literature depends so much on the ear—coming as it does from an oral storytelling tradition—it seems to follow that it does best in the short story. So said Anthony Burgess: "The short story is a form you may listen to, and its length conforms to the span of attention that a listener may give to an oral narrator." Quoting from Edgar Allan Poe, in his Preface to *Modern Irish Short Stories* (Penguin, 1980), Burgess said a piece of writing should be like a piece of music: brief enough for the single uninterrupted session. "Poe didn't write novels and the Irish don't write them either."

I'll spare you much of what Burgess admitted was his "harebrained" reasoning for insisting the Irish don't write novels (he described Joyce's *Ulysses* as a "grossly expanded short story"), but I will agree with one of his comments. Burgess noted that in the Irish short story a character is revealed, not through the "imposition upon him of a large number of vicissitudes" but in some single incident. The truth about human nature comes out whenever the individual "responds to the fumes of the tenth whiskey, or a chance word about his sister Kate."

In this collection, I have tried to identify the particular point in time when each character had what Joyce called the *epiphany*, meaning a moment of sudden revelation or insight. Ralph Klein decided he could make a difference in politics when he realized he'd lost his objectivity as a journalist. Will James decided he could make a future as an illustrator and writer when he was sitting in prison serving time for cattle rustling. Winnifred Eaton decided to assume a fake Japanese identity for her work as a romance novelist when she opted not to compete with her successful novelist sister who had taken on a Chinese identity.

Like the characters I wrote about in *Scoundrels*, all the people in this book are dead. One tongue-in-cheek reason I give for picking only the deceased—especially those who fall into the rogue or villain category—is that dead people famously don't sue. But I should also say I find it particularly satisfying to write biographical profiles of dead individuals because the pieces necessarily have a pleasing symmetry: a beginning, middle and end. Generally speaking, that is. In the case of Edward Wilson, there's some question as to how his story actually ended

As for the other characters in this book, you will note that some are fairly well-known (Ralph Klein) and others obscure (Claire Hedwig Chell). I chose the well-known ones because I wanted to explore aspects of their lives that received scant coverage in the media after their deaths. In Klein's case, I wanted to recall his achievements as a television journalist before he entered politics as mayor of Calgary in 1980. With the more obscure individuals, it was a matter of focussing on particular contributions for which they should be acknowledged and remembered. Claire Chell's singular achievement was that she earned a footnote in the annals of the Canadian hospitality industry when she helped her husband create the Bloody Caesar, the clam-and-tomato infused vodka drink that is now the most popular cocktail in the country.

So what then is the common denominator? What ties Claire Chell together with Ralph Klein, Edward Wilson, Will James, Winnifred Eaton, Peter Pond, Jerry Potts, and the other colourful individuals featured in this book? The simple answer is that, like the characters in *Scoundrels and Scallywags*, they dared to be different. They dared to disturb the universe. They threw away the rulebook, thumbed their noses at convention, refused to take other people's advice, lived impulsively, and relished knowing they had left some distinctive markings on the wall. In the time-honoured words of Nellie McClung—one of the featured individuals in this book—they never retracted, never explained, never apologized. They got things done and let their detractors howl.

I covered the stories of forty individuals in *Scoundrels and Scallywags*. In this book, I feature the stories of thirty-two, which means not that the book is shorter but that the profiles are longer. When I revisited the earlier volume, I felt I had given short shrift to some of the characters. So in this volume I wanted to devote as much space to the telling of their stories as I would if I had written about them for a magazine. And, in fact, I did write about some of them for a magazine, *West*, which came out of High River, Alberta, and served a readership across western Canada from Manitoba to British Columbia. My gratitude goes to former *West* editors Mike McCormick and Bruce Masterman, who were particularly supportive of my work. Their magazine now no longer exists, unfortunately. There were many casualties in High River after the floods swept through southern Alberta in June 2013, and *West* magazine was one of them.

Because I designed this book to be a work of storytelling and popular history rather than an academic work, I have not included an apparatus of references and footnotes. In some instances—for example, in the cases of Ralph Klein, Milt Harradence, Shay Duffin, and Rick McNair—I knew the individuals in question, and simply went back to my interview notes, diaries, and newspaper clippings to refresh my memory. In other instances, I consulted books written about the individuals. I have listed these books at the back of this volume under Sources. Additionally, I combed through newspaper and magazine archives containing feature stories on the individuals. Journalism has been described as history on the run, and I am grateful to the many sprinters and middle-distance runners who reached the finish line before I came trailing along behind. Whenever I found discrepancies in the available information, I tried as best I could to reconcile the differences and to produce the most credible version of the story. As the author, I take full responsibility for any errors that may have resulted.

For helping me with the research, I want to give a big thank-you to Doug Cass, Lindsay Moir, and Jennifer Hamblin at the Glenbow Library and Archives, who always have additional tidbits for me whenever I tell them I'm reading up on a particular subject. Crucial research assistance also came from the helpful staff at the Calgary Public Library, who granted me some valuable writing time to put my research into story form when they brought me on board as writer-in-residence in the fall of 2012.

I've been writing books for the past fifteen years. I could not do this work without the enduring love and support of my wife, Zelda Brennan. Forty-seven years ago, when I worked as a wandering minstrel, she encouraged me to try combining my music with writing for a living. I will always be grateful to her for giving me that much-needed boost.

B.B. 2015

PETER POND
Explorer, Fur Trader, and Brawler
1740-1807

When Peter Pond in 1778 became one of the first non-Aboriginals to cast his eyes upon what is now Lake Athabasca, the fur trade was the biggest commercial enterprise in North America. Pond clearly could not have known it at the time, but that black slime he saw oozing from the banks of the Athabasca River was the first visible evidence of a huge resource that—when eventually developed—would make the fur trade look like a footnote in the history of commerce. Lying below Pond's feet was what we now know to be the richest oil reserve in the world. The Athabasca oil sands contain as much as 300 billion barrels, or six times the known recoverable oil resources of Saudi Arabia.

A pugnacious Yankee with a penchant for settling arguments with his pistol, Pond came to the Athabasca region at age thirty-eight to make his fortune in the fur trade. While he also mapped and made notes on what he found in this hitherto unexplored part of the Canadian West, Pond was in no hurry to record his findings. In fact, he never got around to writing about his exploring activities until he was into his sixties and long removed from the trade.

He joined the fur trade after serving in the military for five years. Born in Milford, Connecticut, Pond became an apprentice shoemaker at age sixteen but soon decided—as he later

Peter Pond. *(Drawing by Howard Hatton, Saskatchewan Archives Board, R-D1859)*

wrote in his irregularly spelled journal—that he really wanted to be a "solge" (soldier). He enlisted as a private in the British colonial army and took part in four campaigns, the last bringing him into what is now Canada for the 1760 capture of Montreal from the French.

After being demobilized in 1761, Pond sailed to the West Indies with the idea of becoming a professional mariner. However, he soon was called back to Milford to look after eight younger siblings after his mother died of a fever and his father moved to Detroit to become a fur trader. Three years later, in 1765, Pond moved to Detroit to become a trader himself. He conducted his business throughout the Minnesota River country for the next six years and was—by all accounts—a master trader, recognized for his diplomacy when negotiating with the Sioux. He also was recognized as a rough man with a violent temper. This, too, may have contributed to his success as a trader. At one point during his six-year stint in the Detroit region, he killed a fur-trading rival in a duel. Though he subsequently confessed his crime to Detroit authorities—he claimed he was abused and threatened by the other trader—Pond was never prosecuted. This would be the first of many violent confrontations with fellow traders. Two more resulted in death and none in charges being laid against the seemingly unassailable Pond.

In 1775 Pond made his first foray in western Canada as a Loyalist fleeing the American Revolution. After two years of trading with mixed results in present-day Manitoba and Saskatchewan, he formed a loose coalition with a group of independent traders, mostly fellow Loyalists or Scottish immigrants. They pooled resources to lessen competition among themselves, and to counter the inland advances of the mighty Hudson's Bay Company. When informally established as an ad hoc business partnership in 1779, they called themselves the North West Company (NWC), and they became known as the Nor'Westers. Pond became the NWC's agent in the Athabasca region, where he had built Alberta's first fur-trading post—Fort Chipewyan—in 1778. He also became the first white man to cultivate soil in present-day Alberta when he planted a garden near Fort Chipewyan. Pond's second-in-command at the post was a twenty-four-year-old Scotsman named Alexander Mackenzie. He would later succeed Pond as the NWC's Athabasca factor and write his name into the annals of the Canadian West as the first white explorer to cross the Continental Divide—the watershed formed by the Rockies separating rivers flowing east from those flowing west.

Pond first reached the Athabasca region by way of the Methy Portage, at the north end of Lac La Loche in northwestern Saskatchewan. As one of the first white men to traverse it, Pond later promoted the ease and convenience of this twenty-kilometre route, which crosses the height of land between the Hudson Bay drainage basin and the rivers flowing northwest into the Arctic Ocean. But it was, in fact, a challenging series of eight hills, each so steep that it took his freight-burdened voyageurs a total of eight days to traverse them. Notwithstanding the difficult nature of the terrain, this portage was to become the northern crossing of choice for fur traders and other trans-continental travellers until the Canadian Pacific Railway pushed through western Canada in the 1880s.

The Athabasca region proved to be a lucrative fur-trading district for Pond. In 1778–79 he collected considerably more beaver pelts than his three canoes could carry—more than ten times the normal load, according to Mackenzie—so Pond stock-piled the surplus furs in winter huts and returned the following year to bring them out.

Pond went back to the Athabasca several times during the early 1780s. But he was now no longer the only trader in town. Word of his success had spread to Montreal, the bustling headquarters of the Canadian fur trade, and that brought competition into his ter-ritory. One of his rivals was Jean-Étienne Waddens, a Swiss-born trader with whom Pond got into a fight while wintering at Lac La Ronge, Saskatchewan, in 1781–82. Waddens was shot and fatally wounded, and Pond was questioned about the shooting by a judge in Montreal. But he was never brought to trial, seemingly because the killing had occurred within the territory of the Hudson's Bay Company, beyond the jurisdiction of Quebec's legal system.

Pond's next homicidal encounter with a competitor was the last straw as far as his fellow Nor'Westers were concerned. It occurred during the winter of 1786–87, when Pond was win-tering in the Peace River country. A rival named John Ross was shot to death in a scuffle with Pond's men, and two of the men were brought to Montreal for trial. This time there seems to have been no issue regarding Quebec's legal jurisdiction. The men were acquitted and Pond, despite being fingered as the instigator, was never charged. The senior partners in the NWC decided, however, that Pond had been responsible for one death too many. They fired him at the end of 1787 and replaced him with his second-in-command, Alexander Mackenzie.

Pond spent his last winter in Athabasca showing Mackenzie a map he had drawn based on his travels through the unchar-tered territories of the Canadian northwest and the conver-sations he had with Natives along the way. On the map he marked sites along the Athabasca River where he had seen tarry deposits that Mackenzie would later describe as "bituminous fountains." Inspired more by wishful thinking than cartographical expertise, the map suggested that a river existed between the Rockies and the Pacific that would complete the transcontinental inland water link from the shores of Hudson Bay to the west coast. Starting with some coastal charts drawn by Captain James Cook, Pond had pinpointed an inlet at the site of present-day Anchorage, Alaska, indulged in some fanciful speculation, and extended the inlet on his map until it reached hundreds of kilometres inland. He named the mythical extension "Cook's River" and made it appear to come within a few kilometres of a river flowing westward out of Great Slave Lake, thus suggesting a navigable freshwater route from the interior to the coast. In a second major mapping error, Pond grossly underestimated the distance from Lake Athabasca to the Pacific, placing the lake one thousand kilometres west of its true position.

After leaving the employ of the North West Company, and selling his one share in the company for £800, Pond went to Montreal and tried to get money from the British government to finance an expedition to the west coast. When that proved unsuccessful, he headed back to the United States. It was then left to Mackenzie to follow the route that Pond had mapped from Great Slave Lake to the Pacific.

In June 1789, with Pond's map in hand, Mackenzie led a party of four canoes north from Lake Athabasca to Great Slave Lake, and then westward along a river that he assumed would take him to the Pacific. He envisaged the river carrying him to a western port that would open up a lucrative trade route to China and Russia. But this westbound river, which would later be named after Mackenzie, turned suddenly north after 480 kilometres, just as the explorer was coming within sight of the Rockies. Though he knew it was now heading in the wrong direction, Mackenzie followed the river regardless, hoping it might eventually turn west again. On July 14, 1789, he reached the frozen waters of the Arctic Ocean. It was a remarkable piece of trailblazing but clearly the wrong ocean on which to found an economic empire. The vast expanse of water, as Mackenzie sadly observed, was "eternally covered with ice."

Pond was widely discredited when it turned out that his map—approved by a mariner who accompanied Cook on his voyage around the world—was so inaccurate. But Pond was somewhat vindicated—at least in terms of showing that it was possible to get from the Rockies to the Pacific by water—when Mackenzie returned to the Athabasca region in 1793 to make his second attempt at crossing the Continental Divide. This time Mackenzie and crew travelled west and south from Fort Chipewyan along the Peace River until they reached a quiet tributary of the Peace later named the Parsnip for the wild sprouts that grew along its banks. From there the voyageurs carried on by paddling and portaging, crossing the Continental Divide at what is now Portage Lake, and continuing south along what is now the Fraser River toward present-day Williams Lake, British Columbia. The last part of the journey involved slogging westward on foot for two weeks until they finally reached the Native coastal settlement of Bella Coola, about five hundred kilometres north of Vancouver. Once again, Mackenzie had achieved a remarkable piece of trailblazing, but this east-west passage would never prove profitable as a trade route.

While Pond's mapmaking earned him few plaudits in Canada, it did strike a chord with some members of the United States Congress when he gave them a chart showing the Missouri River extending from the Rocky Mountains of western Montana to the Mississippi, and a second great river that he called "Naberkistagon" (now Columbia) flowing westward to the coast on the far side of the mountains. Because of this first charting of the American northwest, Pond was invited by the International Boundary Commission—shortly before his death at age sixty-seven in 1807—to suggest where the border should run between Canada and the United States. Pond proposed a line along the St. Lawrence River through the Great Lakes and then westward. This unlettered Yankee adventurer thus helped in some small way to determine the final boundary between the two countries.

He died in poverty like many fur traders. But he left his mark and is remembered with respect notwithstanding his various run-ins with the law. Today Peter Pond has a shopping centre named after him in Fort McMurray, the oil-rich site of his first Alberta trading activities. There's also a national historic site near Prince Albert and two interconnected lakes—Big Peter Pond and Little Peter Pond—in west-central Saskatchewan. An American swashbuckler who prospered as a fur trader in the early Canadian West, Pond was the spiritual forefather of the gambling rogues and rebels who came to Alberta a century later to seek their fortunes in the petroleum industry.

JERRY POTTS
Metis Warrior and Police Scout
1838-1896

J erry Potts was a multilingual warrior of Blackfoot[1] and Scottish parentage who bridged the cultural gap between Natives and white settlers, and helped the fledgling North West Mounted Police (NWMP) bring law and order to the Canadian West during the 1870s.

He was tough and fearless, and he brooked no criticism from anyone. He was proficient with rifle and revolver, and with bow and arrow, which enabled him to survive in a frontier region occupied by warring Natives and trigger-happy traders. He killed his first opponent in a gun duel when he was twenty-three and received the name Bear Child (Ky-yo-kosi) from his Blackfoot brothers as a testament to his bravery.

He received his Anglo-Saxon name from his Edinburgh-born father, Andrew Potts, a former medical student who came to North America in 1832 in search of frontier adventure. After stopping for a while in Philadelphia, Andrew headed west toward the Upper Missouri, where he heard there were

---

1   Please note that for the sake of readability I use the term Blackfoot
    to refer both to the collective name given to the Native peoples of the
    Alberta-Montana border region (formerly Blackfoot Confederacy, now
    Niitsitapi) and to the three main tribes comprising that collective. For-
    merly the Blood, Peigan, and Blackfoot tribes, they are known today as
    Kainai, Piikani, and Siksika.

Jerry Potts. (Saskatchewan Archives Board, R-B1328)

opportunities in the fur trade. When he reached Fort McKenzie, near present-day Lorna, Montana, Andrew landed a job as junior clerk with the American Fur Company, trading with the Blackfoot tribes. He took as his "country wife" a Blackfoot woman named Crooked Back (Namo-pisi). Their son, Jerry, was born in 1838.

Jerry Potts was just two years old when a Blackfoot hunter named One White Eye (Ah-pah) shot and killed his father. The hunter had been thrown out of the fort for troublesome behaviour, and he returned after dark carrying a musket, seeking revenge. He shot at the first person he saw, who happened to be Andrew Potts. When members of his tribe learned he had murdered a well-respected white trader they executed One White Eye and made sure the other traders saw his corpse. One of those traders, Alexander Harvey, became Crooked Back's new bedmate and Jerry's surrogate father for the next four years.

Harvey was a ruthless bully, hated by the Blackfoot for killing their members at will, and disliked by fellow traders for making enemies of the people they were trying to do business with. There's no evidence his cruelty extended to physically abusing Jerry or his mother, but there is evidence of neglect. At age six, Jerry suffered from stunted growth due to generally poor nutrition and frequent periods of starvation.

Harvey's fellow traders finally lost patience with him in 1844, by which time the Blackfoot had stopped trading at Fort McKenzie and taken their business to the rival Union Fur Trading Company at Fort Cotton, a few kilometres upstream. The traders evicted Harvey from Fort McKenzie, and in retaliation he burned the fort to the ground. Crooked Back, no longer able to care for her six-year-old son, returned to her tribe camped near what is now Lethbridge. Jerry ended up in Fort Benton, later dubbed "the birthplace of Montana," where the fort manager was an educated and gentle Scotsman named Andrew Dawson.

Dawson took a fatherly interest in Potts, taught him to read and write in English, and encouraged him to mix with Blackfoot and other Native hunters to learn their customs and languages. He also encouraged the boy to spend time with his mother and her people north of the 49th parallel. In the process, Potts came to know much about the ways and culture of the Blackfoot, as well as something about their traditional enemies, including the Cree, Crow, and Assiniboine peoples. At Fort Benton, meanwhile, Potts learned how to shoot a pistol, how to trade, and how to drink and gamble. He proudly showed off his mixed-blood heritage by wearing the buckskin jacket of the white frontiersman paired with the leggings and moccasins of the Blackfoot.

Potts's first gunfight resulted from a drunken barroom confrontation with a French-Canadian brawler named Antoine Primeau, who thought—mistakenly—that the slight and unimposing Potts would be an easy mark. After shooting Primeau to death, Potts returned to the bar and coolly finished off his bottle of red-eye. He had left a clear message that nobody should mess with him, especially when he was drinking.

In 1864 Andrew Dawson retired from Fort Benton due to ill

health and returned to his native Scotland. American Fur sold the fort the same year. Jerry Potts, at age twenty-six, decided it was time to reconnect with his mother's people. He left the fort, settled in a Blackfoot camp close to the old Fort McKenzie site where he was born, married a young Crow woman named Mary, hunted buffalo, and raised horses. Over the next four years he gained fame as a warrior of the Blackfoot, battling with their enemies and bringing honour to the people.

Potts was thirty when he and Mary had a son named Mitchell. At that point, he decided to return to the trading world he had known at Fort Benton. The fur trade was in decline, but there were other opportunities for a man with his tracking skills and knowledge of the region. From his frequent travels throughout the Blackfoot ancestral hunting grounds, ranging northward from the Missouri to the South Saskatchewan River and westward from the Cypress Hills to the Rockies, Potts had come to know the territory well. That made him an asset for the new breed of whisky traders who wanted to push deeper and deeper into what would eventually become known as "whoop-up country."

In the fall of 1869, Potts signed on as a guide, hunter, and Aboriginal translator for two Montana hustlers, Alfred Hamilton and John Healy, who wanted to build a whisky-trading post in today's southern Alberta. With the United States Army moving to contain the illegal liquor trade in the western states, Hamilton and Healy wanted to establish their business in the unpoliced lands north of the invisible line separating the American and Canadian frontiers. They built what they initially called Fort Hamilton near present-day Lethbridge, only to see it burned to the ground by its unhappy Blackfoot customers after one trading season. The Blackfoot felt they were getting a poor return from the whisky racketeers for their valuable buffalo hides. Undeterred, Hamilton and Healy used the profits from their first season to build a second, more substantial stockade that would soon become known as Fort Whoop Up. Potts kept the building crew well fed through his hunting activities.

The commercial success of Fort Whoop Up gave rise to a number of other illegal whisky forts in the Lethbridge region, including Fort Slideout, Conrad's Post, Robber's Roost, and Fort Kipp. Potts worked for a number of them as a hired hand helping to provide food for the forts. By that time, he had sent wife Mary and baby Mitchell back to her Crow people in Montana, where he figured they would be safe from the growing violence associated with the whisky trade. At the same time, he had taken two sisters as his new wives. After striking a deal with a Blackfoot chief named Sitting-in-the-Middle, Potts welcomed the chief's two daughters—Panther Woman and Spotted Killer—into his tipi. When asked why he needed two wives, Potts replied: "One wife fights her husband. Two fight each other." They bore him several children.

The last great battle between the Blackfoot and traditional enemies, the Cree and Assiniboine, occurred near Fort Whoop Up in November 1870. Potts played a leading role in the battle. The Cree and Assiniboine had been led to believe the Blackfoot were too weak to defend their hunting territory due to the toll taken by alcohol poisoning and smallpox. About eight hundred Cree and Assiniboine warriors attacked what they thought would be a small group of Blackfoot, only to find themselves facing a much larger and tougher contingent than they bargained for. Leading the successful resistance was Jerry Potts, who killed sixteen of the three hundred Cree and Assiniboine casualties, and escaped with little more than powder burns to his left ear. Years later he commented: "You could have shot with your eyes closed that day, and you were sure to kill a Cree."

In 1872 the violence and death that accompanied excessive drinking hit close to home for Potts. His mother, Crooked Back, had remarried twenty-five years earlier and given birth to a second son, No Chief. This son was murdered in a fight with his drunken brother-in-law, who then killed Crooked Back when she went to retrieve the body. Potts took his revenge a year later when the brother-in-law came to do business at Fort Kipp. He shot the murderer off his horse and left him to rot in the prairie dust. Shortly after that Potts quit the whisky forts and returned to Montana to make his living as a rancher. He never worked for the whisky traders again.

The establishment of the North West Mounted Police marked the beginning of the end for the Canadian whisky forts. Prime Minister John A. Macdonald had been slow to react to repeated calls from missionaries and Hudson's Bay Company officials for a military presence to curb the whisky trade in the Canadian West. He said he needed more information. However, Macdonald responded quickly after June 1873, when a group of drunken American wolf hunters killed at least twenty Assiniboine men, women, and children in the Cypress Hills for allegedly stealing the hunters' horses. With the enabling legislation already passed by Parliament, Macdonald ordered that the new police force be mobilized immediately to keep the lawless West under control until the transcontinental railway could be built in the 1880s.

Three hundred red-coated Mounties rode west from Fort Dufferin, Manitoba, in July 1874, heading toward Fort Whoop Up with the help of an inaccurately drawn map from the 1857–60 Palliser Expedition. The map took them to a place near today's Coutts-Sweetgrass border crossing, where they found nothing but a few abandoned log cabins. Demoralized, hungry, and exhausted, several of them detoured south to Fort Benton to buy supplies. There they were fortunate to find Jerry Potts, who took the desperate troops in hand and led them to Fort Whoop Up. After the tragedies in his family, Potts was keen to see an end to the illegal whisky trade in Canada.

Fort Whoop Up was almost deserted when the Mounties arrived. The whisky traders had fled to Montana when they heard the police were on their way, and had left no incriminating liquor behind. The Mounties, needing winter shelter, offered to buy the fort for $10,000. Word came back that the owners wanted more than twice that amount. The owners figured the police would go home and the whisky trade would continue without interruption if the asking price were too high. But they were wrong. Potts guided the Mounties farther west, to an island in the Old Man River valley, where they established Fort Macleod, the first police post in Alberta. It was named by and for James F. Macleod, the force's popular assistant commissioner.

Potts worked for the NWMP for the next twenty-one years, functioning in the role of special constable. He showed the recruits how to track, how to hide, where to find shelter in bad weather, and how to find food and water. He facilitated meetings between Macleod and the various tribal leaders that paved the way for the 1877 signing of Treaty Seven. Potts was a pivotal connection for the Mounties: an intermediary the Natives could trust. After listening to his translations of Macleod's remarks, the Natives concluded the Mounties were there to protect, not harm them.

Treaty Seven, like the other agreements between the Crown and Canada's Aboriginal peoples, offered cattle, money, reserve lands, and other compensations to the Natives in return for the surrender of their ancestral hunting territories to Queen Victoria's representatives. Potts was on hand to interpret for the Blackfoot when the Lieutenant-Governor of the North West Territories, David Laird, spelled out the terms of the treaty. But Potts soon bowed out when he realized that Laird was sending mixed messages. On the one hand, Laird was talking about the Dominion government passing a new law to protect the buffalo herds. On the other, he was saying the buffalo "will probably all be destroyed in a very few years." Potts refused to try and make sense of these contradictory statements, and a replacement translator was quickly recruited.

Despite Potts's misgivings about the mixed messages, the Blackfoot, Sarcee, and Stoney tribes of southern Alberta did sign Treaty Seven. During the 1885 Northwest Resistance, Potts convinced the Blackfoot chiefs not to join the Metis, Cree, and Assiniboine in their stand against government forces. Instead, he had them endorse a letter affirming their loyalty to the Crown. Some of the chiefs agreed to have their people act as scouts for the Alberta Field Force militia raised to suppress the resistance.

Potts's usefulness to the Mounties as a guide and translator diminished during the late 1880s and early 1890s because of the influx of white settlers, the confinement of the Natives to the new reserves, and his abuse of alcohol. He moved his ranching interests to a reserve near Fort Macleod, continued to do some work for the Mounties as a trainer of new recruits, and married a new young wife, Long Time Laying Down (Isum-its-tsee), when his previous two wives succumbed to illness. He mused about moving to some other country "where buffalo roam and Indians live a life of uncurbed freedom" because "this country is getting too damned soft for me."

"Old Jerry," as he had come to be known, quit his NWMP job at age fifty-seven because pain—caused by throat cancer or tuberculosis, or both—made it impossible for him to ride any more. He died a year later, in 1896, after a long drinking bout caused hemorrhaging in his lungs. He was buried in the NWMP cemetery in Fort Macleod. The *Macleod Gazette* described him as a "very potent factor in the discovery and settlement of the western part of the North West Territories." Potts was a "modern Moses" who had led the Mounties out of the desert and brought them "to the end of their difficulties."

Potts seemed destined to be little more than a footnote to western Canadian history until the late 1960s, when his achievements began to be celebrated in story and song. One of Alberta's most eminent historians, Hugh Dempsey, wrote articles and a short book about him. Several more books followed, including Rodger D. Touchie's *Bear Child: The Life and Times of Jerry Potts* (Heritage House, 2005), which offers both a good synthesis of all the previous writings about Potts as well as a general overview of life in the frontier West. In 1973 songwriters Richard Harrow and Glen Mundy composed a musical, *Potts*, which toured Alberta. Songs from the musical, performed by Harrow, were released on CD in 2005. A Calgary elementary school (since closed) was named after Potts. So was a street in Lethbridge. A mountain in the Rockies received his name in 1974, when the hundredth anniversary of the arrival of the Mounties in Alberta was observed.

Canada Post has also issued a stamp in Potts's honour. Author Guy Vanderhaeghe has immortalized Potts in his best-selling novel, *The Last Crossing*. A chamber music work, *Bear Child*, with compositions by Allan Bell and spoken text by author Fred Stenson, was performed in 2009 to great acclaim in Lethbridge,

Fort Macleod, and Calgary. Meanwhile, three of Potts's descendants—great-grandson Henry Potts, his daughter Janet, and nephew Tyrone Potts—have honoured the memory of their ancestor by becoming full-fledged members of the RCMP. As the *Macleod Gazette* said back in 1896, "Jerry Potts is dead, but his name lives and will live."

JOHN WILLIAM TIMS
Anglican Missionary
1857–1945

When he died in 1945, Archdeacon John Tims was eulogized in the Calgary newspapers as a revered cleric who had brought Christianity to the Natives of Southern Alberta. "His memory will be perpetuated so long as the history of Canada's Western plains development is recorded," said the *Calgary Herald*. The writer added, "That his service was a success and highly appreciated can be judged by the present high standing held by these tribes among Western Indians." The *Albertan* said, "tales of his kindness and good humour were told again and again as the word of his death circulated among farmers, rangers, ministers, Indians and residents." The hymns of praise continued to be sung in the 1980s, when social historian Jack Peach wrote in the *Herald* that the English-born missionary had been a saintly soul who dedicated a lifetime of service to the people of Alberta.

By the 1990s, however, a different song was being sung. Calgary historian Hugh Dempsey, in a 1994 book called *The Amazing Death of Calf Shirt and Other Blackfoot Stories*, characterized Tims as rigid, unyielding, and "virtually closed-minded about any aspects of Indian culture that he considered to be undesirable." University of Saskatchewan historian James Rodger Miller, in a book called *Shingwauk's Vision*, said Tims was overbearing and detested by the Natives. Brock University

John William Tims, circa 1896. (Glenbow Archives, NA-2643-12)

historian Maureen Katherine Lux, in *Medicine That Walks*, described Tims as dictatorial and inflexible.

The roots of Native discontent with Tims can be traced back to July 1895, when the *Lethbridge News* reported that the Blackfoot (now, Siksika) tribe at Gleichen had forced "an obnoxious white missionary" to flee their reserve and "wished to celebrate the feat by holding a sun dance." The missionary in question was Tims, who had clearly outstayed his welcome after twelve years of ministry on the reserve.

The son of an Oxford boat builder, Tims came to Canada in 1883 at age twenty-five when the Anglican Church Missionary Society told him he couldn't go to Uganda as he had hoped. There was a greater need for missionaries in the Canadian northwest, said the society. Tims's first encounter with the Natives at Blackfoot Crossing, one hundred kilometres southeast of Calgary, left a distinctly negative impression. "Morally, they had descended to the lowest depths of iniquity," he wrote.

"Gambling, thieving, lying and adultery were common. They gambled away everything they possessed, even their wives." After watching his first sun dance—a religious ceremony performed during the summer solstice—Tims wondered what in God's name he was doing there. "The fantastic costumes of the people, the paint and feathers, the foreign tongue, made my heart sink within me. If ever I felt the hopelessness of a task, it was then." Clearly, it wasn't going to be easy for him to fulfill the Anglican mandate to "Christianize and civilize."

He seems to have started well. He opened a day school on the reserve shortly after his arrival, learned the Blackfoot language, and worked hard to get food, clothing, and medicine for the sick and starving population. He petitioned government officials to increase rations of beef and flour, and persuaded Anglican parishes in Ontario to send out bales of old clothes. Additionally, he dispensed medicines from a wooden chest he had brought with him from England, although he did admit to having only "a modicum of instruction."

With converting Natives to Christianity as his primary goal, Tims made a concerted effort to lead the population away from what he saw as pagan influences. When one of his female students became seriously ill, he blocked efforts by her parents to remove her from a boarding school[1] he had built on the reserve after the day school proved of little use to the nomadic Native population. The girl subsequently died, but Tims had no remorse. "As a Christian child, I did not wish her to be obliged to undergo the noise and manipulations of heathen medicine men." Besides, he added, a Calgary doctor had examined the child and found her to be in no immediate danger.

Tims also tried, unsuccessfully, to have the annual sun dance outlawed because it required young men to prove their bravery

---

1 Today it would be called a "residential school," referring to the education network set up by the federal government in the 1880s to indoctrinate Aboriginal children into Euro-Canadian and Christian ways of living and assimilate them into mainstream Canadian society. But Tims, as a native of England where those terms were not used, called it a "boarding school."

through self-mutilation. The local North West Mounted Police refused to ban the ceremony outright because they feared reprisals from what they called "these dangerous Indians." But Tims did manage to persuade the local warrior chief, Old Sun, to have the self-mutilation ritual removed from the ceremony. "There will be no more flesh-cutting at the sun dances," declared the chief. This did not sit well with other members of the tribe, who petitioned the Department of Indian Affairs in 1892 for Tims's removal. "They said that the Revd. Mr. Tims was no friend to the Indians," said the reserve's Indian agent, Magnus Begg.

Indian Affairs didn't consider Tims's interference with the sun dance rituals sufficiently serious to warrant his removal from the reserve. Nor did the department quarrel with his decision to stop pupils from leaving the boarding school, even for short holidays, after the Indian Act was amended to make school attendance compulsory for all Native children under sixteen. However, Tims's rigid implementation of the compulsory attendance policy precipitated a tense situation in 1895. The Natives claimed that their children were being held captive in the boarding school during the school year, and only being allowed home when in the last stages of terminal illness such as diphtheria or tuberculosis. After two students died of illnesses contracted at the school, a number of parents demanded that their children be released from the school. When Tims rejected their demands, a council of Blackfoot chiefs met with an Indian Affairs inspector, Alexander McGibbon, and asked that "a kinder man" be put in Tims's place. They hinted ominously that if Indian Affairs didn't remove Tims, the people would do the job themselves.

Tims clearly didn't take the threat seriously because he made no move to leave the reserve during the first three weeks of June 1895. He wouldn't be coerced into abandoning his post, he said. However, when a fellow missionary, Frank Swainson, visited the reserve on June 26 and learned from the Natives that plans were in the works to kill Tims either during the coming sun dance ceremonies or shortly afterwards, Tims agreed to leave. He fled with his wife and two children to the Blood (now, Kainai) reserve, 160 kilometres south.

His departure was recorded in the newspapers as marking the end of a failed twelve-year social experiment to "Christianize and civilize" on the reserve. Thousands of dollars had been spent, said the *Alberta Tribune*, and yet "we find the missionary deserting his post without a single convert. Nay more, he has exasperated the people against Christianity by acts of folly, and they are, perhaps, farther today from the church's fold than they were before ever they had the gospel preached to them." A local mounted police inspector, Joseph Howe, said he believed Tims had made an honest attempt to educate the Native children "but he has undoubtedly a pugnacious, and I might say an offensive manner which undoubtedly jars on the Indians' feelings."

While the Natives, the press, the bureaucrats and the police were highly critical of the way Tims had discharged his missionary responsibilities on the Blackfoot reserve, the Anglican church rewarded him by promoting him to archdeacon and transferring him to the smaller Sarcee (now, Tsuu T'ina) reserve southwest of Calgary, where he served for the next thirty-five years. The church also placed him in charge of all the other Native missions in southern Alberta. This caused the *Macleod Gazette* to wonder if the appointment was some kind of joke, because it involved the promotion of a cleric "who is admittedly hated by the Indians of one of the largest reserves, and was intimidated by threats into abandoning his work there."

Tims didn't receive any threats during his thirty-five years on the Sarcee reserve, but he often found himself at loggerheads with Indian Affairs over the way he dealt with the department's sometimes contradictory policies on sick children. In 1909 he defied an order to send home seven students diagnosed with tuberculosis because, he said, the department's chief medical officer, Dr. Peter Bryce, figured it was all right to keep sick children in the school when the other pupils were suffering from the same condition. Six years later, after Tims was reprimanded by the department for sending sick children home, he suggested that Indian Affairs turn the school into a sanatorium with proper nursing care and better food. The government didn't follow up on this suggestion, however, until conditions on the reserve became so bad that it had to act.

In November 1920 a Regina physician, Dr. F. A. Corbett, reported that the health of the students at the Sarcee boarding school was "bad in the extreme." All but four of the thirty-three students showed the presence of tuberculosis requiring active treatment. Corbett found conditions on the reserve itself—where the population had dwindled from more than three hundred in 1877 to 155 in 1920—to be equally bad. He repeated Tims's suggestion of 1915 that the school be closed and the building converted into a sanatorium with doctors and nurses in charge. A year later, a twenty-eight-year-old Ontario physician, Thomas F. Murray, was appointed Indian agent and doctor to the reserve. Tims stayed on as chaplain while Murray set about turning the school into a sanatorium.

Murray, who worked on the reserve for twenty-five years and is widely credited with eradicating tuberculosis, is now remembered by the Tsuu T'ina nation—where the population has since grown to more than 1,700—as "the man who saved the Sarcee people." Tims, who retired to Calgary in 1930, is remembered less fondly. The Natives feel he worried more about the possibility of losing his mission to the Catholics than about finding a way to stem the ravages of disease on the reserve. But as historian Hugh Dempsey wrote, among the non-Native community Tims was later considered to be "one of the grand old pioneers of Southern Alberta and greatly respected for his work among the Indians." Historian Jack Peach maintained in 1982 that the words spoken at Tims's funeral were still entirely appropriate: "Well done, good and faithful servant."

JOSEPH "FIGHTIN' JOE" CLARKE

Pugilistic Municipal Politician
1869–1941

He acquired his nickname after a brawl at Edmonton City Hall in August 1914. He had been serving for two years as alderman, and he wanted Mayor William McNamara to take the blame for council firing a police chief who had tried to rid the city of prostitution and gambling. "I'll mop the earth with you," Alderman Joseph Clarke yelled at the mayor during one rowdy city council meeting. "You haven't the courage of a rat," McNamara shouted back. The two came to blows, and from that point onward Clarke was routinely referred to in the press as Fightin' Joe.

Clarke already had a reputation for fisticuffs when he arrived in Edmonton in 1908, fresh from a ten-year stay in Dawson City, where he had supplemented his lawyer's income by prize fighting. A versatile athlete from the Cornwall area of eastern Ontario, Clarke also excelled at lacrosse, football, and track and field. During his school years, he invariably pleased his sports coaches but rarely his principals. By the time he graduated, he had been expelled from schools in Prescott, Brockville, Morrisburg, and Athens. But he left his mark in each community as a high-scoring lacrosse player.

In 1892, at age twenty-three, Clarke moved to Regina to join the North West Mounted Police. There his prowess as a

Joseph Clarke, 1919. (City of Edmonton Archives, EA-160-205)

track-and-field athlete made him the toast of the division. In an open competition organized by the Mounties, he entered all the events and won every one, taking home a total of $108 in prize money. Asked afterwards if he really had run the hundred-yard dash in less than ten seconds, Clarke replied, "I wouldn't say that. But I would say that I've beaten more men who claim they *can* run that fast than any other man in western Canada."

Clarke didn't last very long with the Mounties. The strict regimen of marching, drilling, and riding practice proved too restricting for him. By 1893 he was back in Ontario, looking for other things to do. First, however, he had to go to court to answer a charge of desertion from the NWMP. He was convicted on the charge, but escaped with a light penalty because the magistrate happened to be his uncle. "I was lucky to get off with a hundred-dollar fine," he said. "The usual sentence was six months."

He found his calling when he enrolled in the University of Toronto to study law. Ever the sportsman, Clarke made his reputation there as a winger with the university rugby team. During one memorable game against Queen's University, he left the field because of a neck injury and figured he would spend the rest of the game providing moral support for his teammates. However, when Queen's racked up a seemingly insurmountable lead of 19-2, the injured Clarke returned to the game, helped prevent Queen's from scoring again, and led Toronto to a 21-19 victory. Asked afterwards how he could play so well despite his injury, Clarke replied, "I had no other choice, really. I had bet two hundred bucks on the game."

In 1898 Clarke moved to Dawson City to make his fortune in gold. He didn't actually strike gold, but he did make good money from his law practice, and from his extracurricular activities as a gambler, freelance journalist, and prizefighter. His gambling often got him in trouble with the law. It was not unusual to see Clarke defending clients in the morning and plea-bargaining his own misdeeds in the afternoon. He boxed regularly until a freak injury—to his ankle—caused him to hang up his gloves. It happened during a charity match with a Mountie named Kid Owens. Clarke took a strong punch to the jaw and fractured his ankle when he fell to the canvas.

Dawson City was where Clarke first became involved in politics. He served on the Yukon Territorial Council for two years, 1903–1904, and campaigned actively for better sports facilities for the community. He characterized himself as the "stormy petrel of Yukon politics." A reporter for the *Seattle Post-Intelligencer* described him as "perhaps the most striking character the Klondike ever produced."

Clarke continued to remain active in sports and local politics after he moved to Edmonton in 1908, following the subsiding of gold-rush fever. He served as secretary-treasurer of the Edmonton Eskimos baseball team, and qualified as a property owner for civic election purposes when a friendly realtor registered a vacant city lot in Clarke's name.

He was first elected to Edmonton city council in February 1912 and would remain a fixture in civic politics for the next twenty-eight years. He ran as the self-styled champion of the underdogs, specifically the working-class and ethnic residents of east-end Edmonton. When asked by an *Edmonton Journal* reporter about his political affiliations, Clarke replied that he was a "radical conservative with socialist leanings" and also a member of the Liberal party. It sounded like a joke but, in fact, over the course of his political career, Clarke held memberships in just about every mainstream political party in Canada.

Clarke resigned his aldermanic seat after nine months to run for mayor in the December 1912 municipal election. When that election bid failed, he ran again for alderman and regained his seat in the 1913 election. Elected mayor that year was William McNamara, who secretly joined forces with Clarke against the social reformers who wanted to rid Edmonton of prostitution and gambling. Publicly, McNamara and Clarke said they, too, wanted to purge the city of vice, but privately they wanted the city to keep collecting taxes from Edmonton's brothels and gambling dens, which included two of the city's largest hotels.

City council instructed Edmonton police to let the whorehouses run, as long as there were no complaints, but to stage a big raid every so often to show the public that the cops were on the job. McNamara and Clarke believed that most Edmontonians wanted a wide-open town as long as the worst excesses of being wide open were prevented. That meant permitting red-light districts and open gambling under police control. As Clarke would say later, he and McNamara were very much in favour of police tolerance. They seemed to have no problem with some cops blackmailing hookers and pimps, warning them of raids, and taking protection money.

This secret alliance between Clarke and McNamara evaporated when a 1914 judicial inquiry revealed that the mayor and his cohorts had conspired to keep Edmonton as a wide-open city by firing a police chief, Silas Carpenter, who had made a genuine attempt to clean up the city. Clarke wanted McNamara to publicly admit he had told Carpenter's successor—Police Chief George Hill—to leave the brothel owners alone, but McNamara wasn't having any of this. He accused Clarke of trying to control the police department, and that's when the fisticuffs erupted at city hall. The *Edmonton Bulletin* said they were "brawling like two drunken men, pounding each other on their blood-bespattered faces with their fists."

McNamara's days as mayor were numbered after that fight. Two months later, in October 1914, he was convicted on a charge of conflict of interest and ousted from council. Fightin' Joe, too, had his own share of legal and political troubles. In December 1914 he was arrested outside his office and charged with four counts of criminal conspiracy. The charges alleged that Clarke had recruited three convicted safecrackers from Saskatoon to come to Edmonton and commit "crimes and misdemeanors." The motive, according to Police Chief Hill, was to start a crime wave and discredit the police department. Clarke was acquitted when one of the safecrackers recanted his confession. He testified that he had fabricated the confession at the instigation of the Edmonton police "in order to destroy Joe Clarke." Clarke sued the police chief for wrongful arrest and malicious prosecution, and was awarded damages of one dollar. He paid the political price, though, in the 1915 election, when he lost his aldermanic seat. The *Edmonton Journal* devoted reams of space to the speeches of his opponents and left Clarke with just a single sentence: "Joe Clarke delivered his usual harangue."

Clarke ran unsuccessfully as an independent candidate for mayor in 1916 and 1917. He finally made it in 1918, as a Labour candidate, winning the mayor's chair when his opponent came down with the flu and couldn't campaign. At that point Clarke decided to settle some old scores with Police Chief Hill. Every time a citizen felt abused by the police, Clarke would file a suit, naming Hill as defendant. If the chief lost, as in a case where he was fined $177 for raiding a gambling den without a police warrant, Clarke would make it difficult for Hill to recoup his legal expenses from city council.

In 1919 Clarke was re-elected mayor. When the Winnipeg General Strike precipitated a wave of sympathy strikes across Canada, Clarke sided with the workers, convinced them not to be violent on the picket line, and banned the use of strikebreakers despite protests from the Edmonton Board of Trade. For this he was roundly criticized by the *Edmonton Bulletin*: "Better to deal with the Soviet direct and standing alone than the Soviet reinforced by the authority of the mayor's office." This was a common refrain in anti-labour newspapers of the time. Strike leaders were invariably viewed as foreigners in the employ of Lenin and Trotsky.

Clarke's pro-labour credentials failed to get him re-elected as mayor in 1920. He lost to the Citizens' Progress League candidate, David Milwyn Duggan, who would later become leader of the Alberta Conservative Party. Clarke ran again for mayor in 1922 (he didn't try in 1921) and lost to Duggan a second time. In 1924 he ran for alderman as an independent candidate and topped the polls. In 1925 he took another run at the mayor's chair, but lost to a former alderman named Kenneth Blatchford. That marked the start of nine successive years of election losses for Clarke, sometimes running for mayor and sometimes for alderman. All told he ran for mayor seventeen times, and for alderman ten times. He thus set a candidate's record that is unlikely ever to be broken because Edmonton's municipal elections now take place every four years, not annually as in Clarke's time.

While out of office in 1929, Clarke participated in a city bid for some federal land that had once been the site of a penitentiary. Council wanted the vacant land to be developed as a municipal sports park. Clarke was invited to join the city delegation going to Ottawa because he had maintained a friendship with the prime minister, Mackenzie King, ever since the two were in university together during the 1890s. After having lunch with King at the Château Laurier, Clarke returned to Edmonton with a ninety-nine-year lease on the penitentiary property, at an annual rent of one dollar.

In 1934 the perennial candidate finally regained the mayor's chair. At age sixty-five, Fightin' Joe was returned to office by the underdogs he had championed for twenty-two years. They elected him again in 1935 and 1936, but then gave their support to a veteran alderman named John Wesley Fry who seemed to have a better plan for helping the Depression-battered citizens. Clarke made one last unsuccessful run for the mayor's job in

1938, then two more unsuccessful runs for an aldermanic position, in 1939 and 1940.

The former penitentiary property that Clarke had acquired for the city's use remained vacant until 1938, when council found the money to install two wooden grandstands and create a home for the Edmonton Eskimos football club. When it came to naming the new park, there was only one possible contender as far as council was concerned. Clarke Stadium served as the home of the Eskimos until 1978, when the team moved to nearby Commonwealth Stadium. The park remained active as a facility for minor-league sporting events until 2000, when it was remodelled and transformed into a more versatile venue for sports, outdoor concerts, and other events.

Clarke made his final, unsuccessful run for municipal office just seven months before he died, from a heart attack, in July 1941. He was seventy-one. His old nemesis, the *Edmonton Bulletin*, praised him as a staunch advocate who threw "the full weight of his influence and gifts of oratory into any campaign, for any purpose that he considered for the benefit of the city." There was no mention of Fightin' Joe's early efforts to turn Edmonton into a wide-open city like the Klondike of his younger years. His widow, the former Gwendolen Asbury, became a municipal politician after his death, serving as a one-term alderman on Edmonton City Council from 1942–43.

NELLIE LETITIA MOONEY McCLUNG

Writer, Feminist, and Social Reformer
1873–1951

The final, triumphant chapter in the story of the early twentieth-century, Prairie firebrand Nellie McClung was written into the history books on October 18, 2009. That's when she and four other Alberta women who had scored an important 1929 victory for women's rights in Canada were named honorary senators. It was the first time in Canadian history that anyone was appointed posthumously to the Senate.

The appointment was long overdue. Eighty years earlier, on October 18, 1929, McClung and her four fellow activists—Henrietta Muir Edwards, Louise McKinney, Emily Murphy, and Irene Parlby—had won the right for women to sit in the Senate. But none of the Famous Five—as the group became popularly known—was given the go-ahead to take a seat in the Red Chamber. Instead, the nod went to Cairine Wilson, an Ottawa Liberal MP's wife who had played absolutely no role in the Famous Five's battle for gender equality. McClung and her four allies, it seems, were considered too "pushy" by the cautious Prime Minister Mackenzie King, who described Murphy as "a little too masculine and perhaps a bit too flamboyant."

McClung's involvement with the Famous Five came after she had established herself as a bestselling author, temperance advocate, and campaigner for the right of Canadian women to vote.

Nellie McClung, 1910. (Archives of Manitoba, N7694)

The first chapter of her story was written in rural Manitoba, south-west of Winnipeg, where her Irish-born father, John Mooney, and Scottish mother, Letitia, established a homestead in 1880. At age sixteen, with only six years of formal schooling to her credit, Nellie Mooney became a schoolteacher in Hazel, Manitoba, 120 kilometres east of her family's homestead. Eighteen months later, she moved to a four-room school in nearby Manitou. She boarded at the home of a Methodist minister named McClung whose eldest son, Wes, worked in the local drugstore as a pharmacist.

Nellie and Wes were married in 1896. She was twenty-three, and he was four years older. They raised five children, and Nellie began to pursue an interest in writing. She wanted to document the experience of frontier life that was not being recorded in the popular books and periodicals of the day. After publishing numerous poems and short stories in such magazines as *Saturday Night*, the *Canadian Home Journal*, and the *Ladies' Home Journal*, Nellie got her big break in 1906 when a Toronto book publisher encouraged her to turn one of her stories into a full-length book. The resulting novel, *Sowing Seeds in Danny*, was published in 1908 and sold more than 100,000 copies. Written at the kitchen table while her children were sleeping, it appealed to rural readers in particular because it gave them a chance to read about their own world rather than the distant worlds of the English aristocracy and Dickensian London. It was the first of three books Nellie would write about young Pearlie Watson, a farm girl whose experiences paralleled Nellie's own. Thirteen more books would follow, including volumes of autobiography, fiction, poems, and essays.

Coupled with her desire to write was Nellie's aspiration to improve women's lives. The powerlessness of women, and the failure of the law to protect them, deeply offended her sense of fairness and natural justice. More than just being denied the vote and thwarted in their efforts to acquire higher education and professional status, women were being relegated to a secondary role in Canadian society—dependent on the protection of husbands, fathers, or brothers for their very survival.

Nellie used the public exposure provided by her book tours to speak out against these injustices. A gifted orator, she advocated for women's suffrage and prohibition, as well as greater access to education, well-paid employment, and laws recognizing gender equality. She joined the Manitou branch of the Women's Christian Temperance Union because—aside from wanting to rid the frontier of alcohol—the WCTU supported a variety of causes aimed at civilizing and humanizing the Canadian West. Plus, it had the backing of the churches and many political leaders.

While Nellie's career as a writer and speaker took off, her husband Wes suffered a nervous breakdown that effectively ended his career as a pharmacist. He sold the drugstore and used the proceeds to buy two farm properties that he rented out. He worked at odd jobs for about five years and—when his health improved—accepted an offer to run an insurance agency for Manufacturers' Life in Winnipeg. Nellie, then thirty-eight, welcomed the chance to move to the bigger city. She joined the Winnipeg branch of the Canadian Women's Press Club and became active in the Political Equality

League, a group of activist women and liberal-minded men who campaigned to win voting rights for women in Manitoba. One of the league's most powerful tools was political satire. Hundreds of suffrage supporters regularly attended the "mock parliament" sessions of the league to watch Nellie offer a devastatingly accurate impersonation of the huffing-puffing premier, Sir Rodmond Roblin. She had met the premier briefly when he told her, "Nice women don't want the vote." In the mock parliament Nellie satirized the encounter, saying that nice *men* didn't want the vote. "The best burlesque ever staged in Winnipeg," commented the reviewer for the *Winnipeg Tribune*.

On January 28, 1916, Manitoba became the first province in Canada to grant women the vote. But Nellie wasn't there to take part in the Winnipeg victory parade. Manufacturers' Life had transferred Wes to Edmonton in December 1914, so Nellie had taken her causes and her passion to Alberta. She was among the hundreds of women who descended on the provincial Legislature in February 1915 and called upon Premier Arthur L. Sifton to give women the vote. Sifton was not sympathetic. He met them on the steps of the legislature and said, "Did you ladies wash up your luncheon dishes before you came down here to ask me for votes? If you haven't, you better go home because you're not going to get any votes from me."

The women included all the members of the future Famous Five. Two of them, McClung and Emily Murphy, were granted permission to speak. Murphy, like McClung, was a self-taught writer who wrote under the pen name Janey Canuck and worked for a number of women's causes. She was also a self-taught legal expert who, when appointed to the bench in Edmonton in 1916, would become the first woman magistrate in the British Empire.

McClung did not mince words when she addressed the Alberta Legislature on February 15, 1915. "I ask for no boon, no favour, no privilege," she said, her voice echoing through the building. "I am just asking for plain, old-fashioned, unfrilled justice." Sifton later told the press, "Mrs. McClung and Mrs. Murphy are very determined women." He did not commit himself immediately to female suffrage, but relented fourteen months later. On

April 19, 1916, Alberta became the third province in Canada to grant women the vote; one month after Saskatchewan women were enfranchised. McClung, Emily Murphy, and their friend Alice Jamieson—who was about to be appointed Calgary's first female magistrate—celebrated by buying new hats and having their photograph taken at an Edmonton studio. "Being women," explained McClung, "we couldn't very well express our joy and satisfaction by going out and getting a bottle." Her commitment to temperance would have ruled out champagne.

The provincial election of 1917 gave Alberta women their first opportunity to exercise their newly won franchise. It also gave them a first opportunity to run for office at the provincial level. McClung opted not to run in 1917 but did so in the next election, in 1921, because she could "foresee a chance of serving women more than in the past." She won as a Liberal candidate in Edmonton and sat in loyal opposition to the United Farmers of Alberta (UFA) party, which toppled the ruling Liberals in a surprise victory. Two years later, the McClungs moved to Calgary, where Wes took charge of the local Manufacturers' Life office. They lived in the inner-city Beltline district, in a Tudor Revival–style house that would sell for $1.5 million in 2012.

McClung didn't have much time for party politics. Though elected as a Liberal, she spent much of her time working with UFA member Irene Parlby—the only other woman in the Legislature—on laws relating to women and children. Nellie said the issues were what mattered, not the dictates of party policy. One of the bills that Parlby sponsored, and McClung supported, was an act permitting unmarried mothers to sue the father of the child for maintenance.

Though she did not enjoy her five years as an opposition MLA—mainly because she disliked parliamentary rules and procedures—McClung decided to run for re-election in 1926, this time in the Calgary electoral district. She had been greatly disappointed when Albertans voted in a 1923 referendum to end Prohibition, and so she ran on a pro-Prohibition platform. She lost by a mere sixty votes, coming in sixth behind five elected candidates. The defeat upset her, but there was a plus side: now she could spend more time at home with her husband and two youngest children—twenty-year-old Horace and fifteen-year-old Mark—instead of being away for weeks at a time when the Legislature was in session.

McClung never ran for elected office again. Though wooed by the federal Liberals, she opted instead to challenge the system from the outside rather than try to work within it. She had her next opportunity to do this when Emily Murphy invited her to join the campaign to allow women's appointments to the Senate. Murphy's various attempts to have the Senate doors opened to women had been rejected by successive prime ministers who declared that the 1867 British North America (BNA) Act precluded women from being appointed. Section 24 of the act stated that only "qualified persons" could be called to the Senate, and a British court had ruled that women were "not persons in matters of rights and privileges." When Murphy discovered by accident that five citizens could ask Canada's Supreme Court for an interpretation of any part of the BNA Act, she invited four Alberta friends—McClung, MLA Irene Parlby, former MLA Louise McKinney, and National Council of Women co-founder Henrietta Muir Edwards—to lend their names to the petition.

The Supreme Court, on April 24, 1928, ruled unanimously that women were ineligible for Senate appointments. The ruling was based on the fact that under English common law women had always been "excused" from taking part in public affairs, and that nothing in the BNA Act ratified such participation.

Murphy and her co-appellants were disappointed but undeterred. They took the case to the Judicial Committee of the Privy Council in London, then the last court of appeal for Canadians. On October 18, 1929, the Privy Council overturned the Canadian Supreme Court decision, declaring that women were indeed "qualified persons" for the purpose of Senate appointments. Their Lordships ruled that political exclusion based on gender was a "relic of days more barbarous than ours" and that the word "persons" included "members of the male and female sex." The Famous Five celebrated their victory with a tea party at the Palliser Hotel in Calgary.

If McClung was disappointed that none of the Famous Five later made it into the Senate, she never said so publicly. She just carried on with her regular routine, railing in print and on the podium against the impediments that still remained for women who wanted higher education, better wages, or memberships in such male-dominated organizations as the Calgary Board of Trade.

One blot on her otherwise unblemished record of public service was her active and vocal support for eugenics, the junk-science of improving the human species through selective breeding. Like many prominent Canadians of that time, including the inventor Alexander Graham Bell, physician Sir William Osler, pioneering socialist Tommy Douglas, and two of her Famous Five colleagues—Emily Murphy and Irene Parlby—McClung believed in the forced sexual sterilization of mentally disabled individuals. During a time when there were no birth control pills, McClung felt it wasn't fair for handicapped women to be forced into having children they couldn't care for. No defence can be made today for McClung's support of eugenics; she was obviously wrong. But one can find a rationale. She genuinely believed that mentally disabled individuals who were incapable of looking after themselves should be stopped from having children because they would also be incapable of looking after them.

Three years after the judgment in what became known as the "Persons' Case"—when McClung was fifty-nine—she and Wes moved to Victoria. She talked about retiring from everything except writing but soon was accepting speaking engagements, serving on the board of the Canadian Broadcasting Corporation, and supporting Japanese Canadians in their quest for voting rights. During the Second World War she worked hard to make the Canadian public aware of what was happening to Jews in Nazi Germany, and she lobbied for women to take charge of food distribution for the Canadian Army because she felt they knew more about proper nutrition than men. After the war she denounced suggestions by male MLAs that women should give up jobs in stores and offices to make room for returning soldiers. But her voice gradually grew weaker as her health declined because of heart disease, arthritis, and other conditions. By the late 1940s, when in her mid-seventies, she was unable to attend church, walk for any distance, or receive more than one or two visitors at a time.

McClung died on September 1, 1951, at age seventy-seven. The newspaper obituaries focussed more on her writing and conventional family life than on her political achievements, as if her early battles for gender equality had been little more than minor skirmishes. It was only when the women's movement began to gather momentum in the 1960s that McClung's achievements as an early feminist started to be recognized anew. What the early British and American suffragists had obtained through violence and belligerent rhetoric, Nellie had helped achieve with wit and eloquence. "Never retract, never explain, never apologize," she had said in one of her most quoted one-liners. "Get things done and let them howl!"

For close to sixty years the only memorial commemorating the outcome of the Persons' Case was a bronze plaque installed in 1938 in the lobby of the Senate. Then, starting in 1996, there was a flurry of celebratory activity. A Famous Five foundation was launched in Calgary to "inspire women to develop their full potential as persons." One of the Historica-Dominion Institute's *Heritage Minutes* videos recalled Nellie's 1914 "nice women don't want the vote" encounter with Premier Roblin of Manitoba. Larger-than-life bronze statues of the Famous Five were installed on Parliament Hill and on Calgary's Olympic Plaza. Canada Post included the Famous Five in its *Millennium* series of postage stamps. The Bank of Canada issued a Famous Five $50 bill. A Nellie McClung foundation was established in Winnipeg to raise funds for erecting and maintaining a statue of her on the grounds of the Manitoba Legislature. And finally, in October 2009, came the posthumous appointments to the Senate. Together, McClung and her allies had made significant contributions to the advancement of Canadian women during the twentieth century. Now, it falls on their successors to build on their achievements during the twenty-first.

WINNIFRED EATON BABCOCK REEVE

Novelist and Poseur
1875–1954

She was a successful romance novelist in New York who threw it all away for the love of an Alberta cowboy. Winnifred Eaton was a literary chameleon of Chinese extraction who made her mark by assuming a fake Japanese identity and publishing novels under the pen name Onoto Watanna. But after she married Frank Reeve, a rancher with a four-thousand-hectare spread near Morley, Alberta, she turned her back on her flourishing career to settle for the life of a local celebrity. She wrote occasional pieces for the *Albertan* newspaper and became active in the Calgary Little Theatre Association.

The daughter of an itinerant portrait painter from Macclesfield, Cheshire, England, and the Chinese bride he married in Shanghai in 1863, Winnifred was born in Montreal after her parents immigrated to Canada in the 1870s. She assumed the Japanese persona primarily, she said, to distance herself from her Sinocentric older sister, Edith Eaton—also a fiction writer—who adopted a Chinese pen name, Sui Sin Far. Winnifred publicly maintained this deception about her ethnic identity until the Japanese bombed Pearl Harbor in 1941. After that, she frankly admitted to a Calgary newspaper reporter she was "ashamed of having written about the Japanese, because I hate them so." She felt like a hypocrite, she said, because she had betrayed her Chinese ancestry.

Winnifred Eaton as "Onoto Watanna." Publicity shot, circa 1902. (Photo courtesy of Diana Birchall)

She had a love-hate relationship with southern Alberta. It began in 1917 when Winnifred, at age forty-two, married thirty-nine-year-old Frank Reeve, a farmer's son from Long Island who decided to make a new life as a cowboy and rancher after selling his interest in a flourishing New York tugboat company. He chose Alberta because he was told he could fetch good prices there for wheat and beef. He met Winnifred when both were in Reno awaiting finalization of divorces from their first spouses. Frank's wife had left him for another man while Winnifred had fled from the abusive and alcoholic husband who fathered her four children.

Winnifred was ready for a change of scenery when Frank suggested they move to Alberta. While New York had been good for her literary career, it also brought unhappy reminders of her turbulent fifteen-year marriage to theatrical agent Bertrand Babcock, which ended when he kicked and punched her on the front steps of their Manhattan apartment.

Despite the beatings and the challenges of raising four children, Winnifred managed to produce a large volume of published writing while in New York, maintaining a pattern she had established in Montreal as a teenager. The eighth of fourteen children born to remittance man Edward Eaton and his wife Grace—the adopted daughter of English missionaries to Shanghai—Winnifred used writing and storytelling as a way of coping with the poverty of her childhood. Her father was trying to make a living in Montreal as a portrait painter, but he never managed to make a go of it.

Winnifred sold her first story, about a poor young boy's desire to be rich, to Montreal's *Metropolitan Magazine* when she was eighteen. Two years later, she was on staff at *Gall's News Letter* in Kingston, Jamaica, writing poems and short stories as well as reporting and editing the news for the Canadian-owned newspaper. She obtained the $10-a-week job through the journalistic connections of her sister Edith and brother-in-law Walter Harte, who both worked for newspapers in Montreal.

Winnifred spent five months in Jamaica, producing copy for the reading pleasure of white tourists and expatriates. She then moved to Chicago, where she worked as a stenographer and began to achieve success selling Japanese-themed stories to magazines using her Japanese pen name. Her fictional stories were mostly about romantic relationships between Japanese women and American men. The nonfiction stories covered such topics as everyday life in Japan, the miniature trees of Japan, and the lives of Japanese actors. Winnifred had never been to Japan so she relied heavily on library research to sustain her pose as an expert on all things Japanese.

Why did she choose Japan as her subject? Aside from her desire to establish an identity separate from that of her literary sister, it seems Winnifred wanted to capitalize on the public's growing fascination with the Land of the Rising Sun. Japanese culture was then viewed in the West as being superior to Chinese culture, while the Japanese people were more admired and less discriminated against than the Chinese.

In 1899, at age twenty-four, Winnifred scored a major literary breakthrough when Rand McNally published her first novel,

Miss Numè of Japan, a four-way interracial romance about a Japanese man falling for a white woman and a white man falling for a Japanese woman. Considered daring for its time because stories about Caucasian females in relationships with non-white males were not at all popular with white American readers, the book received mixed reviews. *The New York Times* described it as a "charmingly written little story" while the *Brooklyn Eagle* took exception to the depiction of Japanese women as "ignorant, mentally and morally, as six-year-old children." The book sold reasonably well, which led to further magazine commissions for the author.

Winnifred's second novel, *A Japanese Nightingale*, first appeared in the *Ladies' Home Journal* in serialized form—a popular way of publishing fiction at that time. With the money she received from the magazine, Winnifred moved to New York City in the spring of 1901. A few months later, she met and married Bertrand Babcock, then a newspaper reporter and aspiring novelist. A few months after that, in November 1901, Harper & Brothers published *A Japanese Nightingale*. This was the book, later compared favorably to *Gone with the Wind*, which would launch Onoto Watanna's career as a major Asian-American writer. It would be translated into three languages, sell 200,000 copies, be adapted for the stage, and be filmed by Pathé as a silent movie.

Following the conventionally acceptable interracial plot model of *Madame Butterfly*—which tells about the doomed marriage of a white U.S. Navy lieutenant and a Japanese geisha girl—*A Japanese Nightingale* focussed on the relationship between a wealthy white American conducting business in Japan and the Eurasian woman who sings in the teahouse he frequents. *The New York Times* noted admiringly that the book was written "by a young Anglo-Japanese girl whose opportunities for observing her countrywomen have been exceptional, and whose mind has been trained to the European point of view." Winnifred played up the Anglo-Japanese angle by appearing in *Harper's Weekly* dressed in a kimono. The photo caption congratulated Onoto Watanna on her "sudden conquest of the Occident." Another publication, the *New York Herald Tribune,* said she was born in Nagasaki. The myth was growing.

Winnifred's first child, son Perry, was born in June 1903. By that time, she had published a third novel, *The Wooing of Wistaria,* and was finishing work on a fourth, *The Heart of Hyacinth.* Additionally, she was contributing stories to magazines such as *Harper's Monthly, Idler, Saturday Evening Post,* and *Frank Leslie's Popular Monthly.* She kept up this hectic writing pace while giving birth to three more children, sons Bertie and Charley and daughter Doris. She was, as she told a friend, producing "a book and a baby a year." During this period her husband stopped trying to do any serious literary work of his own and took to the booze instead. He quit journalism and went to work for Broadway's Schubert Theaters as a publicity agent.

Winnifred's three sons had physical and psychological problems that brought her considerable grief. Her second son, Bertie, suffered from chronic encephalitis and died of convulsions and heart failure in September 1908, just before his fourth birthday. Her oldest son, Perry, suffered from spinal meningitis and developed a severe mental illness—likely schizophrenia—as he got older. He was institutionalized for most of his adult life. Son Charley changed his name to Paul Eaton Reeve and became the poet that Winnifred unsuccessfully tried to be herself. But he was a hopeless alcoholic who constantly pestered his mother for financial support. Only daughter Doris, who became a key financial trouble-shooter for Winnifred's second husband, Frank Reeve, enjoyed a relatively stable life.

Winnifred's final split with Bertrand Babcock occurred in May 1915, when she was working on a movie serial project with a group of male collaborators. Babcock became jealous, sneered at her for doing what he considered inferior writing work, and assaulted her in a drunken rage one night when she came home late. She moved to a hotel and wrote in her diary, "I'm done with Bert forever, this is the last straw. I've had fifteen years of hell and my goodness has been rewarded in this way. He is a madman." He sent her five letters begging forgiveness, but her mind was made up.

With the royalty returns from her twelve novels, including the autobiographical *Me: A Book of Remembrance* that she published anonymously in 1915, Winnifred had the means to live independently while seeking a divorce. She moved to Reno, where a divorce could be obtained quickly after satisfying the six-month residency requirement. She enrolled her three children in local schools and proceeded to cultivate a relationship with Frank Reeve, the man who was to become her second husband. They married in Greenwich, Connecticut, in March 1917, and moved to Frank's newly purchased farm twenty-five kilometres northeast of Calgary. A year later they moved to Bow View Ranch, a four-thousand-hectare property Frank acquired sixty-five kilometres west of Calgary near Morley. They lived in a comfortable home, with a log-burning fireplace, Navajo rugs on the floor, a player piano, and 2,500 books in the living room. But Winnifred felt terribly isolated, especially during the winters when the children were away at boarding school in Calgary and Frank was away on ranch business for days at a time. Much as she loved the outdoors, she found ranch life stifling. "I feel like an exile in Siberia," she told a friend.

Winnifred wrote no novels during her first four years in Alberta. But she did write occasional pieces for the *Albertan* newspaper and for the Calgary-based *Farm and Ranch Review* weekly. She also took periodic trips to New York to write scenarios for Paramount and Universal Pictures. She rented a small house in Calgary, where she found it easier to write than at the ranch, and she became active in local theatrical and writing circles. She helped establish the Calgary Little Theatre Association, and was a founding member of the Calgary chapter of the Montreal-based Canadian Authors Association.

In 1922 Winnifred published what was to be the last of her Japanese-flavoured novels, a romance titled *Sunny-San*. By that time she had grown tired of writing Japanese stories but reverted to her success formula with the *Sunny-San* novel when Paramount Pictures rejected a proposal she made for a western movie about rape and retribution on an Alberta ranch. Set mostly in the United States, *Sunny-San* tells about the Japanese daughter of a white American senator who comes to New York City to be reunited with her father and to marry the young American student who once rescued her from a cruel geisha house owner.

Winnifred reworked her rejected movie proposal into a novel, *Cattle*, which appeared in North America in 1924. Writing under her maiden name, Winnifred Eaton, she abandoned the delicate, poetic style that had been a feature of her Japanese storytelling to give a blunt account of an innocent fifteen-year-old farm girl raped by a brutish landowner unsubtly named Big "Bull" Langdon. The girl eventually finds matrimonial happiness with a young homesteader while the rapist gets his comeuppance when gored to death by his prize bull.

Critical reaction to *Cattle* was mixed. The *Montreal Star* acclaimed it as a great Canadian novel while the *Ottawa Citizen* scornfully dismissed it as crude and unconvincing. An anonymous writer for *The Goblin*, a University of Toronto humour magazine edited by Stephen Leacock, expressed tongue-in-cheek relief that the author had finally "given up writing for Sunday school libraries." The book sold well, but not as briskly as Winnifred's Japanese-themed novels.

The movie rights to *Cattle* were purchased by Hollywood movie mogul Elmer Clifton, business partner to the legendary director D. W. Griffith. Clifton created a stir when he drove out to visit the Bow View Ranch, jumped out of his car, and loudly declared that the Alberta foothills scenery was spectacular, "immense." Despite his enthusiasm, *Cattle* never did get filmed. But shortly after his visit, Winnifred left her husband to return to New York and get back into the world of big-city writing. "How could I live in Alberta and go on with my work?" she wrote in a letter to Frank. "My business is as important as yours, and yours as important as mine, and neither of us can sacrifice his [*sic*] interests for the other."

Frank, understandably, did not want her to leave. But he was not about to uproot and move with her and the children to New York. He liked Alberta and opted to stay even when the farming and ranching business turned sour. With grain and beef prices dropping, he sold the ranch in 1925 and moved into Calgary to take a job with a brokerage firm. He later bought a seat on the Calgary stock exchange and founded his own brokerage, F. F. Reeve & Company. Through shrewd investments in the newly booming oil patch he eventually became one of the wealthiest men in Alberta.

Within a few weeks of her return to New York, Winnifred obtained a $250-a-week job as screenwriter and story editor with Universal Pictures. This was ten times more than a secretary could expect to earn at the time. A year later, in December 1925, Winnifred was transferred to Hollywood, where she spent the next six years churning out screen adaptations of such stories as *Phantom of the Opera* and Edna Ferber's *Show Boat*.

Winnifred published what was to be her last novel, *His Royal Nibs*, in 1925. Set in the same western landscape as *Cattle*, and written under the name Winifred Eaton Reeve (with, for some inexplicable reason, only one "n" in Winifred), it marked a return to the type of popular fiction her readers had come to expect. It poked gentle fun at the descendants of English aristocracy who moved to western Canada to try their luck at ranching. The book enjoyed modest success but did not lead to more novels because Winnifred was now too busy with her movie work.

Winnifred's children left the nest after she moved to Hollywood. Perry, then twenty-one, had a nervous breakdown and was committed to a state mental hospital. Doris eloped with a New York photographer named Geoffrey Rooney and gave birth to a baby boy named Tim. Charley, at seventeen, moved back and forth between Los Angeles and New York, worked sporadically as a film extra, and published poetry in small literary magazines.

In the summer of 1931, Frank moved to Reno to establish residence for a divorce. He and Winnifred had lived apart for seven years, he had a mistress in Calgary named Edith Hill, and he no longer had any feelings for Winnifred. Or so he initially claimed. When he came to Hollywood to talk to Winnifred about the divorce, though, it turned out the spark was still there. "Frank and I have become reconciled," she exulted in a letter to her sister Rose. "I am so happy about it that I scarcely know what to do. I feel as if I were in a sort of dream." She and Frank had spent a week in Lake Tahoe for what turned out to be a second honeymoon, and they soon were making plans to get back together in Calgary.

There was still the nagging question, however, of how Frank would terminate the affair with the widowed Mrs. Hill. He had placed thousands of dollars worth of bonds and securities in her safety deposit vault, with the understanding they would marry after he obtained his divorce from Winnifred. If Mrs. Hill were to find out about the reconciliation, wrote Winnifred, "Frank would have a heck of a time getting his bonds back." Winnifred also worried that she might never again see some of her own valuable possessions—including an autographed first edition of Mark Twain's *A Connecticut Yankee in King Arthur's Court*—that Frank had stored at Mrs. Hill's house for safekeeping while he lived at the Empress Hotel in Calgary.

Winnifred fretted in Hollywood while Frank took his time about breaking up with Mrs. Hill. In her diary Winnifred recounted a long-distance telephone conversation during which Frank said he had retrieved most of his securities but had not yet taken the delicate next step of telling Mrs. Hill about the reconciliation. "You can't resume intimate relations with her," warned Winnifred. Frank assured her the affair was over.

When Winnifred finally returned to Calgary, in December 1931, she was satisfied that the affair was indeed over. Though she never did retrieve the items Frank had stored at Mrs. Hill's house, she was happy to be back home reclaiming her rightful place as the wife of one of Calgary's most prominent citizens. She took her literary revenge on Mrs. Hill by writing a remarkably confessional semi-fictional account of the affair—with the mistress as narrator—which she published anonymously in the facetiously named *True Story* magazine.

With her credits as a Hollywood screenwriter and celebrity author, Winnifred again became a leading figure in Calgary theatrical and writing circles. She re-established her connection with the Calgary Little Theatre Association, which produced some of her plays. She became president of the Calgary Women's Press Club and wrote an autobiographical manuscript, tellingly titled "You Can't Run Away from Yourself." She contemplated writing another novel but never got beyond making notes for a book to be titled *Boom City*, about Calgary's social scene. "I have a large house and a social position that takes up a lot of my time," she explained. "So I have done little writing since coming up here." Whenever aspiring writers asked her for advice, she invariably told them, "The first thing you have to do is get out of this Cowtown."

Throughout the 1930s and 1940s Winnifred made frequent visits back to California to see her institutionalized son, Perry. She also tried to maintain a connection with son Charley, but lost all patience with him when she discovered he was spending her regular gifts of money on booze. Daughter Doris, who had left her husband shortly after baby Tim was born, struggled to make a living in Hollywood until 1934, when she moved to Calgary and became a stenographer with Frank's brokerage firm. Doris continued to work for Frank until his death in 1956, becoming vice-president of his oil company, Commonwealth Petroleum.

Winnifred died of a heart attack on 8 April 1954 at age seventy-nine, while driving back to Calgary from a vacation in California. Frank, then seventy-six, established the $1 million Francis F. Reeve Foundation as a memorial to her. Proceeds from the foundation were used to support various church and educational charities over the next twenty-four years. In 1978, thanks to prudent investing, there was still more than $1 million left in the coffers. Rather than continue supporting a variety of good works, the foundation trustees decided to donate most of the remaining money to the University of Calgary to build a theatre. Given Winnifred's abiding interest in the stage, it seemed an appropriate bequest.

The 250-seat Reeve Theatre opened in 1981. Initially used only for in-house learning and theatrical experimentation, the theatre was later opened up for use as a public performance space for students and alumni. It remains a living legacy. The university had been scarcely dreamed of when Winnifred died, and it had few amenities for drama when it opened in 1966. Today, thanks to the generosity of her husband, the institution boasts one of the most versatile facilities in Canada for teaching and performing drama. Somewhere up in the rafters, the ghost of a woman who once wore a kimono and called herself Onoto Watanna must surely be nodding approval.

EDWARD ARTHUR WILSON, A.K.A. "BROTHER XII"

Religious Fanatic and Swindler
1878–1934

The gold may still be there. That's why fortune seekers and beachcombers still flock annually to DeCourcy Island in the Strait of Georgia, sixteen kilometres southeast of Nanaimo, British Columbia. They are hoping to find some of the estimated $400,000 in $20 gold coins that went missing after a notorious cult leader calling himself Brother XII fled the island in 1933.

Brother XII was the founder of an occult society called The Aquarian Foundation that—at its height in the late 1920s—claimed more than two thousand followers, including many wealthy Americans and Britons. The name Aquarian, taken from the sign of the zodiac, referred to the coming astrological age when people would live in peace and harmony, be able to recall their past lives, and be spiritually enlightened.

"So, who in the holy heck was the infamous Brother XII?" This was the question posed in a *Vancouver Province* headline in June 1999 when DeCourcy Island was overrun with visitors, carrying metal detectors and looking for any gold coins the cult leader might have left behind. The answers, writer Christina Montgomery reported, "wander literally to hell and back, depending on how scholarly or mythical your bent." The

Edward Arthur Wilson, a.k.a. "Brother XII." (Nanaimo Museum Collection)

scholarly answers came from historians John Oliphant and Charles Lillard, who identified the cult leader as an Englishman, born Edward Arthur Wilson on July 25, 1878, in Birmingham, England. The mythical answers were offered by Herbert Emmerson Wilson, a convicted safecracker and murderer from the Sarnia region of Southwestern Ontario who claimed to be Brother XII's younger brother. He asserted in a 1967 "biography" that "Ed" was actually a Canadian, born in Sarnia in 1871. Herbert Wilson's reliability as a witness became suspect, however, when word circulated in Toronto publishing circles that his purported Brother XII biography was actually written by Thomas P. Kelley, a hack writer who contributed true-crime and fantasy adventure tales to pulp magazines. An archivist's note attached to Herbert Wilson's papers in the special collections library at the University of British Columbia warns that he "often embellished his stories, and the boundary between his fiction and nonfiction is not always distinct."

Regardless of where he came from, there is little disagreement over what happened after Edward Wilson arrived in Nanaimo in the spring of 1927. Claiming to be the twelfth master in a mystical brotherhood said to guide the evolution of the human race—hence the name Brother XII—Wilson told his followers he had been chosen to establish a "centre of safety" where they could prepare for the imminent destruction of the world and achieve enlightenment. They would do this by developing a scheme for a new world order based on "truth," and by propagating the precepts of a doctrine called Theosophy that anticipated what is now called New Age thinking with its declaration that the "universal soul" can be constantly improved through a synthesis of the best of world religions and a belief in reincarnation. Supported by cash donations from the Americans and the British (few Canadians bought into his vision), Wilson established a "city of refuge" in the farming district of Cedar-by-the-Sea, eight kilometres southeast of Nanaimo. There, he told his followers, they would survive the coming Armageddon. With the arrival of more and more followers, Brother XII established three satellite camps across the strait from Cedar-by-the-Sea: one on Valdes Island and two on De Courcy Island. One of the De Courcy camps was for men, the other for women. Married couples were forbidden to stay together, but Brother XII made an exception for himself and the various women he slept with. As with many of his decrees, it was a case of "do as I say, not as I do."

Before arriving on Vancouver Island Brother XII had established his credentials as a mystical seer with a series of articles published in England's *The Occult Review* monthly, using the pseudonym E. A. Chaylor. In some of the articles, Wilson included prophesies that he claimed were "dictated" to him by members of the spirit world, who foretold that a new race of spiritually enlightened humans would emerge from the chaos surrounding the imminent destruction of the world. Wilson referred to these spirits as the "masters of the wisdom." He said he was one of the few individuals chosen to receive their knowledge because he had the intellectual capacity to understand it. He had made regular contact with these spiritual masters during the years he travelled the world as a merchant seaman, and eventually came to believe that he—along with eleven other chosen "brothers"—was destined to fulfill their mission on Earth.

In 1926 Wilson published in London a pamphlet, "A Message from the Masters of the Wisdom," which spelled out the "work" that needed to be done to prepare the world for the coming Age of Aquarius. The pamphlet said the work would be done by a select group of individuals spiritually linked to one another by "the bond of service given in other lives" and known collectively as The Aquarian Foundation. Coming as it did just eight years after the end of the First World War, the message's millenarian thrust seems to have registered favourably with a number of well-educated and well-connected British astrology enthusiasts because several joined the foundation. Wilson announced in a letter to the group that his spiritual masters had chosen Vancouver Island as the place where an Aquarian colony should be established. This planned utopian retreat would become the "centre of spiritual energy and knowledge for the whole continent of North America, and for the whole world in the not distant future."

Wilson indicated to his followers that he knew little about Vancouver Island but he had, in fact, lived in Victoria for about two or three years before the First World War, working first as a delivery wagon driver and then as a clerk in the Dominion Express office. Before returning to Vancouver Island in 1927, Wilson first did a fundraising tour of eastern Canada that met with limited success, followed by a tour of the United States that did much better. With the support of Joseph Benner, an Ohio publisher of astrology and occult books, Wilson succeeded in attracting several prominent Americans into the fold.

When the Aquarian Foundation was incorporated as a charitable organization under British Columbia's Society Act in May 1927, the listed directors included: publisher Benner; a Pasadena novelist named Will Levington Comfort; a Santa Cruz astrologer named Coulson Turnbull; a retired Chicago manufacturer named Maurice Von Platen; and Philip Fisher, the scion of a wealthy Birmingham family. The only Canadian director was Edward Lucas, a Vancouver lawyer.

The Aquarians, described by the *Vancouver Sun* as "typically restless, wealthy people who were schoolteachers, chemists, lawyers, barons, heiresses, executives and authors," flocked to the Nanaimo area between 1927 and 1930. Those who could not come sent money. The *Sun* reported that, at the height of the cult's popularity, more than two thousand people were sending up to $1,000 each a week. The paper added that Wilson's chauffeur-driven car was taking him daily to the Nanaimo banks to make large deposits.

When Brother XII first arrived in Nanaimo, his wife, Elma Wilson, accompanied him. Within a year, however, he had kicked her out and taken up with Myrtle Baumgartner, the wife of a New York physician. To justify the affair, Brother XII claimed that Myrtle was the reincarnation of the Egyptian goddess Isis, that he was the reincarnation of the god Osiris, and that their child would be the reincarnation of the god Horus. When Myrtle became pregnant, he announced that the child would become a "world teacher" who would rise up—somewhere around 1975—and save all true believers. Myrtle suffered a miscarriage, however, and was rejected by Brother XII, who then claimed he was the reincarnation of the Apostle Paul. Divorced by her husband, Myrtle suffered a mental breakdown and left the colony. Brother XII then took up with a woman from Florida named Mabel Skottowe, who used the initial "Z" as her occult name and was called "Madame Zee" by the disciples. Brother XII put her in charge of supervising the day-to-day operations of the colony, and she happily complied, enforcing his decrees with a bullwhip. The craziness was becoming increasingly apparent. The disciples put up with the abuse from Madame Zee, apparently, because they saw it as a rite of initiation. If they failed to follow Brother XII's orders, they believed, they would lose their souls.

Life in the city of refuge became more hellish than utopian. One rule for acceptance into the colony had been "the surrender of personal possessions." The disciples noted, however, that the rule did not seem to apply to either Brother XII or his mistress, the sadistic Madame Zee. While the followers lived in tents on a starvation diet and participated in a daily routine of enforced manual labour—clearing rocks from the land with buckets—Brother XII and Madame Zee lived like royalty in a well-appointed cabin with fine linen and china.

Why the double standard? There's no knowing at this point. Perhaps Wilson may have felt that as the "chosen one" he was entitled to certain privileges. Or he may simply have become mentally unhinged. Medical records unearthed in the 1990s show he was suffering from syphilis, which can cause brain damage when left untreated.

Eventually some disgruntled disciples took Brother XII to court on a charge of embezzling $13,000 in foundation funds. But the trial fell apart when Brother XII allegedly used his "black magic" to strike the prosecutor with an unexplained memory lapse, make the judge start growling like a dog, cause a key witness to disappear without a trace, and have other potential witnesses throwing up in the washroom and unable to testify. As bizarre as it all sounds, that is how the story was reported in the *Vancouver Province* by a writer named Bruce McKelvie.

In 1932 police and immigration officers raided the colony to investigate allegations of mistreatment from a former colony member. Perhaps predictably, Brother XII became increasingly paranoid. He stockpiled food, outfitted his remaining followers with guns and ammunition, set up night patrols, and fired on passing boats. He withdrew money from the Nanaimo banks in $20 gold coins, sealed them in Mason jars, and hid them in various places around the islands. He offered his older and weaker followers the choice of either leaving the islands or remaining behind and being beaten by whips as a form of religious discipline. Some, like self-flagellating monks, chose to stay and be flogged.

The disciples revolted for a second time in 1933, bringing another court action against Brother XII to recover their money. This time they won their case. But they never got a chance to collect because Brother XII destroyed much of his island compound in a fit of anger and fled with Madame Zee to Europe. They took with them—or left hidden somewhere on the islands—an estimated $400,000 in gold coins. When police and local residents searched the compound, all they found was a roll of tarpaper containing a scribbled message from Wilson: "For fools and traitors, nothing." The fortune seekers of later years, according to the 1999 *Vancouver Province* story, found nothing but sea slugs, rock crabs, and "a lot of beer bottles." But still they kept coming, hoping to find some sign of the buried Mason jars, or a boat possibly containing the missing gold that Brother XII was said to have sunk when the police closed in on him.

Nobody knows what became of Madame Zee. Wilson is said to have died penniless in Switzerland on November 7, 1934, at age fifty-six, about eighteen months after fleeing the colony. A death certificate, signed by a Dr. Roger Schmidt, listed the cause as angina pectoris. There are suggestions, however, that Wilson may have faked his death to avoid having to pay his creditors. Like Elvis, he was the subject of various sightings, in San Francisco, Vancouver, and Gibraltar, during the years following his reported death.

As for the disciples, they gradually left the islands and made new lives for themselves elsewhere. One declared that he no longer intended to seek spiritual guidance from self-proclaimed messiahs. "I'm just going to listen to my higher self."

JACK KRAFCHENKO

Career Criminal
1881–1914

Awebsite for the south-central Manitoba community of Plum Coulee reveals the enduring love-hate relationship between the town's 750 residents and a former resident named John "Bloody Jack" Krafchenko: "One of Plum Coulee's most famous past citizens is someone they might rather forget."

But the Plum Coulee residents never forget because Krafchenko's story has been told and retold in books, newspaper articles, history journals, and even a book-length poetry collection by Winnipeg writer Dennis Cooley. Krafchenko is remembered as a career criminal who graduated from petty larceny and cheque forgery to bank robbery and murder before writing his name into the history books as one of Canada's most notorious desperadoes of the early twentieth century.

Raised in Plum Coulee from age seven onward—after his Ukrainian-born parents emigrated from Romania to Canada in 1888—Krafchenko began his life of crime at age eleven when charged with stealing five watches from a Winnipeg jewellery store. He got off with a warning from the judge and stayed out of trouble for the next four years. At that point, he was caught stealing a bicycle in Morden and seems to have been sent to jail, though the record is far from clear. He next showed up in Australia, where he trained as a wrestler. When he came back to North America, he wrestled professionally under the names "Australian Tommy

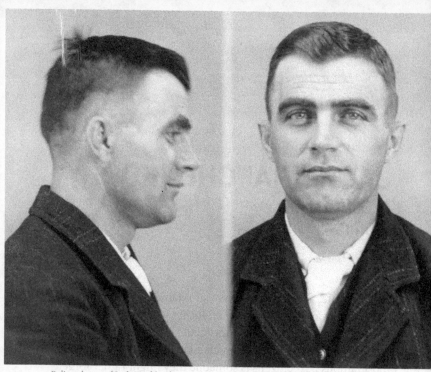

Police photos of Jack Krafchenko, 1914. (Archives of Manitoba, N21204)

Ryan" and "Pearl Smith." Though only 168 centimetres tall, Krafchenko was extremely well muscled for his seventy-three kilograms. He quit the wrestling circuit in 1902 at age twenty-two, and returned home to southern Manitoba, where he posed as a temperance lecturer and started writing bad cheques.

Prairie historian James H. Gray has written there are "at least two or three versions" of every story about Krafchenko. This poses a problem for a Krafchenko biographer, but enriches his legend. So while it is known from court records that Krafchenko was convicted of cheque forgery in Regina in 1903, and sentenced to eighteen months in the Prince Albert Penitentiary, it is not known if—as reported afterward—the handcuffed Krafchenko really jumped from a moving train while en route to the prison, only to be quickly recaptured by a guard who jumped off the train immediately behind him.

The juiciest parts of the Krafchenko legend deal with him first escaping from the Prince Albert Penitentiary in 1904 and then roaming the world from New York to St. Petersburg, robbing banks and leading the life of a gangster and fraud artist. In London (or, some say, Milan), he is alleged to have robbed a bank, locked the manager in the vault, and then joined the crowd outside to watch the excitement when the police arrived.

In Russia, in 1905, Krafchenko is said to have met and married a self-styled "gypsy lady" named Fanicia, and then brought her back to Canada. But another version of his matrimonial story—written by Martin Zelig for the Manitoba Historical Society's 1998 spring-summer newsletter—says Krafchenko may actually have gotten married in the United States, to the daughter of "Gentleman" Jim Corbett, the world heavyweight boxing champion between 1892 and 1897. Or maybe he married both. Nobody knows for sure. The ultimate fate of each possible bride remains unknown.

In 1906 Krafchenko returned to his native Plum Coulee, and soon afterward he robbed the Bank of Hamilton in nearby Winkler. For this crime, he was sentenced to three years in Stony Mountain Penitentiary, a medium-security federal institution located twenty-five kilometres north of Winnipeg. After release, Krafchenko took up blacksmithing, which had been his father's trade. He moved to Graham, Ontario, a remote community located 180 kilometres northwest of present-day Thunder Bay, and worked as a boilermaker at the National Transcontinental Railway's locomotive shops.

Krafchenko seems to have mostly stayed out of trouble during his years with National Transcontinental. However, in the summer of 1913, he was fired for repeated outbursts of violence on the job. He returned to Manitoba, settled in Winnipeg's rundown north end and—because of his criminal connections—was recruited by Winnipeg's police chief, Donald MacPherson, to work as an informant. A former detective sergeant, John Burchill, wrote in the January 1992 edition of the police union newsletter, however, that Krafchenko never actually did anything for his informant's salary. He simply took the money and never reported back.

In November 1913 Krafchenko hatched his last big caper as a bad guy. After several reconnaissance trips to Plum Coulee, he decided the town's Bank of Montreal would be the perfect target for a robbery. He made arrangements with a local taxi driver, William Dyck, to drive the getaway car for him, and scheduled the robbery to occur over the lunch hour on December 3, 1913, when the only person on the premises would be the bank manager, Henry Medley Arnold.

The idea of choosing Plum Coulee for a bank robbery was, as historian James Gray wrote in *The Boy from Winnipeg*, "so transparently preposterous as to immediately indicate serious mental disorder." Just about everyone in town knew Krafchenko. Police would have no difficulty finding witnesses to finger the suspect. Plus, escaping from the town would be very difficult by car, because little maintenance was done on Manitoba's mud roads after the first snow fell. "There was literally nothing about the Plum Coulee caper that made the slightest sense," wrote Gray.

Yet, Krafchenko did proceed with the robbery, masking himself with a handkerchief and wielding a 9mm Browning automatic handgun. He pocketed $4,700 in cash and coldly shot the bank manager to death when the manager tried to prevent Krafchenko from escaping. Three people witnessed the shooting. One, a young woman named Mary Doerksen, recognized Krafchenko and positively identified him later in a police lineup. Krafchenko ordered cabbie Dyck to drive him a few kilometres beyond Plum Coulee, and somehow he managed to make it on to Winnipeg without the police catching up with him.

Arriving in Winnipeg wearing a false beard, Krafchenko took refuge in a boarding house in the north end. He told the landlady he was a teacher at St. John's College. One of his underworld cronies tipped off the police and claimed the posted reward of $1,000 when he saw Krafchenko drinking and gambling at one of his old Winnipeg after-hours haunts. Krafchenko was arrested without a struggle on December 10, one week after the Plum Coulee incident.

Krafchenko was charged with murder and robbery and committed for trial at the spring 1914 assizes in Morden, Manitoba. However, the day after his committal, on January 10, Krafchenko escaped from jail with the help of his lawyer, Percy Hagel, and the police constable, Robert Reid, assigned to guard him in prison. Both accomplices were taken in by Krafchenko's promise to share money, diamonds, and other valuables with them if he ever got out of jail. "They seem simply to have been mesmerized by the bandit, and to have fallen under the spell of his charm," wrote poet Dennis Cooley, quoting from a story in the *Manitoba Free Press*. "He was simply fascinating." Krafchenko escaped through a fourth-floor window, badly injuring his right leg when his escape rope broke and he fell nine metres to the pavement. Despite the injury, he still was able to hobble along the Winnipeg streets until a passing motorist stopped and offered him a lift.

Police launched a massive manhunt that kept the city on tenterhooks for eight days. James Gray, then aged seven, joined the hunt along with his fellow first-graders at Machray Elementary. They played a dangerous game of hide-and-seek in the back lanes of their north-end neighbourhood. "None of us ever had any clear idea of what we would do if we ever blundered into the Krafchenko hiding place," wrote Gray in *The Boy from Winnipeg*. "But if he was a murdering bank robber to our elders, to us he was a hero in the grand tradition of Jesse James, even Robin Hood."

Fortunately for Gray and his pals, they never met up with the fugitive. The Winnipeg police chief, accompanied by a dozen heavily armed constables and a large crowd of gawking onlookers, captured Krafchenko on January 18 at his west-end hideout. Four days later, the police guard who aided Krafchenko admitted to his involvement and was sentenced to seven years in Stony Mountain Penitentiary. Lawyer Hagel was also found guilty of aiding and abetting, and was sentenced to three years. Although disbarred for life from practicing law in Manitoba, Hagel did, in fact, return to the courtroom during the mid-1920s and continued to practice criminal law until his death in 1944. The *Winnipeg Tribune* obituary referred to him as a "colourful" barrister but made no mention of his past connection with Krafchenko.

Krafchenko, represented by another lawyer, was convicted of murder on April 9, 1914. On July 9 he was hanged in the exercise yard of the Vaughan Street Jail. He was thirty-three years old.

According to the *Manitoba Free Press*, he expressed "the most intense sorrow for the pain he caused others." His execution was the last big event to engage the attention of Winnipegers before the First World War started the following month. "John Krafchenko deserved his fate much more than many other murderers over whose hanging the public betrayed little feeling," said the *Free Press* in a solemn editorial. "Interest was chiefly aroused because a large number of people saw in Krafchenko the degeneracy and perversion of a strong, resourceful, and original character."

MORRIS "TWO-GUN" COHEN

**Pistol-Packing Englishman
in the Chinese Revolution
1887–1970**

The Facebook page for Saskatoon's Two Gun Quiche House restaurant said that its chef, Bill Mathews, brought a little piece of the past to the west-side Riversdale neighbourhood when he opened the restaurant there in 2012. He started with fresh, local ingredients, added his passion for cooking, and topped it all off with "a touch of Saskatoon's sordid history." That history referred to a roguish adventurer named Morris "Two-Gun" Cohen, who used to hang out in Riversdale during the years before the First World War.

Cohen emerges as one of the most colourful historical characters ever to spend time in the Canadian West. He became a bodyguard to the Chinese revolutionary leader Sun Yat-sen and earned his nickname, Two-Gun, when he made a habit of always packing two pistols for protection.

Born in Poland to a Jewish couple who fled to England to escape the anti-Semitic pogroms of the early 1900s, Cohen grew up in poverty in East London. He was arrested at age ten for picking pockets, sent to reform school for six years, and then shipped off to western Canada through the auspices of the Dr. Thomas John Barnardo, who set up and found homes for needy

Morris Cohen, Montreal, 1946. (Saskatoon Public Library, PH-98-115-3)

children, to work for a homesteader at a Jewish farm colony in Wapella, Saskatchewan. Cohen abandoned farming after a year and then wandered throughout the West, picking pockets and hustling as he went. He spent much of his time in Chinese gambling dens, worked briefly as a carnival barker, and served six months' hard labour in a Winnipeg jail for pimping and having sex with an under-age prostitute.

Cohen arrived in Saskatoon after his release from prison in October 1909. He headed for the west side of the city, where boozing, gambling, and prostitution flourished. At that point, he might have been destined for obscurity but for an incident in January 1910 when Cohen stumbled upon an armed robbery at a Chinese restaurant on 20th Street West—in the same block where the Two Gun Quiche House was established a century later. It was a freak encounter, and it earned Cohen a permanent place in the history books. He knocked the villain to the floor, recovered the stolen money, and sent the robber packing. His deed earned him the gratitude of restaurant owner Mah Sam and the respect of Mah's fellow Chinese, who were amazed that a white man would go to the aid of one of their own.

Despite his act of gallantry at the restaurant, old habits die hard. Cohen continued to get in trouble with the law after settling in Saskatoon. In August 1910 he was picked up on a charge of pickpocketing and sentenced to a year in the Prince Albert Penitentiary. Mah was arrested at the same time, charged with running a gambling and opium den, and sentenced to six months. The pair reunited in Saskatoon after serving their respective sentences. Mah, who supported the revolutionary movement in China to overthrow the Manchu rulers, talked to Cohen about the possibility of the Englishman playing a role in the revolution. Cohen was agreeable because his own family had suffered greatly under the Russians in Poland. In 1912 he joined Mah on a trip to Calgary's Chinatown, where the Englishman was granted membership in Sun Yat-sen's secret Tung Meng Hui Society, an organization seeking to create a Chinese national state in the form of a republic.

Cohen remained in Calgary after that and made an illegal living as a gambler until the local vice squad made things too hot for him. He moved to Edmonton, sold real estate for the National Land Company, continued gambling on the side, contributed to the local branch of the Chinese Nationalist League, and became recognized as a spokesman for Edmonton's Chinese community. One Edmonton newspaper reported: "Mr. Cohen is in close touch with Chinese affairs here and knows the men of the orient probably better than any man in Edmonton or in western Canada." Another newspaper spun a fabulous tale relating to his background: "Mr. Cohen is a highly intelligent American with a long residence in China, who speaks fluent Cantonese and is a mason of high degree."

Having sway with the Chinese helped Cohen secure important political connections in Edmonton. He became friendly with Charles W. Cross, Alberta's first attorney general, who paved the way for Cohen to become a commissioner of oaths. Cohen used that office to help Chinese immigrants become naturalized.

The bottom dropped out of the Edmonton real-estate market at the start of the First World War. That left Cohen without any income except for the limited amount he could still make from gambling. However, the war opened up a new opportunity for him. He joined the 218th Overseas Battalion, was made an acting sergeant, and moved to Calgary to do his training. He had numerous skirmishes with the law while learning to be a sergeant at the Sarcee Camp, located on the southwestern outskirts of Calgary. The local newspapers referred to "his weekly appearance" whenever he went to court to answer a charge of disorderly conduct after a night of carousing at the King George Hotel.

In October 1916 Cohen was one of thirteen soldiers charged with disturbing the peace after a tussle with Calgary city police. He conducted his own defence. "Sergt. Cohen shows surprising knowledge of court procedures," reported the *Calgary Herald*. The knowledge paid off. Cohen was acquitted.

Cohen served overseas during the last part of the war. He saw action in Belgium before returning to Edmonton and opening his own real-estate office. He dabbled in oil and mining investments and tried to achieve a measure of respectability by serving on the executive of the Great War Veterans' Association. However, his old habits soon caught up with him. In 1920 he was tried and acquitted on a charge of using his office as a gambling den. In 1922 he was tried and again acquitted on a charge of illegal gambling. By that time Cohen was ready to move on. He packed his bags and set sail for China, where he hoped to work for Sun Yatsen. Sun was attempting to unite the various political forces in China into a Leninist-style party after he had been toppled from power by a warlord named Yuan Shikai. Cohen arranged a meeting with Sun in Shanghai through a New York–born journalist who worked for Sun's English-language newspaper, *Shanghai Gazette*. He was given a job as one of Sun's bodyguards.

Cohen quickly became one of Sun's main protectors, saving his boss's life on several occasions. After being hit in the arm by a bullet during an attempt on Sun's life, Cohen began carrying two guns for protection, one on his hip and one in a shoulder holster. This attracted attention among Shanghai's Western community whose members were already intrigued by this Westerner who consorted with the Chinese. They started calling him "Two-Gun" Cohen.

In 1925 Cohen came back to Canada to buy weapons for the revolutionary cause. He inflated his credentials to make himself a general in the nationalist army—despite the fact that he spoke not a word of Chinese—and impressed the Edmonton newspapers, which described him as "the right hand man of the president of the South China republic."

Sun Yat-sen died while Cohen was in Canada, at which point Cohen switched his loyalty to the new Chinese leader, Chiang Kai-shek. To the Western press, Cohen made it seem as if he were an important force in southern Chinese politics. In reality he was little more than an errand boy, delivering messages for a series of revolutionary bosses in Canton and acting as a courier to accompany important officials passing through Canton and Hong Kong.

When Japan invaded China in 1937, Cohen joined the war effort, smuggling arms and raising money for the China Relief Fund. When Hong Kong fell in 1941, Cohen was captured and sent to an internment camp. He was released two years later in a prisoner exchange and came back to Canada, settling in Montreal, where he met his fiancée. In 1944 he married Ida Judith Clark, the owner of a Montreal dress shop. They spent their honeymoon in Lake Louise and Calgary, and spent much of the trip promoting the beleaguered Chinese government.

That was Cohen's last visit to western Canada. He spent the next few years making frequent trips back and forth from Montreal to China until the Communists took over in 1949. Since he spent so little time at home, his marriage understandably failed. During the early 1950s, he and Judith divorced. Cohen moved permanently to England to live with a sister, and collaborated with ghostwriter, Charles Drage, on a memoir, *The Life and Times of General Two-Gun Cohen*, that proved to be mostly fictitious. He made a few more trips to China during the years following the publication of his memoir, and helped Rolls-Royce negotiate sales of its aircraft engines to the Chinese. In

May 1960 he made one final visit to Canada, to appear as a mystery guest on the television show, *Front Page Challenge*. Panelist Pierre Berton recognized his voice immediately because he had interviewed Cohen for the *Toronto Star* during the 1950s.

Cohen died in London in 1970 at age eighty-three. In 1997 New York author Daniel S. Levy published a well-researched, well-documented biography, *Two-Gun Cohen: A Biography*, which corrected all the errors in Cohen's own account and concluded that he was drawn to China in much the same way that he had been drawn to western Canada a dozen years earlier. "China between the wars was the Wild East," wrote Levy. "It was the last great frontier, filled with adventurers and fortune seekers, offering them the freedom to range and look for what they could take. Cohen seemed made for such a land."

MIKE MOUNTAIN HORSE
First World War Veteran
1888–1964

Like his fellow Canadian Aboriginals, Mike Mountain Horse didn't have to enlist for service in the First World War. Treaties between the Crown and First Nations had designated Natives wards of the government—in effect, minors—and thus they were deemed exempt from military service. Despite this exemption, Mountain Horse and more than 3,500 others—representing more than one-third of Canada's Native male population of military age—volunteered to become warriors for King George V.

Why did they undertake to fight the white man's war? Historian James Dempsey, a great-nephew of Mountain Horse, offers three possible reasons:

1. The war afforded a legitimate excuse for the traditional Native warrior ethos, long frowned upon by Ottawa, to be revitalized and to again play a central role in a young male's life.

2. The Natives retained their loyalty to the British Crown. They viewed any deceptions or unfulfilled promises after the treaties to be the fault of the Canadian government, not of the monarch. So they were fighting for the Great White Father, not for Ottawa.

Mike Mountain Horse, 1959. (Glenbow Archives, NB-44-92)

3. Adventure beckoned. The war provided an escape from the psychological choke of residential school and reserve life.

Mountain Horse had a fourth, more personal, reason for wanting to go to war. His younger brother, Albert, had been gassed three times in Europe after volunteering for service with the Canadian Expeditionary Force in 1914 and had died of tuberculosis at age twenty-two shortly after returning to Canada. "Reared in the environment of my forefathers," wrote Mountain Horse, "the spirit of revenge for my brother's death manifested itself strongly in me as I gazed down on Albert lying in his coffin that cold winter day in November 1915."

Mountain Horse was twenty-eight and working as an interpreter and scout for the Royal North West Mounted Police in Fort Macleod when he enlisted as a private for service overseas with the Canadian Army. Before that, he had worked in various jobs around the Blood (now, Kainai) reserve, located between Lethbridge and Cardston. Born on the Blood reserve in 1888, he revealed a rebellious streak in childhood when he and a group of fellow six-year-olds were caught piling railway ties onto the tracks near his home. Because of that infraction, his parents sent him away to the Anglican-run St. Paul's mission boarding school[1] near the reserve so he would be "kept out of mischief and get educated as well."

Because St. Paul's didn't have facilities for vocational training, Mountain Horse transferred at age fourteen to the Anglican-run Calgary Indian Industrial School (St. Dunstan's) to learn carpentry and how to live a "clean and cultured life." He graduated in 1905 at age seventeen. Two years later, he was hired as a scout by the mounted police detachment at Kipp, between Fort Macleod and Lethbridge. His duties included interpreting and helping suppress illegal liquor traffic on the Blood reserve. He went on routine patrols with the mounted police, keeping an eye on the activities of suspected whisky traders, and he also was responsible for checking on the sick and elderly Natives in the district.

Mountain Horse had indicated no interest in army life before his brother's death spurred him into action as a private in the First World War. Albert had trained as a cadet in his teens and was taking an instructor's course in musketry when the war broke out. Mountain Horse, however, was more interested in soccer and sprinting than in learning how to shoot a service rifle. For a couple of years, he raced professionally under the name Mike Deerfoot.

Mountain Horse told a friend he felt like "an old-time warrior going to war" when he enlisted in 1916. After basic training in Canada and England, he was sent to France in 1917, where he joined the 50th Canadian Battalion and was part of the assault

---

1   *Today it would be called a "residential school," referring to the education network set up by the federal government in the 1880s to indoctrinate aboriginal children into Euro-Canadian and Christian ways of living and assimilate them into mainstream Canadian society. But at the time, such schools were called "boarding schools."*

on Vimy Ridge in April of that year. "As I listened one night to an enemy bomber droning like a huge bumblebee over the Allied lines," he wrote, "the thought came to my mind, 'where is the God that the white man has taught the Indian to believe in? Why does He allow this terrible destruction?' And I prayed that He might yet bring the nations to their senses."

After surviving Vimy Ridge, a battle that left 3,598 dead and 7,004 wounded, Mountain Horse participated in the Battle of Passchendaele (Belgium), between July and November 1917. He suffered shell shock during the first phase of the battle but recovered quickly and returned to duty. During a subsequent phase, on August 21, 1917, he was wounded by a German bullet and then trapped for four days in the cellar of an old building after a shell hit it. When he was rescued, he was taken to an English hospital where he wrote a letter that was subsequently published in the *Macleod News*. "I hate the idea of staying here doing nothing," he wrote, "but they've told me that I've got to stay for another two months before I am again fit for active service."

Mountain Horse returned to the continent in early 1918, and took part in the 100 Days Offensive that ultimately led to the end of the First World War. He adopted a habit of marking captured German artillery with designs of the Blackfoot Confederacy (now, Niitsitapi), a collective of First Nations from the Alberta-Montana border region that included the Blood people. When he was discharged in 1919, he enlisted the help of a friend to paint twelve of his wartime experiences onto a cowhide robe that is now on display in the Medicine Hat Museum and Art Gallery. "The war proved that the fighting spirit of my tribe was not quenched through reservation life," he wrote. "When duty called, we were there, and when we were called forth to fight for the cause of civilization, our people showed all the bravery of our warriors of old."

He came home a war hero, with battle scars, the rank of acting sergeant, and a Distinguished Conduct Medal. He resumed employment with the mounted police and spent the next fourteen years with the force in various detachments around southern Alberta, lecturing on Native legends. He left the force in

1933 to devote all his time to writing and lecturing. He published many articles in the *Lethbridge Herald* and visited schools in Alberta and British Columbia to talk about his war experiences. However, there wasn't enough money in writing and lecturing to sustain him, and he returned to the mounted police job, based in Lethbridge.

A Lethbridge magazine journalist, Thyrza Young Burkitt, encouraged Mountain Horse to write a book about the life and culture of the Blood nation. He completed the manuscript, *Indians of the Western Plains*, in 1939. Burkitt then tried to get a publisher for the manuscript, but no publisher in Canada would take it on. A London publisher, Macmillan, did indicate some initial interest but eventually turned it down "because it lacks any special qualities which would ensure its success in the English market." After that rejection, Mountain Horse filed away the manuscript and forgot about it.

His failure to find a publisher weighed heavily on him. So did the financial difficulties that came with raising a family of seven children. Mountain Horse inherited an instant family when he married a woman from the reserve, Mary Healy. Reduced to the misery of a poverty-stricken existence, Mountain Horse sank into a slough of unhappiness and problem drinking.

Because he preferred to live away from the reserve and imagined himself as a writer, he was often treated with scorn, even disdain, by his fellow Bloods. One characterized him as a "windbag" who made a show of using "big words" whenever he attended a reunion of St. Paul's school. The Bloods didn't have much time for Mountain Horse's newspaper writing, because it was produced for a white readership and not many Natives read newspapers in those days. But they did acknowledge Mountain Horse had made a significant contribution when he served his country in the First World War.

Throughout his life, Mountain Horse was recognized as a war veteran. He helped form a Native war veterans' association, and he was often invited to speak at schools and service clubs. When his wife died, he returned to live on the reserve and was elected to the Blood Tribal Council in 1959. There, his reputation as a war veteran transcended any petty criticisms that his fellow councillors might have had about his newspaper writings or the marginal life he had lived in Lethbridge. "The fact that he had been in battle was more important to the tribe," wrote historian Hugh Dempsey, the father of historian James Dempsey. The Dempsey family connection with the Mountain Horse clan relates to the fact that Mike's wife, Mary Healy, was an aunt of Hugh Dempsey's wife.

Mountain Horse served just one term on council before dying at age seventy-five in 1964. At the time of his death, he no longer had a copy of his manuscript, *Indians of the Western Plains*. But a Lethbridge lawyer, A. B. Hogg, did have a copy, and in 1979 it was published under the title *My People, the Bloods* as an initiative jointly sponsored by the Blood Tribal Council and the Glenbow Museum. "It was unfortunate that his manuscript was not published during Mountain Horse's lifetime, for it undoubtedly would have raised his stature both on and off his reserve," Hugh Dempsey wrote in the Introduction. "Not only is it a valuable document for the recollections of his own childhood experiences, but it also contains a wealth of primary information about the life and customs of his tribe."

MARGARET "MA" MURRAY
Newspaper Publisher
1888–1982

Ma Murray was an adventurer, a romantic, and one of the quirkiest voices in the history of Canadian journalism. At age twenty-four, she left her native Kansas and moved to Canada in hopes of meeting and marrying a handsome cowboy of mythic proportions. She did not find her cowboy, but she did find a husband: newspapering entrepreneur George Murray, who became her partner for life. Together, they published community newspapers that achieved a kind of mythic status. Though they broke all the conventional rules of journalism, and also shattered the rules of grammar and syntax (Ma Murray used to say jokingly that "sin tax" was "something you pay the church"), the newspapers were widely read and much talked about in political circles across Canada.

The seventh of nine children born to Irish-Catholic immigrants from County Cork, Margaret Lally had no formal training as a journalist. Nor did she have much formal education. She never got beyond Grade 8. She quit school at age thirteen after an argument with her teacher in Windy Ridge, Kansas, over who was going to clean the classroom stove. "It's not fair, I've done my turn," Margaret said, and stormed out. After struggling for four years to support herself as a farmhouse kitchen maid, she enrolled in a business school in Fremont, Nebraska,

"Ma" Murray in Fort St. John, 1952. (Fort St. John North Peace Museum, 1988.05.181)

to learn typing and double-entry bookkeeping. That led to a job maintaining the books for the Shipley Saddlery and Mercantile Company in Kansas City, where Margaret amused herself by including personal notes with the saddles being shipped to Alberta. When some of the cowboys replied and sent photographs of themselves, she decided she should move to Canada to marry one of them.

After working her way west and north as a freelance office typist, Margaret arrived in Vancouver in 1912. First she sold subscriptions for the *British Columbia Federationist*, a labour newspaper. Then she landed a $15-a-week job as bookkeeper with the *South Vancouver Chinook*, a neighbourhood weekly owned by twenty-five-year-old George Murray, an Ontario-born businessman, former *Ottawa Citizen* reporter, and Liberal party supporter.

As well as keeping the books, Margaret did some writing for the *Chinook*. Recognizing her natural ability to string sentences together, George assigned her to cover local political gatherings and ratepayers' rallies. "For a little newspaper, it's sure exciting," she wrote in a letter to her family in Windy Ridge. "My boss is a nice young man, a little vague and annoying maybe, but real handsome. He loves this country so much and talks so much about northern British Columbia that you forget what time it is and listen."

Margaret worked at the *Chinook* for a few months and then left for Calgary, in January 1913, to take a job selling advertising for the morning *Albertan*. She still had this notion that she might meet and marry an Alberta cowboy. But she returned to Vancouver after a month, having decided she could not stand the frigid Calgary weather. She reunited with George, who promptly asked her to marry him. After receiving a dispensation from the local Catholic archbishop, Timothy Casey, Margaret the Catholic and George the Presbyterian were married in Vancouver's Holy Rosary Cathedral on February 5, 1913.

Margaret Murray became Ma Murray in the winter of 1913 when daughter Georgina (Georgie) was born. Son Dan arrived a year later. The year after that, the Murrays filed on a $10 acreage of Crown land in the woods near Burrard Inlet, east of Vancouver, where George planned to homestead. They cleared the land, built a cabin, and planted a garden.

By that time the *Chinook* had fallen on hard times. George sold the paper in 1919 to pay off his debts and went to work for Vancouver's daily *Province* as a reporter. Two years later he became managing editor of the rival *Vancouver Sun*. The salary from that job allowed him to rent a cottage near today's Pacific National Exhibition site in east-end Vancouver, which was a much more comfortable home than the makeshift cabin on his homestead property.

Though he appreciated the regular salary George was not happy working for someone else. He quit the *Sun* after a couple of years and became publisher of a trade journal called the *Western Lumberman*. At the same time Margaret founded her own publication, *Country Life in British Columbia*. She gathered the stories, about pig raising, bee keeping, and poultry marketing, while George did the editing and layout.

Country Life folded in 1928 due to lack of advertising. The *Western Lumberman*, by contrast, did so well that the owners—the H. R. MacMillan Export Company—sold the publication for a profit. After George stepped down as publisher, MacMillan commissioned him to travel to Japan to scout out potential export markets for the company's lumber.

George spent four months in eastern Asia, exploring potential export opportunities for MacMillan. Margaret put the children into boarding school, moved to the homestead, and learned the craft of rug hooking. She taught others how to make rugs, sold her own creations, and used the proceeds to buy a cow, pig, and a few chickens. That small farming operation would prove to be a godsend during the Depression when their only income was the small salary George could earn from the *Province* as a reporter.

In the fall of 1933, George entered provincial politics. The Conservative government of the day could offer no solutions to the problems of the Depression, and George figured a Liberal government would do better. However, as a homesteader of modest means, he didn't think he would have much chance of securing a party nomination in an urban Vancouver riding. Instead, he chose the Cariboo constituency of Lillooet, 260 kilometres north of Vancouver, where he promised the voters he would start a newspaper if elected. He won handily in the November 1933 election, and the *Bridge River-Lillooet News* was born.

With George away in Victoria on legislative business, Margaret took over the running of the *News*. Nineteen-year-old daughter Georgie was her editorial assistant. Georgie looked after the social news and the proofreading while her mother churned out the provocative opinion columns that would become her trademark. Written in what she liked to call "flapdoodle vernacular," they were sprinkled with such salty expressions as "damfool critters" and "that's fer damshur." In one column Margaret editorialized in support of the prostitutes who ran a bawdy house in the nearby mining community of Gold Bridge. "They were here first and don't bother anybody." That drew from the paper's female readers a spate of angry letters, every one of which Margaret published in the following week's edition. "Shows they're reading my stuff," she said proudly.

The *News* was a community weekly like few others. Margaret's unconventional practice of printing the registrations from the hotel in town led to at least one divorce case. She also printed names from the local police blotter so that the readers would know which of their neighbours had been arrested on morals- or liquor-related charges.

Aside from courting controversy, Margaret supported various causes that helped her husband's political career. He topped the polls in the 1937 provincial election because Margaret had used the newspaper's editorial page to campaign for improved workplace safety in the mines. True to his word, George crafted the first plan in British Columbia to compensate miners who were injured or fell sick on the job. Part of the plan involved imposing a 9 per cent tax on the mining industry to cover the medical costs of miners stricken with lung disease. The mining companies did not like the legislation, but the miners were happy.

George's political luck ran out in 1941, when he failed in his second bid for re-election. He and Margaret had refused to lend their editorial support to a miners' strike held during the war, when strikes were illegal, and that cost him the votes of his key constituents. He also alienated his fellow provincial Liberals when he spoke out against their proposal to prop up their sagging political fortunes by forming a coalition with the opposition Conservatives. After losing the election, George decided he and Margaret needed to make a fresh start somewhere else.

They chose Fort St. John, where the United States Army had recently established a construction camp for the building of the Alaska Highway. When the Americans realized after the bombing of Pearl Harbor that the only protection for the entire northwest coast of America against another Japanese attack was an abandoned cannon (converted into a flowerpot!) on the grounds of the territorial courthouse at Juneau, Alaska, they took immediate steps—with the blessing of the Canadian government—to build a highway supply route linking airfields from Dawson Creek to Fairbanks. More than 10,000 American troops poured into Fort St. John with their bulldozers, front-end loaders, and graders; the town became the staging ground for this gigantic construction operation. To George and Margaret Murray, it seemed like the perfect place to start another newspaper. They named it the *Alaska Highway News* and launched it while still keeping the *News* going in Lillooet. George took charge of the Fort St. John paper while Margaret looked after the Lillooet weekly.

When son Dan came home from the Second World War in 1945, he took over the running of the Lillooet paper and Margaret moved to Fort St. John. George, meanwhile, decided to take another run at provincial politics. He ran in Lillooet as an independent, calling himself a Liberal Progressive because he could not support the Liberal-Conservative coalition of Premier John Hart. Margaret, too, entered provincial politics at that time. But, perversely, she ran in the BC constituency of Peace River under the banner of the Social Credit Alliance, a party about which—she freely admitted—she knew virtually nothing. "But it does offer an alternative to that lame-brained outfit we have in Victoria."

George, understandably, was shattered by his wife's defection. "I feel very much like the man who invented the atomic bomb," he wrote in a letter to her. "It was a great idea at the time, but now what to do with it? It may destroy all of us." Dan was also unimpressed by his mother's decision to join this little-known political party that had not existed prior to 1937. "Margaret Murray is related to our family only by blood," he declared on the front page of the *News*.

Perhaps predictably, both Murrays failed to win seats in the 1945 election. Each came a distant third in their respective races, losing in each instance to a coalition candidate. Bloodied but unbowed, the couple returned to newspapering. They had turned over control of the papers to their children—Dan in Lillooet and Georgie in Fort St. John—but they still wanted to be involved. Margaret, especially, wanted the readers to know that "Ye Ed," as she called herself, was still active behind the scenes.

On the editorial masthead of the Lillooet paper she included the notice: "Printed in the sagebrush country of Lillooet every Thursday, God willing. Guaranteed a chuckle every week and a belly laugh once a month, or your money back. Subscription, $4.00 in Canada. Furriners, $5.00. This week's circulation 1,643, and every bloody one of them paid for."

While Georgie resented her mother's interference, she had to acknowledge that the Fort St. John paper's growth in circulation and advertising were due in large part to Margaret's widely read columns. During a water shortage, Margaret wrote: "We sure as hell need to use less if we are going to have this modern convenience. To head off this catastrophe, only flush for number two, curtail bathing to the Saturday night tub, and go back to the washrag, which could always move a lot of B.O. if applied often enough." The water crisis ended in a week.

In 1949 Georgie married a soldier named James Keddell and left the Fort St. John paper. Dan took over as publisher after selling the paper in Lillooet. George entered federal politics as the Member of Parliament for the Cariboo riding, which then included Fort St. John. Margaret continued to interfere in the operations of the Fort St. John paper, so much so that Dan eventually gave up and left for California. That left Margaret, at age sixty-one, running the paper by herself. It was not a role that she particularly relished. In her letters to George, she complained bitterly about the difficulties of getting reliable staff.

George lasted just one term in Ottawa. He returned to Fort St. John in 1952 and assumed responsibility for the business operations of the paper. That allowed Margaret to concentrate on what she did best, afflicting the comfortable with her outspoken critiques of government. Her editorials were reprinted widely in newspapers across Canada, giving her a national profile rarely achieved by those who write for community weeklies. The eastern media sat up and took notice. In 1952 a writer for *Chatelaine* magazine, Earl Beattie, published a personality profile, "The Rebel Queen of the Northwest," depicting Margaret as a "frontier hell-raiser who could chew gunpowder and wash it down with whiskey." The legend of "Ma" Murray was born.

Notwithstanding her short-lived, early infatuation with the Social Credit Party, Margaret became highly critical of the Socreds, and their leader W. A. C. Bennett, after the party assumed power in British Columbia in 1952. She routinely denounced Bennett as a "gangster," "crook," and "that old bugger." When he greeted her at a Prince George function with a kiss on the cheek, a surprised CBC reporter asked if she was going soft. "Sonny, you didn't see me kiss him back, did you?" she snapped.

In the summer of 1960, when in their early seventies, George and Margaret retired to Lillooet. Dan came back from California to take over the running of the *Alaska Highway News*. But it wasn't a retirement for his parents in the conventional sense. George and Margaret bought back their old newspaper, the *Bridge River-Lillooet News*, with the intention of breathing new life into what had become a moribund publication. Then disaster struck. George drove his car off the road while returning to Fort St. John to complete the retirement move. He survived the automobile accident but succumbed, on August 19, 1961, to the cancer he had hidden from his family for years. Margaret wrote the obituary and had it published in both papers. "He was our light, our life, and inspiration."

Margaret settled back in Lillooet as planned, ran the paper with Georgie's assistance, and delighted a new generation of readers with her cheeky prose. "Agnes Campbell has gone to her reward," she wrote in a tongue-in-cheek obituary. "She used to be a beautiful singer. I remember her around Vancouver, 40 years ago. She would inflate those bellows of hers, and almost knock the steeple off Mount Pleasant Methodist." Not all of the readers were enchanted by her salty salvoes, but she had no time for her critics. "They don't like me because I call them a bunch of idiots, and they are a bunch of idiots."

Her birthdays became occasions for grand celebrations in Lillooet. On her eightieth she told a Vancouver reporter, "Looking back on my life, I wouldn't change a thing—'ceptin' maybe my underwear." On her eighty-fifth she deplored the lack of Bible education in the schools: "What the hell's the matter with Beatitudes?" At that point, failing health forced her to sell the paper. But she continued to write a local gossip column that she called *Chat out of the Old Bag*. She made frequent guest appearances on the CBC television show, *Front Page Challenge*, received the Order of Canada, was awarded an honorary doctorate from Simon Fraser University, and was the subject of a play by Vancouver humorist Eric Nicol, simply titled, *Ma*.

On her ninetieth birthday, Margaret disclosed to a Vancouver reporter that she had started smoking again. "These days, everybody, even your own children, seem too busy to sit down and have a talk. So you have a cigarette. You can light it, and at least you can see the smoke. It hangs around awhile, and it's company of a sort."

She died in Lillooet on September 25, 1982, at age ninety-five. She was buried in Fort St. John, next to her beloved George. Asked shortly before her death about the secret to a long and happy life, she replied: "I like a little bit of everything, a little bit of loving, a little bit of drinking, and a little bit of working. I watch out pretty careful every day for banana peels. Apart from that, I'm damned if I know why I'm so lucky."

WILL JAMES
Cowboy Artist, Author, and Masquerader
1892–1942

Think of great cowboy novelists and the names Zane Grey and Louis L'Amour invariably spring to mind. Think of great cowboy artists, and the names Charlie Russell and Frederic Remington usually top the list. For Old West aficionados, however, the leader in both genres will always be a masquerader who called himself Will James.

His name is barely remembered today. During the 1920s and 1930s, however, Will James was as well-known as Will Rogers or Tom Mix. He hobnobbed in Hollywood with celebrities such as Bing Crosby and Randolph Scott. Two of his books were made into major motion pictures during his lifetime, and his drawings were praised as masterpieces of western art.

He carefully fashioned an identity for himself that hid his true origins. His real name was Ernest Dufault. He was born in a village east of Montreal and he grew up wanting to be a cowboy when other young boys dreamed of becoming firemen or locomotive engineers. Dufault had never seen a cowboy, but he had seen pictures of them, and he had read French translations of western adventure novels.

His talent was revealed early. At age six, Dufault was drawing—from memory—pencil sketches of farm animals with an accuracy that belied his years and astonished his parents. His younger brother, Auguste, said Dufault's mind "could photograph

Will James, circa 1923. (Courtesy of University of Nevada, Reno, Special Collections, UNRS-2270-01)

any thing, action or movement, and that photograph was the model on which he would draw."

Dufault quit school after Grade 8 and got a job in Montreal as a hotel dishwasher. He saved his pennies, bought a .32-calibre revolver, and spent many hours in an abandoned quarry practicing target shooting and quick draws. At the same time, he constantly pleaded with his parents for permission to go west and become a cowboy.

His parents finally relented in 1907, when Dufault was fifteen. He travelled west on a one-way train ticket with $10, his revolver, and a bag of his mother's cookies. He knew nothing about riding or stock tending, and he couldn't speak English. But he was determined to learn. He served his apprenticeship on ranches in Manitoba and Saskatchewan, learning to ride, rope, break horses, and herd cattle.

By the time he arrived in Alberta in 1909, Dufault had left his French-Canadian identity behind. A real cowboy, he believed, could only be a native of the American West. He told fellow bunkhouse dwellers he was a drifter from Montana, raised by a Metis trapper in the bush country of the Canadian northwest after his parents died. He called himself Will James.

James spent about two years in Alberta. He worked for the Imperial Ranch near Olds, which was later owned by the cattle king Pat Burns, and for a ranch owned by the Long Lake Cattle Company near Botha, east of Stettler. Then he rode straight into trouble. While drinking in a Calgary barroom, he got into an argument with a sheepherder. The man flashed a knife, James drew his gun, and the man was found dead the following morning. James was arrested and briefly jailed before he convinced the judge the herder had been killed in a second brawl later that night. He then fled to the United States. He rode into Montana with a walletful of aliases, including Clint Jackson, Stonewall Jackson, and William Roderick James.

The law caught up with him again in 1914 in Nevada, where James was jailed for cattle rustling. The fifteen-month incarceration did have a positive outcome, however. It gave James time and opportunity to use his wrangling skills to look after the prison horses and exercise his talent with pencil and paper. His artistic output was prodigious. His jailers were so impressed they sent some of his sketches to the local newspaper in Ely, Nevada. The paper reported, "His work is especially good on ranch scenes, and with proper training he would soon be able to do first-class work."

One of the last drawings James did in prison was a three-part sketch that he titled, "The Turning Point." The first depicted James roping a longhorn. The second showed him sitting in jail, thinking. The third showed him at an easel, drawing a picture of a cowboy on horseback. The caption said, "Have had ample time for serious thought, and it is my ambition to follow up on my art."

He did not follow up on his art right away, however. Instead James drifted around Nevada and California, breaking horses and herding cattle. After being kicked in the jaw by a particularly violent horse, James headed to Los Angeles for dental repairs. He paid for his treatment by working as a movie extra and stuntman. When he concluded his affairs in the movie capital, James hit the rodeo circuit as a broncobuster. He made an appearance at the Calgary Stampede and also appeared in such southern Alberta communities as Taber, Hardisty, and Medicine Hat, where he and four rodeo colleagues put on a spectacular street show, riding and trick roping. James and his colleagues also wanted to ride a bucking bronc down the main street of Medicine Hat, but the police put a stop to that.

In May 1918 James enlisted in the United States Army and served as a scout with a mounted infantry unit stationed near San Diego. He was discharged in February 1919. He returned to Nevada and took his first step in the direction of becoming a professional artist when he sold a sketch of a bucking bronc to the organizers of Reno's First Annual Nevada Round-Up. They paid him $50 and used the sketch for the rodeo poster and the cover illustration on the rodeo catalogue.

James quit the rodeo circuit during the summer of 1919 after being thrown from a bucking horse and suffering a concussion. He recuperated at the ranch home of a Reno friend, Fred Conradt, whose fifteen-year-old sister, Alice, became infatuated with the twenty-seven-year-old range rider. With her encouragement, James started taking drawing classes at the California School of Fine Arts in San Francisco, but he soon dropped out because he felt that formal instruction was cramping his style. After selling six full-page drawings to the popular west coast magazine *Sunset*, James decided he had a future as an artist.

He also decided he had a future with Alice Conradt. He courted her by mail and on horseback, wearing a woollen shirt and cowboy chaps. "She didn't see me in a regular suit of clothes till the day before we was married." They married in Reno in July 1920. He was twenty-eight and she was sixteen. They lived initially on a ranch in Kingman, Arizona, where James tended stock while trying unsuccessfully to sell his sketches to New York magazines. His body told him he could no longer be a broncobuster, yet his failure to crack the eastern art market seemed to be putting his future as an artist in doubt.

Troubled by their lack of income, Alice suggested that James broaden his scope by combining his illustrating abilities with a gift for storytelling he had revealed during his convalescence. If he could write those stories down, she said, he might have more success. Her instincts proved correct. In the fall of 1922, James sold an illustrated short story, "Bucking Horses and Bucking-Horse Riders," to *Scribner's Magazine* for $300. This was the eastern breakthrough he had been seeking. Seven stories later, he had enough material for a book. It was titled *Cowboys North and South* and was published in 1924 by Charles Scribner's Sons, owners of the magazine that gave him his first break. The *New York Herald Tribune* described it as "a gorgeous and almost unbelievable book" with illustrations as "brilliant and as filled with violent action as an exploding dynamite stick." *The New York Times* said that James stood apart from "synthetic manufacturers of oat operas like the moon competing against a streetlight."

Here, for the first time it seemed, was the authentic voice of the American cowboy. James wrote in a kind of stylized cowboy vernacular, and his editors wisely opted not to change it. "Good English is fine," he said in the preface of his first book, "but it don't git there." In manufactured western lingo, James wrote not about saloon brawls and gunfights—standard fodder for Wild West novels in those days—but about the look of the rangeland in the early morning, the smell of hot biscuits in the pan, and the experience of sitting astride a "good-feeling" pony.

James's second collection of stories, *The Drifting Cowboy*, consolidated his reputation as an accomplished and popular writer of illustrated westerns. His third book, an illustrated children's novel titled *Smoky the Cowhorse*, won the American Library Association's 1927 John Newbery Medal for outstanding children's literature, was translated into six languages, reprinted nine times in four months, and used as the basis for three Hollywood movies. *The New York Times* called it "the *Black Beauty* of the cow country."

With the proceeds from *Smoky*, James put a down payment on an 3,238-hectare ranch called the Rocking R, located in the foothills of the Pryor Mountains, south of Billings, Montana. Here he wanted to preserve the image of the traditional cowboy culture he had dreamed about in Quebec. He wanted to see from his windows a rugged western landscape like the one he described in his novels—a vast, open range dotted with cattle and ponies, not with fences and tractors. "I want to see a rider once in a while," he told his publisher, "and not a farmer hauling a load of grain—you savvy what I mean?" Scribner's savvied that James needed to be in some kind of frontier setting to sustain his artistic vision at a time when cowboys were no longer riding the range. But this was going to be expensive, and James didn't yet have the kind of money needed to maintain a large spread. To earn it he would have to sell many more books.

James committed himself to a gruelling schedule to pay for his new ranch, producing a book a year to keep the money flowing. In 1930 he published a largely fictionalized autobiography, *Lone Cowboy: My Life Story*, which became almost as successful as *Smoky*. It was chosen as a Book of the Month selection in 1931 and made into a movie in 1934. In it James wrote that he was born on a wagon train travelling from Texas to Alberta, where his American parents hoped to establish a cattle business. His birth occurred beside a creek in central Montana, and James observed with a certain touch of irony, "If I'd been born a month later, I'd been a Canadian." He wrote that his California-born mother died of the flu when he was one year old, and that a longhorn fatally gored his Texas-born father when James was four. He was raised after that by a French-speaking trapper named Jean Beaupre who was on the run from the law in Canada for crimes he never spoke about.

James worked on the "autobiography" with Alice, who received no publication credit for her contribution and was mentioned only in passing as the unnamed "girl I married." By the time it was published, James was in the throes of alcoholism due to the pressure of having to produce thousands of words and hundreds of illustrations, and because of his inability to handle the demands of instant fame. James had for years been a binge drinker, like many cowboys whose work required that they go for long periods without a drink. However, when his career as a writer and illustrator took off, James never worked without a full tumbler of whisky sitting on his desk next to his bag of Bull Durham cigarette tobacco. He told Alice he needed the booze to help his concentration, and for a while she believed him.

The couple moved to Hollywood in 1931 after 20th Century Fox bought the movie rights to *Smoky*. James appeared briefly as himself in the first version of the film, released in 1933. With his handsome, hawk-faced profile, his thick, dark hair and smouldering brown eyes, he was a natural for the movies. He was supposed to open the film with the words, "Me, I prefer horses," and then periodically embroider the storyline with what *The New York Times* called "human little asides on the psychology of horses." However, James slurred his words so badly that the voice of another actor had to be dubbed in. The star of the film, Victor Jory, later recalled that James was always so drunk on the set that he would start a conversation, nod off in mid-sentence, later regain consciousness, and then begin again on a totally different topic.

Some of his drunken exploits were colourful, almost amusing. A favourite stunt of James was to ride his pony into a hotel lobby and shoot out the chandeliers. He showed his dislike of cities by pitching his tent and building campfires on hotel roofs, and he told reporters he always wore his boots and spurs to bed to keep from sliding off. But the incidents grew uglier as his alcoholism progressed. James became violently abusive to Alice, and he frequently cheated on her.

In 1934 James made his only trip back to the province of his birth when he travelled to Montreal—without Alice's knowledge—to make sure his mother destroyed every letter and photograph he had ever sent her. If his mother ever wrote letters back to him, Alice never saw them. The following year, James lost the Montana ranch due to unpaid bills. Alice gave up on the marriage, determined to save herself, at least. She returned to Nevada to live with a sister. James drifted back and forth from Hollywood to Billings, where he lived with a friend who accidentally discovered the Canadian's true identity from letters written to James by his brother, Auguste. James swore the friend to secrecy, explaining that not even Alice knew about his Quebec origins. The friend agreed, and the masquerader's secret remained safe.

He carried his secret to the grave. James died on September 3, 1942, from cirrhosis of the liver and kidney failure, at age fifty. His ashes were scattered from an airplane over the Montana ranchlands where he had become what he lied about: a true American cowboy. In what seemed like a final stroke of irony, James left his estate to one Ernest Dufault of Montreal, Canada. It was only when she contested the will that Alice learned from Auguste who her ex-husband really was.

James was quickly forgotten after his death. His books disappeared from the shelves—though new film adaptations of his novels continued to appear—and his sketches disappeared into private collections. He might well have remained in obscurity after that had not a Nevada writer named Anthony Amaral emerged in 1967 with a well-researched biography, *Will James: The Gilt-Edged Cowboy*, which finally revealed the true identity of the storekeeper's son from Quebec who reinvented himself as an icon of the American West. The book was written with the help of Alice, who at last received due credit for her role in documenting the story of her talented and troubled ex-husband.

The Amaral biography sparked a resurgence of interest in the life and work of Will James. More biographies followed, including Jim Bramblett's *Ride for the High Points: The Real Story of Will James*, and William Gardner Bell's *Will James: The Life and Works of a Lone Cowboy*, both published in 1987. The Yellowstone Art Museum in Billings began to assemble what is now the largest collection of James's art in North America. A Will James Society was established in Billings, with about six hundred members across North America, to keep his memory alive and donate reprints of his books to rural libraries and schools. A Montana publisher, Mountain Press of Missoula, was commissioned to do the reprints. First editions of the books, which had sold originally for three dollars a copy, began fetching up to $1,000 apiece.

Canada, too, saw a resurgence of interest in the life and work of its fabled expatriate son. Jacques Godbout's 1988 National Film Board documentary, *Alias Will James*, reasserted the identity that Dufault had spent a lifetime denying. Singer Ian Tyson wrote in his 1994 autobiography, *I Never Sold My Saddle*, that James was a major influence on his songwriting: "If whiskey was his mistress, his true love was the West." A Medicine Hat historian, Allan Jensen, organized the first Canadian conference of the Will James Society in his hometown in October 2007. And Millarville, Alberta, author Wendy Dudley donated copies of all twenty-four of his published books to her local community library on behalf of the society in October 2008. "This is where it started for him," she said. "A lot of his work came out of southern Alberta and Saskatchewan." In a way, Will James had finally come home.

TOMMY DOUGLAS
Political Leader
1904–1986

The television program was a one-hour documentary produced as part of a CBC series called *The Greatest Canadian*.
It began with a scene at a drive-in movie theatre. On the
screen, the actor James Dean was emoting. "You're tearing me
apart," he wailed as his parents argued over what they thought
best for their rebellious son. Watching the movie from a red con-
vertible was CBC talk-show host George Stroumboulopoulos,
casually dressed in a dark shirt with rolled-up sleeves.

"1950s' Hollywood was a happening time," intoned Stroumboulopoulos in characteristic deejay vernacular. "And James
Dean was a happening dude. He made a big impression playing
a rebel without a cause."

"But is that really what a rebel looks like?" asked Stroumboulopoulos, nodding toward the drive-in screen. "James Dean, after
all, was just an actor. And while he was faking it out on the big
screen, we had a real rebel up here in Canada. He wasn't playing
a part. He was living it. His name was Tommy Douglas, and he
fought for a better Canada, one where nobody got left behind."

"Tommy Douglas is best known as the man who gave us
medicare," continued Stroumboulopoulos. "But he left us a legacy far larger than that."

Part of that legacy is something many historians often mention only in passing as they focus on the significant achievement

Tommy Douglas. (Saskatchewan Archives Board, R-WS13228.1)

of Douglas bringing universal health care to Canada.

The story goes that long after he had retired from public life, Douglas was flying over Saskatchewan one night with fellow political leader Roy Romanow. "What would you consider your greatest political accomplishment?" asked Romanow.

Douglas replied, "I expect you will think that I will say medicare, and there's no question that I'm enormously proud of that. But a lot of other people besides me had a big hand in that."

It was a clear summer evening and the small charter plane was flying between Lloydminster and Regina. As they peered out the window, Romanow and Douglas could see a pattern of twinkling lights, like jewels on a black canvas, where darkness had once stretched endlessly. "The thing I am most proud that I did you can see in all the lights down there," said Douglas. He was referring to a provincial program, started by his government in 1950, which had brought power to 50,000 Saskatchewan farms over a period of ten years.

Rural electrification had become a priority for Douglas during his first term in office as Saskatchewan premier, starting in 1944. Formerly a Baptist preacher in Weyburn, Saskatchewan, this Scottish-born clergyman entered politics reluctantly at age twenty-nine in 1934, when members of his congregation urged him to run provincially as a member of the newly formed Farmer-Labour Party to fight for the unemployed during the depths of the Great Depression.

Douglas lost the 1934 race and was all set to return to his church work. But his congregants continued to insist there was no other person in the region capable of representing them effectively. And so he ran federally in 1935 as a member of the socialist Co-operative Commonwealth Federation (CCF) Party. This time he was victorious.

Douglas served two terms as the Member of Parliament for Weyburn. But as a representative of the tiny third party in the House of Commons, he left virtually no impression on what one Ottawa journalist called "the rhinoceros skin of government." The CCF's provincial Saskatchewan wing, on the other hand, seemed to offer more possibilities for positive change. Douglas won the leadership of the provincial party in 1942 while still serving as an MP, and he resigned his Ottawa seat before leading the CCF to victory in the 1944 election. It was North America's first social democratic government—"a beachhead of socialism on a continent of capitalism," as Douglas called it—and it came with a broad economic reform plan for postwar Saskatchewan.

During its first sixteen months in office, the Douglas government passed 192 bills aimed at improving the province's roads, health, welfare, and education services. Additionally, the government introduced North America's first government auto insurance plan, integrated rural and municipal telephone networks into a single system, introduced Canada's first universal hospital insurance program, and launched a provincial bus company.

But Douglas realized that continually improving services without raising the economic base to pay for them would be folly. So when the Saskatchewan voters renewed his government's mandate in 1948, he set out to increase the productivity of the province. "This meant generating more power," he told journalist Chris Higginbotham. "Every time we got power on the farms, we were giving the farmer another hired man and giving his wife a hired girl. This would increase agricultural productivity, particularly for dairy and poultry farmers and mixed farmers."

Many people, including members of Douglas's own party, were deeply skeptical about the electrification program. Potential customers were scattered across great distances, which meant the program would service only one farm per 1.6 kilometres of power line. But Douglas was not about to let anything stand in his way. When unionized electrical workers threatened to stall implementation of the program because of a dispute over wages, Douglas expressed his determination to press ahead. "It would be an act of complete irresponsibility for us to stand idly by and permit a strike," he said.

Rural electrification was a tough sell in some places. Farmers greeted the Saskatchewan Power Corporation workers with guns and threats when they showed up to install power poles. The farmers had never used electrical appliances before and were simply afraid of electricity. But the company hired a home economist, Lillian McConnell, to show rural homemakers how to use the new electrical gadgets, and the women quickly embraced the new technology. "The first thing homemakers wanted was an iron," said McConnell, who went by the pseudonym "Penny Powers." "The second thing was a refrigerator."

Because of the effectiveness of the "Penny Powers" publicity campaign, most of the electricity consumed initially in farming districts was for domestic purposes. However, the farmers were soon won over when they discovered that electricity could power their pumps, lights, milk coolers, water heaters, and other machines. The result, as Douglas noted afterward, was increased productivity and efficiency. "When we took office we were getting a little over $1.5 million from resources," he said. "This eventually increased to about $25 million. This was revenue we were able to spend on welfare programs."

When rural electrification began contributing to an improved standard of living in rural Saskatchewan, Douglas set out to introduce the universal health care program for which he is mainly remembered. It, too, was a tough sell. Doctors opposed it and went on strike for three weeks to stop the bill from being enacted into law. By that time, in 1962, Douglas had left provincial politics and returned to the federal scene as leader of the newly created New Democratic Party (NDP). But his successor as premier, Woodrow Lloyd, was as determined as Douglas had been to make medicare a reality. With the help of a British mediator, Lloyd struck a deal with the doctors and Douglas's dream was realized. Six years later, in 1968, the Saskatchewan plan was adopted as a model for the federal medicare program that would make Canada the envy of the world.

Douglas got off to a bad start as first leader of the NDP. He failed to win a Regina seat in the 1962 federal election—mainly because of residual doctor anger over the medicare bill—and had to move to British Columbia to find a riding where he could run in a by-election. He won a seat in Burnaby-Coquitlam later in 1962 but lost the redistributed seat of Burnaby-Seymour in the federal election of 1968. He then moved to Vancouver Island, where he won a by-election in 1969 representing Nanaimo-Cowichan-The Islands, and he retained that riding through two federal elections before retiring from politics in 1979 at age seventy-four.

He wasn't in the best of health when he retired. In 1975 Douglas was rushed from the House of Commons on a stretcher after he collapsed with a bleeding ulcer while making a speech opposing the Liberals' energy policies. In 1981 he was diagnosed with inoperable cancer. He died five years later at age eighty-one and was remembered by NDP leader Ed Broadbent as "a great man, a truly rare individual who changed the course of history."

The CBC Television series, *The Greatest Canadian*, was broadcast in 2004. After six months of polling by e-mail, letter, telephone, and website, CBC revealed the bottom forty of the top fifty "greatest" choices, listed in order of popularity. The remaining ten were revealed in alphabetical order so as not—the network said—to unduly influence the final vote.

The second round of viewer voting was conducted over a six-week period while documentary profiles of the top ten were

presented on TV. Such Canadian celebrities as Stroumboulopoulos, Mary Walsh, Rex Murphy, and Paul Gross championed
the finalists. Aside from Douglas, the finalists included former
prime ministers John A. Macdonald, Lester Pearson and Pierre
Trudeau, as well as hockey celebrities Wayne Gretzky and Don
Cherry, cancer crusader Terry Fox, environmentalist David
Suzuki, inventor Alexander Graham Bell, and Sir Frederick
Banting, the co-discoverer of insulin. According to the network,
more than one million viewers cast votes in the contest.

When Douglas was named the winner of the television
poll, his advocate, George Stroumboulopoulos, observed there
was no monument in Ottawa dedicated to the memory of this
Saskatchewan rebel who "came in on a Prairie wind with a
vision of a better, brighter country." But Douglas had an answer
for that. "Let us raise monuments all over Canada," he once said.
"Monuments in the form of schools and hospitals and libraries. These are monuments of which we can be proud. These are
monuments that in the days to come our children will see. And
they will bless us and thank us for those kinds of monuments."

GLADYS ARNOLD
War Correspondent
1905–2002

When one thinks of Canadian correspondents in the Second World War, the names Ross Munro, Matthew Halton, and Greg Clark spring immediately to mind. One doesn't usually think of Gladys Arnold because the big wartime events such as the London Blitz and the D-Day landings at Normandy were invariably covered by men. Yet Arnold, too, deserves a place in the Canadian News Hall of Fame because not only was she the sole accredited Canadian journalist writing from Paris during the first months of the Second World War but she was also—notwithstanding severe limitations imposed by her chauvinistic Canadian editors and French government staff—as adept a reporter as any of her male colleagues.

Saskatchewan-born Arnold had been working as a wire-service correspondent in Europe for four years when the war began. Five years before that, in 1930, she left a teaching post in rural Saskatchewan to become a secretary at the Regina *Leader-Post*. She wasn't particularly interested in secretarial work but was drawn to journalism. The *Leader-Post* job gave her a foot in the door. She quickly graduated from taking dictation to writing a column about women's issues, with occasional ventures into covering such events as the Regina Riot of 1935, which involved striking residents of federal unemployment relief camps.

Gladys Arnold in Paris, 1938. (University of Regina Archives and Special Collections, file 711, box 32, 98-54)

She was twenty-nine years old when she decided, in 1935, to spend a year in Europe. She later said she wanted to check out all the "isms": fascism, socialism, and communism. After seeing the misery the Great Depression was causing in Saskatchewan, she wanted to know if any of these political movements could provide answers to the question of why more than a million Canadians were unable to find work. But her editor at the *Leader-Post*, D. B. MacRae, told her it wasn't appropriate for "a Canadian girl" to be writing on such topics and that most readers wanted articles about "love, food, the movies, clothes and family affairs." So for $10 per weekly column Arnold spent her first months in London writing about such soft subjects as the reading habits of the English, the appeal of cheese shops, and the latest fashion designs from the House of Schiaparelli.

In early 1936, Arnold moved to Paris, where she heard that the Canadian Press (CP) wire service didn't have a correspondent. She couldn't speak French but was a quick learner and soon became proficient in the language. For three months she submitted to CP's Toronto office a weekly article "with a Canadian angle" that the wire service routinely distributed to its member newspapers. She received no payment for the articles, however, nor any commitment from CP to take her on as a paid contributor. Finally, she wrote to CP serving notice that unless she received a job offer soon, she would stop contributing to the wire service. She soon received a letter from CP editor Gillis Purcell. "You're our Paris correspondent," he wrote. "We're paying you $15 a week."

By that time, in May 1936, Arnold had realized that a year wasn't long enough to learn about the "isms" she had come to study, and so she decided to extend her stay indefinitely. Over the next three years, she reported from several European countries, including Germany, Spain, Italy, Hungary, and Czechoslovakia, as well as France. She sent stories home to the *Leader-Post* in addition to filing her regular dispatches to CP. After taking a first-hand look at how socialism, fascism, and communism functioned in the different countries, Arnold eventually concluded that none offered a better way forward than the Canadian democratic system when it came to dealing with the larger socio-political and economic issues of the day.

While most of her stories were the kinds of feel-good pieces for a Canadian readership that her CP editors required, Arnold occasionally filed harder-edged articles designed to inform if not to alarm. Thus in October 1936, she observed that Canadian women in Italy were "tense under fascist rule." Eighteen months later, it was France's turn to feel tense, when the Nazis took over Austria. Five months after that, in September 1938, Arnold wrote about how "close we came to destruction; how near we were to the brink" when Britain's Neville Chamberlain and French Prime Minister Édouard Daladier met in Munich with Adolph Hitler and Benito Mussolini to conclude the controversial "peace in our time" agreement on the future of Czechoslovakia.

Arnold became convinced war was imminent at the end of 1938 when she visited Germany and saw the internment camps and the factories producing munitions. She became even more convinced when she came across a wall map—that she managed to smuggle out of Germany—showing a future "Greater Germany" that encompassed most of Europe. But she didn't think war was going to happen right away, so in August 1939 she took a trip back to Canada to visit her parents in Victoria and friends in Saskatchewan. "I had been homesick for the sight of the big night sky and the golden haze of windborne chaff, and for the smell of wheat baking in the sun."

When Canada entered the Second World War in September 1939, Arnold decided she had to return to work in Paris. "We can't be responsible for you if you go back," Gillis Purcell warned. But Arnold couldn't imagine staying home while the conflict between fascism and democracy played out on the battlefield. "It would be like leaving a theatre just after the curtain rises." Purcell knew she was not about to change her mind so he gave Arnold a $5-a-week raise and wished her well.

When she got back to Paris, by passenger ship from New York and by train from Bordeaux, Arnold received a reminder from her CP bosses about her mandate: "Stick to human interest stories....The boys in the London bureau will look after political and military stuff." If she was offended by their patronizing attitude, she didn't say so.

Although she received wartime accreditation from the French information ministry, Arnold was not allowed to attend the daily briefings at the war office. Nor was she given permission to see the Maginot Line, the fortification France built along its northeastern borders after the First World War as a defence against future German invasion. These constraints, she discovered, were imposed not because she was female but because she was Canadian. "Canada figured far down on the list of important countries in the eyes of those doing the news briefings," she wrote in her 1987 memoir, *One Woman's War*. "The correspondents of the British and American press were the ones that counted."

Though restricted in her reporting to matters peripheral to the military activities, Arnold found plenty to write about during the so-called phony war: a period of comparative inaction between the German invasion of Poland in September 1939 and the invasion of Scandinavia in April 1940. She wrote about the food supply stations set up across France to feed millions of mobilized French soldiers, and about the hundreds of thousands of women recruited to work on farms and in factories while the men were at the front. She described the pride the women had in their work when she visited an armament factory and saw employees putting in extra hours to achieve a mirror-like shine on artillery shells. When their supervisor said the extra effort could be better spent on increasing productivity, the women replied: "But these are *French* shells. No German can make a shell that looks like ours."

In May 1940 the Germans launched a blitzkrieg (lightning war) against Belgium and the Netherlands. Arnold saw bullet-ridden refugee trains pouring into Paris with dead and wounded passengers aboard. "Blood was spattered everywhere," she wrote in her memoir. "I rushed to a washroom and retched. It was the first and only time I vomited. Such scenes were to become familiar." After filing her story to CP, she went to the Red Cross office in Paris to offer her services as a volunteer.

On June 10, 1940, Arnold learned from an American colleague that the Germans had smashed through the Maginot Line to enter northern France and would invade Paris in the next few days. She also learned that the French government had packed up and moved from Paris to Tours. To get her articles to CP she, too, had to move to Tours, because her stories had to be censored by government staff before they could be dispatched to Toronto. On June 12, two days before the Germans arrived, she and two friends fled Paris in an old two-seater Ford. "I was leaving not of my own free will; I was being pushed out," she wrote. "Pushed out by the Germans. It made me furious but I was also broken-hearted."

From Tours, Arnold followed the French government censorship staff south to Bordeaux where—in the absence of Canadian consular officials—she tried to get press credentials from the American consulate for front-line coverage as a freelancer for U.S. newspapers. When that application was turned down, she asked the British embassy to be accredited as a freelancer for the British papers. That bid was also unsuccessful. "I was told flatly that I could not remain in France. Ships were leaving for England, and I was told I had better get on one."

Back in London, Arnold's fluent French helped her secure the first Canadian interview with General Charles de Gaulle, the leader of the Free French resistance forces in Britain. He captivated her, and she quickly became a convert to the Free French cause. When she asked if there might be a place for her in de Gaulle's movement, he said she could help him best by writing about his efforts to build an army that would be "present at the liberation of our country." Arnold readily agreed. She had been a committed pacifist before moving to Europe but had since become convinced that it was "better to die fighting than to allow the world to become subject to the fascist terror."

In August 1940 CP's London bureau chief, Sam Robertson, assigned Arnold to accompany a shipload of British children en route to Canada for safety while their parents worked back home for the war effort. She didn't want to leave, "it seemed like running away a second time," but she had no choice. She asked about returning to London after she had done some follow-up stories on the British children in Canada. But that door was firmly closed, she said, after Robertson was killed in a torpedo attack off the west coast of Ireland. Arnold was assigned to CP's Ottawa bureau where she wrote feature stories about the Canadian war effort and covered the parliamentary committee on veterans' affairs.

Arnold found the Ottawa job boring after the excitement of London and Paris. She left CP in 1941 to become a spokesperson for the Free French movement in Canada. This proved to be a challenge because the Canadian government still supported Marshal Henri Pétain's Vichy regime even after it became clear it was nothing more than a puppet government installed by the Nazis. But Arnold was passionate about the cause and continued to work for the French after the war, serving as director of information at the French embassy in Ottawa until her retirement in 1971. She had considered moving back to Paris after the war because she loved living there before the occupation.

But ultimately she decided, "What I had to do must be done in Canada. I wanted to help other English-speaking Canadians share my experience."

She lived quietly in Regina after retirement until publication of her 1987 memoir put her in the media spotlight. After that came a television documentary about her life as a war correspondent, *Eyewitness to War*, and a featured spot in the CBC Television series, *Canada: A People's History*. To those who said her wartime correspondent work had been courageous, Arnold responded that what she did was nothing out of the ordinary. "I simply told the story."

She died in Regina a few days short of her ninety-seventh birthday. When she was in her early twenties, Arnold had made a pledge to herself to "someday see every country in the world [and] get everything out of every day." At the end of her life, she said she had fulfilled that dream.

JAMES H. GRAY
Social Historian
1906–1998

Though he called himself "the boy from Winnipeg" in his best-selling memoir of that name, renowned prairie historian James H. Gray was, in fact, a boy from Whitemouth, Manitoba. He was born in that rural municipality on August 31, 1906, and lived there for five years when his father worked as a timekeeper with the National Transcontinental Railway. And while he spent the rest of his life in the urban surroundings of Winnipeg, Ottawa, and Calgary, pursuing a career as journalist and author, Gray never forgot what it was like for a person to carve a living out of tough prairie soil.

His abiding memory of Whitemouth, Gray recalled in *The Boy from Winnipeg*, was "etched by terror." He and his younger brother were helping their mother pick berries along the tracks near their railway-siding home when a black bear with cub emerged from the bush thirty metres ahead of them. His mother screamed, grabbed the two boys, and fled in panic up the path toward their home. "The bear, fortunately, chose to ignore us," wrote Gray, "but for the next several weeks our fear of bears kept us all very close to our front yard."

The family moved to Winnipeg in 1911 when Gray's father, Harry, landed a timekeeping job at the Canadian Northern Railway's Transcona locomotive shops. But that job didn't last very long because Harry had a recurring problem with alcohol.

James H. Gray. Publicity photo, circa 1955. (Matthews Photo Lab photo, courtesy of Patricia and Bill Fennell)

It wasn't until Prohibition closed the bars in 1916 that Harry was able to keep a job for longer than a few months. He then got a low-paying clerical job at city hall that lasted for five years. However, when the hotels reopened their bars for beer sales, the temptation to drink again proved too strong for Harry. He managed to hide his problem from his city-hall bosses for a few months but was eventually fired for fuelling his addiction by stealing from the petty cash.

Because his father could not be relied upon to support the family, Gray dropped out of school at age sixteen to work as a messenger at the Winnipeg Grain Exchange. By the time he was in his mid-twenties he was earning good money as a book-keeper. Then came the Depression and a year on unemployment relief, after which Gray became a freelance writer. Through sheer persistence he landed a full-time reporting job at the *Winnipeg Free Press* where he worked for twelve years, including a year as parliamentary correspondent in Ottawa.

In 1947 Gray was fired by the *Free Press* for refusing to write articles from Ottawa supporting the paper's editorial opposition to federal government subsidies for wheat farmers from the Prairies. He moved to Calgary, became editor of the *Farm and Ranch Review* monthly, and subsequently did a twice-weekly talk show on radio station CFCN that he called, *I'd Rather Be a Farmer*. The program name was not a gimmick. At the time, Gray was living on an acreage on the western outskirts of Calgary and telling friends that he was "fascinated by everything about production from the soil." Though he never made any serious attempt to grow anything aside from oats for his horses, Gray always talked about "the farm" as if it were a place where he eventually planned to have chickens and cows as well as pasture for the horses.

During his time with the *Farm and Ranch Review*, Gray changed from objective reporter to what he called an "inflamed zealot—a partisan polemicist in the intellectual controversies that enveloped my subject." As he described it in his autobiographical book *Troublemaker!: A Fighting Journalist's Personal Record of the Two Booming Decades that Followed The Winter Years*, Gray became a rabble-rousing commentator "caught up in the currents that were changing the face of western Canada, and became a partisan shouter against the tide."

Gray published his first book, *The Winter Years*, in 1966 when he was sixty years old. A chronicle of the Depression on the Prairies, it was a national bestseller and favourably reviewed in newspapers across Canada. But Gray was stung by one review that said he did a poor job of conveying the impact of the Depression on the rural population. "Gray has told the story as a city man," Barry Broadfoot wrote in the *Vancouver Sun*. "Some day, some farmer will sit down and tell his story." This upset Gray because, in fact, he had included the story of the rural population in the 40,000 words he had to cut from the manuscript during the editing process. He rectified that omission in his next book, *Men Against the Desert*, which was all about the farmers who had battled dust-bowl conditions during the 1930s, working in tandem with agricultural scientists to control soil erosion in the area known as the Palliser Triangle—a great swath of semi-arid farmland stretching eastward from Calgary to Morden, Manitoba, and southward from Saskatoon to the Canada-U.S. border. For years afterward, Gray maintained that *Men Against the Desert* was "not only my best book but probably one of the most important books ever written about Canada," though its sales were modest compared to some of his other eleven titles.

During the 1970s, the prolific Gray published six best-selling books of popular history—an achievement matched only in Canada by Pierre Berton with his classic books about the Klondike and the building of the Canadian Pacific Railway—documenting aspects of our heritage never covered before by chroniclers of the post-settlement era in western Canada. The most successful of these was *Red Lights on the Prairies*, which told the story of prostitution in the frontier West. In it Gray quipped that if other historians were to be believed, only "monks, eunuchs and vestal virgins" had settled the West. When published in the United States in 1973, *Red Lights* was placed on the paperback racks next to *The Happy Hooker*, Xaviera Hollander's racy memoir of her life as a New York call girl. This greatly bothered Gray, who had written what he considered a serious sociological study of prostitution. He resented being associated with what he called the "garbage end of the publishing trade." But he was somewhat mollified when the American distributor put 350,000 copies of *Red Lights* on sale in drugstores and corner groceries.

Although Pierre Berton had a higher national profile than Gray because of his regular appearances on such popular television shows as CBC's *Front Page Challenge*, Gray was seen by eastern media commentators as being equally significant in terms of his efforts to show that the early Canadian West—while tamer than the American frontier—had a colour and flavour all its own. Doug Fisher, writing in the *Toronto Sun* after the publication of *Troublemaker!* in 1978, characterized Gray as a "distinctive yet well-matched complement to the better known Pierre Berton in the East. Strong personalities and popular historians, each is a great exponent of what I sense is Canada."

Under the circumstances, it seemed only fitting that when the second Pierre Berton Award for "distinguished achievements in popularizing Canadian history" was presented in 1995, it went to James H. Gray. Berton, who agreed to have his name attached to the award after being declared the first winner in 1994, wrote in a short letter of congratulations to Gray that he could not think of a more worthy recipient.

Aside from the Berton award, Gray earned three honorary doctorates, the Order of Canada, and the honour of being appointed adjunct professor of history at the University of Calgary. All told, he sold more than 400,000 copies of his twelve lively and engaging popular histories. Not bad for a public-school dropout, as Gray used to say.

When Gray died, in November 1998 at age ninety-two, his contributions to popular history were recognized in newspapers and magazines from coast to coast. "He was unquestionably the best writer of history in Western Canada that we ever produced," wrote Ted Byfield in a full-page tribute in the *National Post*. "The whole of the Canadian West is the beneficiary." As if to echo that sentiment, the *Literary Review of Canada* in November 2005 chose *Red Lights on the Prairies* as one of the one hundred most important books in Canadian literary history. Not bad for a boy from Whitemouth, Manitoba, I would say.

CLYDE GILMOUR
Broadcaster
1912–1997

For more than forty years, Clyde Gilmour had the best-known and most mimicked hello—"huh-LO"—in Canadian broadcasting. As the host of CBC Radio's popular *Gilmour's Albums*, he used that trademark greeting—which seems to have anticipated Jerry Seinfeld's famous "hell-OOO" routine of later years—to forge a personal connection with the half million listeners who tuned in every Saturday and Sunday to hear what kinds of classical arias, train whistles, novelty songs, animal sounds, and comedy routines Gilmour had pulled from his 10,000-plus record collection that week.

He wasn't a trained broadcaster, but Gilmour knew what *not* to do on the air from having listened as a child to any number of phony-sounding announcers on local radio in Medicine Hat. He recalled being constantly exasperated by disc jockeys with fake American accents who addressed their between-song remarks to "all you folks out there." "Dammit," Gilmour would mutter to himself. "Just talk to *me*. I'm the only one here."

The Calgary-born son of a CPR clerk, Gilmour lived in the railway town of Medicine Hat from age nine to twenty-four. His mother sang mezzo-soprano in local amateur musicals, and his father did operatic burlesques as a joke. The young Gilmour developed his eclectic musical tastes listening to the opera, vaudeville, and novelty-song 78s his parents brought home to play on the family's windup RCA Victrola gramophone. "It seemed natural to me to listen to Caruso singing an operatic aria or an Italian song, John McCormack doing a Handel aria or an Irish ballad, and then go on and play comedy records, pops and jazz."

After finishing high school, Gilmour wanted to take law at the University of Alberta, but the Depression wiped out his father's savings, making university education unattainable. Gilmour compensated by educating himself through reading, mostly from the encyclopedias in his local library. He worked as a junior clerk with the Maple Leaf Milling Company in Medicine Hat, and then freelanced for the *Calgary Herald* as the paper's Medicine Hat stringer and local circulation agent. The newspaper work paid him just $7 a week, while the mill had been paying him $15 weekly. But he didn't mind the drop in salary. "By that time I knew I didn't want to stay in the business world, and newspaper work appealed to me. It was terrific experience. I was only 19 and doing every kind of reporting there was: covering city hall meetings, sports events, and even murders once in a while."

After two years as a *Herald* stringer, Gilmour landed a full-time job at the *Medicine Hat News*, earning $20 a week as a general reporter. To earn added experience, he moonlighted as an unpaid entertainment reviewer for the *News*. He then applied to the *Herald* for a full-time job. He travelled to Calgary on the train, brought along some of his *News* clippings, and checked into a downtown hotel while awaiting his 3:00 pm appointment with the *Herald*'s managing editor. His watch malfunctioned, however, and he missed the appointment by forty-five minutes. As a result, Gilmour never got the *Herald* job. The experience taught him a valuable lesson. He vowed never to be caught in a similar situation again. "Since then I've been a punctuality freak," he said afterward. "I always wear two watches now because I like a *second* opinion."

In 1936, at age twenty-four, Gilmour spent a summer working as an unpaid intern at the *Edmonton Journal*. He was hired on as a full-time staffer at the end of the summer and remained there until 1942, when he joined the Royal Canadian Navy as a press officer. At war's end, he moved to Vancouver, working first as an entertainment columnist with the *Province* and then as a movie critic with the *Sun*. At the same time, he did his first broadcasting as a movie reviewer on CBC Radio's *Critically Speaking*.

The big disappointment of Gilmour's early journalistic career occurred in 1951, a few years after joining the *Vancouver Sun*, when a lunch interview he had arranged in Hollywood with the young Marilyn Monroe was cancelled by *Sun* managing editor Hal Straight. "Forget the lunch," Straight said. "Go to San Francisco and cover the return of General MacArthur. Cover it like a movie." Douglas MacArthur's return to the United States from Korea was expected to draw huge outpourings of public support for the popular army general and condemnations of President Harry Truman for firing him. MacArthur had angered Truman by publicly calling for an extension of the Korean War to China, and Truman had responded by relieving MacArthur of his post as commander of the United Nations forces. MacArthur came home as a war hero, but not to Gilmour, who couldn't get the disappointment of the cancelled Monroe lunch out of his mind. He later said that MacArthur must have wondered about this young reporter at the airport who just stared at him with "such a fixed state of malevolence."

Back in Vancouver, while still working at the *Sun*, Gilmour took his revenge on editor Straight by lampooning the paper's practice of routinely mentioning the wealthy and the prominent in its social notes columns—just because they had been seen out on the town attending black-tie cocktail parties. Gilmour invented an alter ego named "Kosmos Kagool," created a tongue-in-cheek identity for him as a "Greek diplomat, freelance nuclear physicist, and oxyacetylene welder," and got him listed in the Vancouver telephone directory. With the help of a fellow conspirator on the *Sun*'s copy desk, Gilmour then saw to it that his alter ego's name was mentioned in every society column. At the end of each list of cocktail party guests, there would appear, "Also attending was Kosmos Kagool." Gilmour enjoyed his little joke so much that he took his alter ego to Toronto in 1954 when he was hired as movie critic by the *Telegram*. He listed Kagool in the Toronto phone book and frequently conned *The Globe and Mail's* gossip columnist, Zena Cherry, into mentioning Kagool as a regular attendee at society events around town.

Having an alter ego—Gilmour created several for himself over the years—gave him the freedom to say the kinds of things people say nowadays when they cloak themselves in anonymity and contribute to Internet chat sites. Thus, whenever he wanted to phone and complain about "shoddy" service at a restaurant, Gilmour affected an upper-class British accent and identified himself as "Colonel O. B. Blassingame." Whenever he wanted not to be disturbed at home, he answered his private phone in an eastern European accent, said he was the electrician, and "dat Mr. Glimrope" was out of the house. His colleagues at the *Telegram*, and later at the *Toronto Star* cherished as souvenirs the personal notes he sent them, written in longhand, filled with anecdotes and amusing commentary, and signed either by Kagool or by Ed Schnarff, another of the pseudonyms Gilmour adopted with his W. C. Fields–style affection for unusual names. "Schnarff" was his catchall hypothetical name for people whose real names he couldn't remember. His other pseudonyms were actual names that Gilmour found in newspaper stories and telephone books. To preserve the names for his own use and enjoyment, he founded what he called the Society for the Verification and Enjoyment of Fascinating Names of Actual Persons, and listed the names along with whatever information he could find about the individuals. Some of his favourites included Polly Wanda Crocker, Sexious Boonjug, and Philander Philpott Pettibone.

As a movie critic, Gilmour positioned himself as the everyman who liked the same kinds of shows he thought his readers might enjoy. His tastes were decidedly mainstream, which meant that Gilmour was generally in tune with the likes and dislikes of the movie-going public at a time when movies were still being marketed as entertainment for the whole family. The novelist Malcolm Lowry characterized him as "the most reliable and entertaining judge of movies in Canada." Another commentator,

Hye Bossin, noted that Gilmour came from Medicine Hat, "which is best known for two products—corn and natural gas." This was a tongue-in-cheek reference to the fact that Gilmour sometimes used corny humour in his columns, and he occasionally came across as windy in his writing. But Gilmour preferred to think of Bossin's comments as being literally true. "The golden bantam corn grown in Medicine Hat was indeed the most delicious corn on the cob I've ever eaten," he said. "And the natural gas was so plentiful the streetlights were never turned off."

Gilmour's Albums began in October 1956 as a thirteen-week experiment for CBC Radio, and carried on without interruption for the next forty years. It was the perfect vehicle for Gilmour's creative talents, allowing him to develop a special intimacy with his public that he was never able to achieve as a newspaper writer. He now had an opportunity to speak directly to his listener in Medicine Hat, using the informal, conversational style he had wished the local announcers would have used when he was growing up. His ideal listener, he said, was an intelligent individual living in small-town Alberta who enjoyed listening to music and comedy not otherwise available on local radio. This person would have "a good sense of humour, real curiosity, and an open mind," Gilmour said. "I would not talk down to such a person, or talk up. I would just talk straight." His famous "huh-LO" welcome came from one of Gilmour's singing heroes, bass-baritone Paul Robeson, who eschewed showy introductions. Robeson would simply come on stage, say "hello," and start singing. That impressed Gilmour.

Classical music aficionados were upset with Gilmour initially because he seemed to thumb his nose at them by playing a mock aria by the caterwauling novelty singer Jerry Colonna immediately after a serious operatic performance by Enrico Caruso. But Gilmour had no desire to restrict his programming to a particular format, serious or otherwise. "A specialist misses so much," he said. "It's like saying you only read books with green covers." He attracted a devoted following, who shared his all-embracing enthusiasm for tenor Jussi Bjorling, contralto Kathleen Ferrier, Italian castrati who sounded like stuck pigs, Calgary banjo player

Johnny Thorson, Scottish music-hall star Harry Lauder, moose mating calls, and "the ever-popular Nate Glantz and his Sobbing Saxophone." Nothing pleased Gilmour more than to introduce his imagined listener to undeservedly neglected music that had been consigned to what he called "cut-out limbo." One kind of music that Gilmour never played, however, was rock 'n' roll. "All branches of rock are alien to me," he said. "When I hear it, it sounds to me like Attila the Hun and his Barbarians breaking through the living room window. Most of the people who play it have no more skill than a toad on a rock."

A self-styled workaholic, Gilmour went on the air fifty-two weeks a year with no reruns, and he proudly boasted that everything he played came from his own private collection of vinyl albums and shellac 78s. When the collection grew to 10,000 and took over the entire basement of his Toronto bungalow, including the laundry room, Gilmour stopped keeping count. He said his insurance agent advised him not to talk about the size of the collection. He put together the radio program with the help of his wife, Barbara—former head of book sales for The Hudson's Bay Company in Vancouver—whom he described affectionately as his "mail-bag queen, research chief, and finder of lost albums." As tempted as he might have been to use the CBC's extensive record library as a safety net whenever one of his own discs went missing, Gilmour never borrowed from the radio station. He wouldn't even borrow from his own son, Paul, when he discovered that Paul had a copy of a recording Gilmour had mislaid. "There wouldn't be anything wrong with taking it," Paul insisted. "After all, the show is called *Gilmour's Albums*. I'm Gilmour, and this is my album." The father hesitated for a moment and then politely declined the offer. "I have to believe I really mean it when I say the records come from my own collection," he said. "My aim is to create the feeling that I've invited the listener to drop by my house and hear my favourite music. If that were happening in real life, I wouldn't go borrowing from the CBC, or borrowing from anyone else."

Every program was carefully researched and scripted. Gilmour and his wife would spend weeks tracking down birth dates of obscure performers and composers so he could honour them on their anniversaries. He offered prizes to anyone who could prove he had the wrong dates and rarely had to admit error. He rehearsed the shows in his basement, with Barbara timing him on a stopwatch, and highlighted suggested script deletions for the producer when he went to the CBC studio to record the programs.

Occasionally he got into trouble for his descriptions of "buxom" sopranos and female performers, such as the German violin virtuoso Anne-Sophie Mutter, who bared their shoulders for their publicity photos. However, as Barbara pointed out patiently in a form letter she created to answer the criticisms, her husband described *everyone* on air, including men, for whom his favourite description was "handsome devil."

Gilmour continued to write movie reviews for the *Telegram* until the paper folded in 1971, and then for the *Star* until he retired in 1980 at age sixty-eight. At that point, Gilmour wasn't seeing many movies that he liked. Most of them he characterized as "lousy." "They're written for people with an attention span of seven seconds," he said. "I quit the *Star* at just the right time for me because I found I was panning most of the pictures I saw. Movies were becoming cheaper and sleazier, with more explicit violence by people who were geniuses at special effects instead of storytelling. It bored me to expound this opinion in review after review."

During the early 1980s, Gilmour considered donating some or all of his record collection to the University of Calgary, because of his Alberta connections. But the transfer never came to pass. After discussions with the director of libraries for the university, Gilmour decided he still needed the LPs, and even the 78s, for his weekly radio show. The rest of the radio world might have moved on to compact-disc technology, but Gilmour would never forsake his trusty turntable. "That would be like abandoning a good, old book."

In October 1996 Gilmour celebrated forty years of broadcasting with the CBC. It was a bittersweet anniversary because Barbara, "my lady love and working partner," had died a year earlier, from bone marrow cancer at age seventy-five. The listeners had never heard her voice on the air, but chances are they had received a handwritten letter from her if they ever asked a question about something played on the show. She wrote at least 1,500 letters a year, answered the telephone, and maintained her husband's archive of radio scripts (more than two thousand of them), albums, and reference books.

Gilmour continued doing the show until June 1997, but his heart was no longer in it. His health was declining, and he missed Barbara's involvement and the private jokes they had shared while compiling the show. On one occasion he decided to open the program with "howdy" instead of his trademark "huh-LO" because Barbara had chosen a country song as the opening selection. However, she had to go into hospital after he taped the show, so she never got to hear him.

He died of respiratory heart failure in November 1997 at age eighty-five. His entire album collection, scripts, reference books, and the old wooden desk from his basement, were donated to the CBC. A new program of miscellaneous recordings, *Collector's Corner*, replaced *Gilmour's Albums* on weekends, but it suffered from being too much like the original, without the saving grace of Gilmour's dry wit and his fascinating collection of research trivia. *Collector's Corner* never came close to matching the popularity of its predecessor because the mould had been broken when *Gilmour's Albums* went off the air. *Collector's Corner* faded from the weekend airwaves after a couple of years and was replaced by a very different kind of music-and-talk show, Stuart McLean's *The Vinyl Cafe*, which continues to this day.

RUTH PEACOCK GORMAN

Social Justice Advocate
1914–2002

In the Victorian world that was the Alberta of the 1930s, it was conventionally agreed that a married woman's place—especially if she came from the upper echelons of society—was in the home. She might join the Junior League, embrace volunteerism, and do good works, but, at the end of the day, her main job was to stay home and look after the needs of husband and children. Ruth Peacock knew this and accepted it. In fact, when her father encouraged her to follow in his footsteps and become a lawyer, she intentionally failed her high-school Latin exam to make herself ineligible for law school. Her ambition was to marry well and become a debutante in Mount Royal, Calgary's most exclusive residential district. She had never even met a woman lawyer, she said, so why would she want to become one?

Her father's will eventually prevailed. Mark Peacock was from the fourth generation of his family to practice law in Canada, and he was determined that his daughter—his only child—should be from the fifth. He had fought injustice throughout his legal career, including a landmark 1932 case in which he convinced the Alberta Supreme Court to overturn the conviction of a Stoney deer hunter charged with killing animals with antlers smaller than the law allowed. Peacock knew there were many more legal battles still to be fought, and he urged his daughter to become involved.

Ruth Peacock Gorman. (Thomas A. Edge Archives at Athabasca University, 2009.004/2254(1))

Ruth really didn't want to be a lawyer. She flunked the Latin exam for a second time and that put her on the road to a general arts degree, which she earned from the University of Alberta at age twenty-two in 1936. However, when her father discovered that the arts degree actually fulfilled the law-school entry requirements—even without the Latin—he sent her back to the university. Three years later, she graduated from law school.

Her father's law firm gave her the opportunity to article, but practicing law was not high on Ruth's priority list. She saw the courts as being dominated by men with little time for women lawyers. In 1940 she married a law-school classmate, John Gorman, gave birth to a daughter named Linda, and left the courtroom behind. From that point onward, she confined her legal activity to working as unpaid "convenor of laws" for the Calgary Local Council of Women. This was an umbrella group of women's organizations formed in 1895 to become what co-founder Lady Isabella Lougheed called a "mothering society," working to improve the living conditions of women and children through advocacy and education. They had never been able to find a qualified woman lawyer to help them achieve their reforms because few women went to law school in those days. Ruth became the answer to their prayers.

Like her father before her, Gorman took on the cause of fighting injustice when she joined the Local Council as legal counsel in 1942. She did so with a passion that was to burn in her for the rest of her life. Her first major initiative was to put together a brief calling for an amendment to Alberta's Dower Act, a law that seemed equitable on paper because it prevented a husband from selling the matrimonial home without his wife's consent. In practice, however, the law provided only limited protection for the wife because her only recourse if the husband sold the home without her permission was to sue him. If the husband then disappeared, noted Gorman, "the wife found herself and her children penniless and on the street." She proposed that the law be broadened to allow the wife to sue the purchaser as well as the husband. To press her case, she went directly to Social Credit Premier William Aberhart and he, to her surprise, agreed to personally introduce the amendment in the Legislature. He surprised her further by inviting her to become his new Attorney General, because he couldn't find a suitable replacement for a lawyer he had fired for refusing to support some of his fiscal-reform legislation. Ruth declined the offer, saying, "I have a husband and small baby to care for."

Her success with the Dower Act amendment proposal whetted Gorman's appetite for more advocacy. "I realized how powerful the Local Council of Women was, and how valuable to the community and the women of Calgary," she wrote afterward. "For the next twenty years, I gladly served as their laws chairman." She lobbied successfully for separate washrooms for men and women in buildings where they worked together. She convinced the justice authorities to hire more women police offers and prison matrons, and to institute improvements in the police lineup system to shield women witnesses from possible reprisal. Above all was her mounting concern for the social problems of

Native women, especially those caught up in a prison system that had no basic facilities or programs for women in custody. When her father was made an honorary chief of the Stoney in 1937 and Gorman was named a princess of the tribe, she had not fully appreciated the honour. Now, as an advocate for Native women's rights, she was totally committed to working on their behalf. After her father's death in 1943, she felt obliged to carry on the work he had started.

In 1944 Gorman accepted an invitation from fellow Aboriginal rights activist John Laurie to become the unpaid lawyer for the newly formed Indian Association of Alberta. Laurie was a white Calgary schoolteacher who brought Stoney teenagers in from the Morley reserve, sixty kilometres west of Calgary, and boarded them in his home so they could go to high school. As volunteer secretary of the Indian Association, Laurie worked to secure better living conditions and educational opportunities for the Stoney, and for other Natives throughout Alberta.

Gorman, already busy with her volunteer work for the Local Council of Women, was initially reluctant to accept Laurie's invitation because of the time commitment it would entail. "But whereas my work would only take up a few weeks of the year, Laurie worked every spare second of his days, and often all of his nights." For the next ten years, she travelled with Laurie, holding information meetings across the province, explaining the intricacies of the Indian Act to Native leaders so they could make effective submissions to the federal government for needed changes. The Indian Act was an archaic piece of legislation designed and administered on the false premise that the Natives were a vanishing race. Among its more odious provisions was an "enfranchisement" clause, which gave Natives the right to vote federally as long as they gave up their treaty and statutory rights and their right to live on reserves.

In March 1952 Gorman and Laurie attracted widespread media attention when they took up the cause of 122 Cree residents of Hobbema who faced expulsion from their reserve—ninety kilometres south of Edmonton—because their ancestors had allegedly sold their treaty rights back in the 1880s. If successful, the eviction order would have forced the 122 residents—one-tenth of the reserve population—to forfeit all claims to the royalties they were then receiving at the rate of $25 each per month following the discovery of oil and gas on the reserve. Beyond that, it would have set a very disturbing precedent. As Ruth noted, it would have meant that all descendants of individuals who had ever accepted a payment known as "scrip" as compensation for loss of Aboriginal land titles could face removal from their reserve homes. "If put legally into force, it could drive half of all the Indians off our western reserves."

Gorman and Laurie fought the Hobbema case for five years, with Gorman representing the 122 residents for the nominal fee of one dollar per person, and Laurie acting as her unpaid court reporter and assistant. The media-savvy Gorman made sure that *Time* magazine, the *Times* of London, the *Calgary Herald*, the *Toronto Star*, and other Canadian newspapers knew about the case, especially during those times when it looked as if the eviction order might stand. While arguing the case before two inquiry commissioners appointed by Ottawa, Gorman was also active in the court of public opinion, giving dozens of speeches to community groups and securing support from church leaders and members of the Canadian Bar Association. She later wrote about the case in her own *My Golden West* magazine, a publication in which she characterized Laurie as the "Doctor Schweitzer of the Western Plains," dedicated to helping others less fortunate than himself.

The final appeal of the Hobbema eviction order was heard in an Edmonton district court in February 1957. The Natives won on a legal technicality. Their supporters sang and danced in the streets of Edmonton, CBC Radio captured the sounds of the victory celebration, and a taxi driver was heard to say, "We stole the country from them in the first place. We're not going to steal from them the little we paid." By that time, Gorman had become prominent as a national media figure, a role she did not particularly relish because of the stress it placed on her family life. She told a reporter she considered herself primarily as a housewife, with Canada's Natives as her major outside interest. However, when a press photographer tried to reinforce the stereotype by having her pose in her kitchen stirring a pot, she refused to have her picture taken. "I made them go out and photograph the Indians and show the poverty," she said afterward. She thought a more appropriate public recognition of her achievement was the honour she received from the Hobbema Cree when they adopted her as their tribal mother and named her Queen Mother Morning Star.

John Laurie was seriously ill with heart problems at the time of the Hobbema appeal, which meant he could not be in Edmonton for the resolution of the case. He died in April 1959 at age fifty-nine. That left Gorman to carry on the struggle, which at that juncture meant lobbying Parliament for elimination of what she called the "worst sections of the iniquitous Indian Act." Removal of the enfranchisement provision was her first priority, while clauses about education, welfare, and hunting and fishing rights were on her list of provisions that needed to be improved. It was all about, as Gorman put it, bringing Natives out "from behind the buckskin curtain" and giving them the dignity and respect they deserved.

Gorman gathered plenty of support from Alberta Native leaders before making her submission to the Joint Senate-Commons Committee on Indian Affairs in 1960. She visited six of the most populous reserves in the province then met in Hobbema with appointed delegates from these reserves, and she commented afterward that embarking on this campaign was the high point of her twenty-five years with the Indian Association of Alberta. Understandably, she did not find consensus on every issue. Some of the Native leaders maintained, for example, that getting the unfettered right to vote in federal elections would mean more taxation for them. They were all agreed on one point, however: the section of the Indian Act making voting rights contingent on forfeiting treaty rights was an unfair provision that had to go.

The Diefenbaker government amended the Indian Act in 1961 to remove the contentious enfranchisement clause. It's probably fair to say that Gorman's brief to the Joint Senate-Commons Committee—signed by several prominent Native leaders, including future Alberta Lieutenant-Governor Ralph Steinhauer—strongly influenced the passing of the bill. It's probably also fair to say her previous publicity campaign on behalf of the Hobbema Cree had helped bring Diefenbaker's Conservative Party to power in the 1957 federal election. Diefenbaker did, in fact, admit to Gorman that the threatened expulsion of Natives from their reserves might have contributed to him winning the five crucial seats in western Canada that made the difference between victory and defeat in his election campaign against the Louis St. Laurent Liberals. To show his appreciation for her advocacy efforts, Diefenbaker offered Gorman a Senate seat. But as she had previously done when asked to choose between formally entering public life and attending to what she saw as her duties as a wife and mother, Gorman turned down the appointment. The Senate job went instead to James Gladstone of the Blood reserve; he was the first Native to be appointed to the Red Chamber. It seemed that Gorman's destiny, for the time being at least, was to be known nationally—as a March 1961 headline in Toronto's *Star Weekly* magazine described her—as "the housewife who fights for the Indians."

Gorman's next public battle, however, did not involve Natives, and it did not put her back on the national stage. It was a local skirmish involving an attempt in 1963 by the Canadian Pacific Railway to move its main tracks from the centre of downtown Calgary to a location along the south bank of the Bow River, paralleling what is now a much-used bicycle path. At first glance, it seemed like a win-win proposal for all concerned. For the railway company, it afforded an opportunity to convert the existing trackage into prime commercial building lots. For the city, it presented an opportunity to eliminate traffic bottlenecks caused by a railway line cutting through the heart of downtown. The Downtown Business Association stood squarely behind the proposal, as did most of city council. "Track removal could open up city centre," said the *Calgary Herald* headline.

Gorman was not impressed by the CPR proposal. For more than two decades, she and other members of the Local Council of Woman had been lobbying city hall to preserve areas along the Bow River for public enjoyment. On at least two occasions, council had voted to clean up and landscape the riverbank, and rid the area of unauthorized garbage dumps, slum properties, and other forms of urban blight. Putting railway tracks along the waterfront was not an answer to this problem, said Gorman.

She found an ally in Alderman Jack Leslie, who also had his doubts about the CPR proposal. He said that riverbank improvement was already in the city plans and suggested that the railway line be rerouted to the city's outskirts. The CPR flatly rejected this proposal, saying that such relocation would cost twice as much as the company could hope to gain from its downtown real-estate holdings.

As she had done with her initiatives on behalf of Alberta's Natives, Gorman enlisted the support of community groups in her bid to have a green buffer zone established between the river and any proposed track relocation. They held meetings, bombarded city hall with letters, and drew up a petition demanding that a plebiscite be held before council proceeded with the project. With the CPR making the occasional concession in terms of improving northbound road access to the city centre across the railway company's east-west right-of-way through the downtown, council became increasingly divided on the issue. After more than a year of debate, aldermen considered following Gorman's suggestion and asking taxpayers to vote on a plebiscite for approval of $9 million in estimated city spending on the project. Before this could happen, however, the other big railway company in town—Canadian National—upped the cost of the project by two-thirds. CN announced that it intended to charge the city $6 million to move its east-end warehouse to make room for the new CPR line. That unanticipated cost overrun went to an emergency council meeting for debate on June 22, 1964, and the majority of aldermen decided they didn't want to spend the extra money. They voted 10-3 to kill the track relocation project for once and for all. It was never revived again. Once again, the Local Council of Women had proved you could fight city hall—or any other legislative body, for that matter—as long as you had a sharp legal counsel like Gorman in your corner. She later characterized the battle as one of the most effective ever waged by the Local Council, with positive and lasting consequences for the city.

Gorman turned to a quieter project after marshalling Calgary's community groups to fight the CPR track relocation. In 1965 she founded a quarterly magazine, *My Golden West*, to celebrate western heritage and Native culture. "We never published on time," she said years later with a laugh. "If we had some money, we ran off a few issues." With no publishing experience and no grants from government funding agencies, Ruth set out to foster pride in the West through essays, poems, photographs, and pen-and-ink sketches by local artists. She did much of the writing herself and soon had a readership that spanned the Dominion. She told reporters that while the magazine took up much of her time, she was still vitally concerned with the problems of Canada's Natives. "She sees them as a forgotten people who must have their rights restored, and be allowed to benefit from those rights," reported *The Globe and Mail*.

In 1968 Gorman received the Order of Canada for her work on behalf of Canada's Natives. At that point, she seemed content to stay out of the public spotlight and live the life of a Mount Royal matron. But, as the *Calgary Herald* was to report some years later, she still "had this habit of getting involved in fights—fights over issues of major consequence; fights that have a lasting impact."

All of her fights were linked by a desire to remedy what she saw as a significant wrong. "I never wanted to be a lawyer or a writer," she told the *Herald*. "I just wanted to help people. That's the only thread I can find." She fought against patriation of the Constitution of Canada because she thought it would invalidate Aboriginal property rights. She fought for Senate reform because she thought the upper chamber lacked effective regional representation. She even fought for the separatist Western Canada Concept political party, although she insisted, paradoxically, that she was not a separatist herself. She just viewed the party as being involved in a struggle to rectify the injustices associated with living in a part of the country mostly ignored by Ottawa. That was reason enough for her to become involved.

The Western Canada Concept, for which Gorman developed a constitution and did much of the legal work, was the last of her big causes. The last of her smaller causes was a fight to have John Laurie's name officially attached to a Bow River Valley mountain popularly known as Yamnuska. She achieved victory in 1984 when a government panel decided to let the mountain bear the name Mount John Laurie (Iyamnathka). "Hooray, it satisfies everything," said Gorman when told of the decision. Iyamnathka is a more accurate phonetic spelling of Yamnuska, the Stoney word for "wall of stone."

Gorman died in December 2002 at age eighty-eight. At the time of her death she was working with historian Frits Pannekoek to complete a biography of Laurie, for which she had started compiling notes and research materials many years earlier. When Pannekoek read through her early drafts, he realized it was as much a story about Gorman as it was about Laurie. She acknowledged that, indeed, the manuscript was largely autobiographical and added that she hoped this would not be too obvious: "Women of my class and my generation don't write about themselves; they write through men."

Behind the Man: John Laurie, Ruth Gorman and the Indian Vote in Canada was published by the University of Calgary Press in 2007. Inspired by the example of Gorman, who had never taken a penny for her legal services, editor Pannekoek decided that all proceeds from the book should go to Red Crow Community College, a tribal post-secondary institution in Cardston.

STU HART
Wrestling Promoter
1915–2003

Professional wrestling took Stu Hart around the world, made him wealthy, and gave him the chance him to rub elbows with the likes of Bob Hope, Prince Philip, Muhammad Ali, and Arnold Schwarzenegger. In a business that often gets no respect, Hart was a well-respected figure.

Wrestling became part of his life starting in 1929 when he was fourteen and living in Edmonton, where the local YMCA provided free opportunities for youngsters to become involved in sports. For four years before that, Hart had been living with his parents and two sisters on a farm near Tofield, about sixty-five kilometres southeast of Edmonton, where survival took precedence over all else. The family camped year-round in two tents because Hart's father, Edward, was involved in a legal dispute over the ownership of the homestead and did not want to build a cabin until the problem was resolved.

Tent living began as a grand adventure for Hart at age ten as he milked cows with his father in an open corral, and hunted birds and small animals with his slingshot to put food on the table for his mother, Elizabeth. But he soon found it difficult to deal with the black flies and sweltering heat of a prairie summer and the long dark nights and subzero temperatures of a prairie winter. With no heat in the tent, he cuddled up next to his dog to stay warm at night and prayed that the rocks his mother

Stu Hart at the Cornwallis naval base in Nova Scotia, circa 1943. (Courtesy of Alison Hart)

heated in the campfire before bedtime would keep his toes from freezing.

In late 1926, eighteen months after the Harts moved to Tofield from Stu's birthplace in rural Saskatchewan, the courts finally ruled that Edward was legally entitled to the homestead he had purchased. However, he now had to face a new problem, dealing with the property taxes that had accumulated while the ownership issue was in dispute. He did not have the money to pay the taxes, so the family continued to live in the tents while Edward tried to make his peace with the taxman.

The taxman had little patience. In late 1928 the RCMP moved in and Edward was sentenced to six months for what Stu called "trespassing on his own land." The police scooped up Stu, his mother and two sisters, burned their tents, and put them on a train for Edmonton where they became wards of the court. They were placed in the custody of the Salvation Army, which lodged them in a hotel and paid their expenses for a few weeks until Edward was released on appeal. He moved them to a small, two-room shack in Edmonton's low-rent Bonnie Doon district, where they slept on the floor on mattresses under a pile of flannel blankets and tanned cowhides. It was there, said Hart, that he first became "blessed or cursed with ideas of grandeur." He gazed with envy at the mansions in the ritzy neighbourhoods around Bonnie Doon "and dreamed that if I applied myself, I would be able to live there too." One mansion that left a particularly strong impression on him was a fourteen-room home built by millionaire developer William Magrath in the city's Highlands district. With its wings, towers, gables, and balconies, it resembled one of the Queen Anne Victorian mansions built in New Orleans during the early part of the twentieth century.

At the YMCA, Hart learned how to wrestle the hard way, taking on bigger and heavier opponents who used him as a guinea pig, pinning him to the mat and "trying to see how far they could twist my head without pulling it off." He kept coming back for more punishment "because I wanted to do the same to them." Gradually, and mostly on his own, he learned how to turn the bigger size of his opponents to his own advantage: "You had to get their legs up so that they got in the road of their own bodies." He developed his strength by lifting weights and by doing thousands of squats, chin-ups, and push-ups.

Using submission holds that were mostly of his own invention and unknown to those he fought against, Hart moved up through the competition ranks, winning municipal and provincial amateur championships. At the same time, he went to school and paid for his upkeep by working part-time as a newsboy, selling copies of the daily *Edmonton Journal* and the sensationalistic *Liberator*, a weekly propaganda sheet published by Edmonton-based Ku Klux Klan leader John J. Maloney. By this time, Hart's father was earning good money as a landscaper, but Hart wanted to establish a measure of independence for himself by having his own income sources.

Hart got his first taste of professional wrestling at age sixteen when he saw Jack Taylor, the Regina-born British Empire champion, defeat Tiger Daula, the self-styled "Hindu champ" from

India, in a match in Edmonton. Hart loved the theatricality of the pro sport, with its flashy off-the-mat moves, good-guy-versus-bad-guy match-ups, and two-way involvement with a hyped-up audience. He dreamed of becoming a pro himself, but first he wanted to see how far he could go as an amateur.

In 1937, at age twenty-two, Hart won the Dominion amateur welterweight wrestling championship and took silver in the middleweight class. With hands as big as dinner plates and a body like Adonis (five-foot-ten and 190 pounds), he cut a striking figure on the mat. The following year, he qualified for the British Empire Games in Sydney, Australia, as a light heavyweight, but the Depression-battered federal government didn't have the funds to send him. He also missed out on opportunities to compete in the Olympics when the 1940 and 1944 games were cancelled because of the Second World War.

A versatile athlete, Hart not only wrestled but also played soccer, baseball, and cricket. He played hockey after teaching himself how to skate, and he tried out for the Edmonton Eskimos football club after spending a couple of seasons with the Edmonton Athletic Club, the Eskimos' farm team. Hart delighted in telling how he challenged Eskimos' coach Bob Fritz to a wrestling match when the coach suggested he didn't have the physique for a football player. He stretched Fritz into submission and ended up playing centre with the Eskimos for two seasons.

After high school, Hart entered business school for two years. To support his various sporting activities and education, he worked at a variety of different jobs. He worked as an installer for a glass company in Edmonton, journeyed to Yellowknife to cut timber supports for a mineshaft, and moved down to Calgary to work as a bouncer at a dance hall. When he returned to Edmonton, he coached wrestling at the University of Alberta for the nominal wage of $75 a year. He did his bit for the war effort by working as a sheet-metal technician with Northwest Industries, an Edmonton company that maintained military aircraft.

In 1941, on Christmas Eve, life almost ended for Hart when a fire truck hit him while he was cycling home from work at Northwest. He was thrown ten metres into the air and suffered broken elbows and thumbs and a serious spinal injury. Luckily for him, the injuries caused no lasting damage. He spent three months recuperating at Royal Alexandra Hospital and then went back to the YMCA to resume his wrestling training. He enlisted in the Canadian Navy, trained a crack baseball team that defeated the previously unstoppable American services team in 1942, and transferred to the Cornwallis naval base near Digby, Nova Scotia, where he staged exhibition wrestling matches for the entertainment of his fellow sailors.

While on furlough in the Unites States in 1943, Hart had a chance meeting with the man who was to get him into professional wrestling. Joseph "Toots" Mondt was a promoter who had revolutionized wrestling in the 1920s, taking it from its slow-moving, mat-confined carnival roots to a more exciting and popular form of arena entertainment that combined elements of the boxing ring with Greco-Roman, freestyle wrestling, and old-fashioned, lumber-camp fighting. Mondt called it "slam-bang western-style wrestling." He promoted it successfully in New York, Philadelphia, Boston, and Washington. Always on the lookout for new recruits, Mondt approached Hart at a restaurant in Washington, listened to what he had to say about his career as an amateur wrestler, and suggested that Hart get in touch with him after the war. Three years later, at age thirty-one, Hart was on his way to New York to make his debut as a pro wrestler.

The New York newspapers took professional wrestling seriously in those days. The results of the bouts were reported as if they were actual athletic contests rather than scripted matches with predetermined outcomes. In one newspaper report, Hart was credited with "pounding for the count" four opponents in an eighty-minute elimination match. One of the "losers" was a former world champion, "Texas Babe" Sharkey, a former college football player whose real name was Charles Kemmerer. The "classy Canadian," as the newspaper dubbed him, vanquished Kemmerer and the other opponents with a combination of "power crushes, flying crosses, and hard-driving slams."

The newspapers also took note of Hart's pretty-boy looks and movie-idol build. "Stu Hart gets gals in a fluster," reported one sports scribe. "He possesses a boyish charm, and I know the girls will just love his slow-dimpled smile." Hart hadn't sought female companionship while in Edmonton "because you can't be romancing and taking wrestling seriously." But now he was ready to start dating. A friend introduced him to Harry B. Smith, a retired long-distance runner who had finished seventeenth in the marathon competing for the United States at the 1912 Olympics in Stockholm. Smith, in turn, introduced Hart to his five marriageable daughters. "They all had scholarships and were all Miss Something-or-other, like Miss Long Beach," Hart noted approvingly. He chose daughter Helen, a petite, dark-haired, twenty-two-year-old, Rita-Hayworth lookalike who worked as a secretary for the public school board in Long Beach, New York.

Because he was busy wrestling six nights a week, Hart dated Helen only on Sundays. He did so for a year, and married her on New Year's Eve, 1947, at Long Beach's St. Ignatius Martyr Catholic Church. "We were married in a blizzard," Helen joked for years afterward, "and I've been snowed under ever since." This was a tongue-in-cheek reference to the fact they ended up raising twelve children, who all, in some manner, became involved with wrestling, either inside or outside the ring. Sons Smith, Bruce, Keith, Dean, Bret, Ross, and Owen all wrestled professionally. Son Wayne was a wrestling referee. Daughters Ellie, Georgia, Alison and Diana all married pro wrestlers.

Stu and Helen made their first home in a trailer park in Great Falls, Montana, from where he became involved as a promoter in a professional wrestling venture covering the Pacific Northwest circuit. He was not the best-paid wrestler in the "Toots" Mondt stable, and so he moved into promoting to make better money. Within a couple of years, while still active as a wrestler, Hart was promoting matches in Edmonton through a company he named Klondike Wrestling.

Hart made enough money in Great Falls and Edmonton to put a $10,000 down payment on the Calgary wrestling franchise when it became available for $50,000 in 1951. By that time, he and Helen had three children—Smith, Bruce, and Keith—and so they looked around for a big house in Calgary to accommodate their growing family. They found one on the western outskirts of the city, a twenty-two-room, rundown, Edwardian mansion that had been an orphanage during the 1920s and was surrounded by thirteen hectares of weeds. For Hart, it was the equivalent of the Magrath mansion he had admired in Edmonton as a young teenager. He bought the redbrick house from a Calgary judge, Henry Patterson, for $25,000. Fifty-nine years later, it would be on sale for an asking price of $4.95 million. Three years after that, when it failed to sell, it would be listed online for rent for $10,000 a month. Helen would jokingly tell visitors she could never remember "if we bought the house to justify the kids, or had the kids to justify the house." Every room, she said, was a rumpus room. She filled the house with books, while Hart decorated it with antique chandeliers, Persian rugs, maroon velvet curtains, and Chippendale chairs. She looked after the financial side of the business, and Hart handled the publicity. On the domestic front, they shared the cooking and cleaning duties. Hart drove the kids to school in one of the many ancient Cadillacs he kept stored in the front yard.

Calgary proved to be a lucrative market for professional wrestling. Hart staged most of his tournaments in the two-thousand-seat Victoria Pavilion, moving to the larger, seven-thousand-seat Stampede Corral whenever he had a card featuring such big names as Walter "Killer" Kowalski or "Whipper" Billy Watson. In 1954 Hart struck a deal with the new Calgary television station CHCT (later, CFAC and now, Global Calgary) to promote the matches in one, fifteen-minute program called *Meet the Wrestlers* and in a second weekly program called *Mat Time*. The standard gimmick was for the wrestlers to tell the TV audience what kind of damage they planned to wreak on their opponents during their coming matches. The fans would then flock to the pavilion to see the wrestlers follow through on their threats. Microphone skills, the wrestlers discovered, were just as important as ring skills.

As his business grew, Hart changed the original name of his company from Klondike Wrestling to Big Time Wrestling, then Wildcat Wrestling, and finally Stampede Wrestling, the name by which it became best known around the world. Some of the early stars included Gene Kiniski, Lou Thesz, Earl McCready, and Al "Mr. Murder" Mills. Guest referees included such well-known figures from the sports world as former boxing champions Joe Louis, Jack Dempsey and Rocky Marciano, and former American track star Jesse Owens. Also featured, both as wrestler and as referee, was Phil "Killer" Klein, father of future Alberta premier, Ralph Klein.

For young wrestlers wanting to turn pro—including his own sons as they got older—Hart converted the basement of his home into a gym, put in a training ring, and taught them the moves that had brought him success as a wrestler. The room became popularly known as "the dungeon" because it was dark and close, with rusty ceiling pipes and clammy walls. Experienced wrestlers, friends of Hart, also taught in the dungeon, helping launch the careers of such future stars as Archie "The Stomper" Gouldie, Greg "The Hammer" Valentine, and Jake "The Snake" Roberts.

The house was a regular menagerie, filled with cats, dogs, and other animals, including Terrible Ted, a 650-pound grizzly bear that wrestled humans and slept under the front porch when hibernating. Putting circus animals such as bears and tigers into the ring was a common gimmick in those days. On his property, Hart also kept a Jersey cow, chickens, and a goat. Visiting wrestlers who made the Hart house their temporary home-away-from-home included the Great Antonio, "Sweet Daddy" Siki, the Dynamite Kid, "Bad News" Allen, Abdullah the Butcher, and the two McGuire brothers, Billy and Benny, who together weighed close to 1,500 pounds and were listed in the *Guinness Book of World Records* as "the world's heaviest twins." André the Giant (seven-foot-four and 450 pounds) was a frequent babysitter at the home.

Hart's business took a turn for the worse during the early 1960s, when he lost his regular CFAC television spots, and some of his top wrestlers moved to eastern Canada to work for better money. Audiences dwindled at the Pavilion, and Hart's plans to do some needed improvements to his house were put on hold. However, with the support of ringside announcer Ed Whalen, who initially agreed to work for a nominal $25 a night, and a $1,000 loan that Hart obtained to cover the set-up costs for a new weekly show telecast from the Pavilion, he was able to carry on. He loved wrestling so much he could never give it up. Within a few years, Stampede Wrestling was being syndicated internationally, becoming as well-known in Honolulu and Tokyo as it was in Calgary. It was so popular in Uganda that dictator Idi Amin sent a letter to Whalen inviting Hart and the troupe to Kampala for a tournament at his palace. "We politely declined," Whalen said afterward. "We wanted to keep living and we weren't about to endorse Amin."

The 1970s and the early 1980s were the glory years for Stampede Wrestling. The biggest matches were always held to coincide with the annual Calgary Stampede, when Hart would get to dine with the celebrities brought in to put on white cowboy hats and lead the parade. "I've always liked the regular guys," he told a *Calgary Herald* reporter who visited the Hart house during the 1983 Stampede. "Bing Crosby, he seemed like a regular guy. Old Babe Ruth, he seemed like a good guy too. See that guy on the wall (pointing to a picture of Robert Kennedy)—I met him too." Then, feeling sheepish about his name-dropping, Hart smiled and added, "You know, there's nothing more boring than watching an old fart going through his clippings."

Stampede Wrestling closed its doors in September 1984, a few months after Hart turned sixty-nine. "It's time to get off the treadmill," he said. "I'd hate to die knowing I stayed on too long." The end came for many reasons: The Calgary Boxing and Wrestling Commission had imposed a six-month ban on his wrestling operations for excessive violence both inside and outside the ring. Increased operating costs, his advancing age, and a buy-out offer from New York boxing promoter Vince McMahon also contributed to Hart's decision. But McMahon's Titan Sports (later, World Wrestling Federation [WWF] and then World Wrestling Entertainment) never caught on in Calgary. A year after closing its doors, Stampede Wrestling was back at the Victoria Pavilion under the leadership of Hart's thirty-four-year-old son, Bruce. "Sometimes, you live to eat your words," said Hart.

Stampede Wrestling reopened for business, but it was not without its problems. Its biggest stars, including Hart's son Bret "Hitman" Hart, and his sons-in-law Davey Boy Smith and Jim "The Anvil" Neidhart, had joined the McMahon stable, and were wrestling in the larger venues of Boston and New York. Replacing them was, in the words of a *Herald* scribe, "an assortment of blond heroes, Hitleresque managers, masked men, and southern rednecks." Stampede Wrestling limped along for another four years before closing its doors for the second time at the end of 1989. "It's hard for us to compete with the big-money shows the WWF can put on," said Hart. "The rest of us, the small promoters, are like the minor leagues. I don't know if there's room for all of us." By that time, Hart's youngest son, Owen, had joined the WWF, wrestling as the masked "Blue Blazer" without revealing to the public that he was actually a member of the famous Hart clan. In the backrooms of pro wrestling, it had been decided the sport should have just one Hart at a time, and that was to be Owen's well-known brother, Bret.

Throughout the 1990s, Hart was regularly featured in the news as the aging patriarch of Alberta's first family of wrestling, declaring contentedly that the wrestling life had been good to him and that he had no regrets. Helen was often in the news as well, talking about the account of their lives that she hoped to write someday, and which she would title "Harts and Cauliflowers." (She never did write the book.) By the end of the decade, however, life was no longer good for Stu and Helen. Their youngest son Owen had been killed in a wrestling stunt that went tragically wrong, Bret had suffered a concussion in the ring followed by a stroke that spelled the end of his pro career, and Hart had been denied permission by city hall to develop his acreage property to create a retirement nest egg for himself and Helen. "I'm set up for life if I don't live too long," he said bitterly. "We've been had by the city."

Helen died in November 2001 at age seventy-six from complications from diabetes. "She was the glue that held us together," said Hart sadly. "I don't have my 'Tiger Belle' to push me along any more." Then, in failing health himself, he died two years later at age eighty-eight. Premier Ralph Klein, promoter Vince McMahon, Olympic wrestling champion Daniel Igali, former Calgary Flames star Lanny McDonald, former Calgary Stampeder Ezzrett "Sugarfoot" Anderson, and a host of pro wrestling stars, past and present, including "Killer" Kowalski, Harley Race, Chris Benoit, Ángel "Cuban Assassin" Acevedo and "Bad News" Allen Coage, were among the one thousand mourners who came to pay their respects at Calgary's First Alliance Church. Bret Hart delivered the last of the eulogies. "This wasn't just the end of my father's life, this was something deeper," he wrote afterward. "This was the day pro wrestling died for me—for good." For Bret, his father's Stampede Wrestling had represented the best of what pro wrestling had to offer—athletic prowess and myriad submission holds—until McMahon's big-budget cartoon extravaganza came along and put the mom-and-pop Hart enterprise out of business.

The Hart house, with its fabled dungeon, went on the block in 2004 and sold to Calgary restaurateur Dario Berloni for $1.5 million. The last occupant was oldest son Smith Hart, then fifty-five, who wanted to live in the house forever. However, his siblings dug in their heels and said the ongoing costs of maintaining the place would be prohibitive. When the new owner announced plans to convert the house into a duplex and surround it with twenty-two townhouses, the siblings joined with local heritage advocates to lobby for preservation of the home as a historic resource. Owner Berloni then threatened to demolish the house, but he eventually compromised and agreed in 2006 to have it restored as a heritage home, ringed by thirteen condos. Daughter Georgia Hart expressed satisfaction with this agreement. "This house represents the spirit of Calgary in some ways," she said, "and it needs to be preserved." When the restoration was completed in May 2010, owner Berloni put the Patterson Heights mansion up for sale at an asking price of $4.95 million. It never sold. At last report, in January 2013, the house was being listed for rent at a cost of $10,000 a month.

MELVIN CRUMP
Musician and Civil Rights Activist
1916–2009

As a first-generation black Albertan, Melvin Crump learned early about racial discrimination. His father, Bobbie Crump, was one of the black immigrants who left Oklahoma between 1908 and 1911, lured by Canadian government advertisements targeting potential American homesteaders. Bobbie and his fellow immigrants—including his parents and nine siblings—thought they were leaving for a better life, escaping the infamous Jim Crow segregation laws of the American South. It was only when they arrived in Alberta that they discovered Canada wanted only *white* settlers to populate the region. This wasn't spelled out in the government ads, of course. In fact, the first ads spoke directly to black farmers: "No better opportunity affords itself to the agricultural Negro than in Western Canada." However, when the Edmonton and Calgary newspapers and the local boards of trade started claiming that "desirable" white settlers were refusing to homestead in Alberta because of the influx of black immigrants, government agents travelled to Oklahoma and told the black farmers to stay home. "The land is unproductive and the climate harsh," said the agents, clearly contradicting what they were telling white American farmers at the time. "Go to Washington or Montana instead."

Bobbie Crump, who was twenty when he arrived in Alberta, chose not to homestead with his parents in Amber Valley, a black

Melvin Crump performing with Kashmir's Jazz Jam in Calgary, circa 1980. (Glenbow Archives, PA-3439-8)

settlement located thirty kilometres east of Athabasca. Instead he settled in Edmonton, where he met and married fellow immigrant Esther Day, and fathered five children. Melvin, the third child, was born in August 1916. Bobbie earned a subsistence living working as a cattle butcher and skinner at the Swift meatpacking plant in Edmonton. "Because we were black, most doors were closed to us," Melvin would recall years later. "Swift's employed black men to do the bloody, dirty work that white men wouldn't do. The clean jobs, like those in the butter and cream rooms, went to the white men."

In 1926, when Melvin was ten, Esther died following a shooting accident. She was shot in the knee while travelling back to Edmonton by car with Bobbie, after visiting with family in Radway, ninety-five kilometres northwest of the provincial capital. Bobbie kept his rifle cocked and loaded in case he might see some "wild chickens" along the way. The car hit a bump, the gun went off, and Esther's resulting wound became infected.

She died a few months later, and Bobbie left Edmonton to find farm work in Saskatchewan. He sent his five children to live with other family members and had very little involvement with them after that. Melvin stayed in Edmonton with his maternal grandmother, his aunt, and three male cousins who would become like brothers to him.

Melvin left school in Grade 8 to contribute to the family income. He shovelled snow, cut grass, shined shoes in a shoe parlour, slaughtered and plucked chickens at Swift's, and, at age eighteen, applied for a job as a sleeping-car porter with the CPR—the best job available to a black man in those days. "How old do you have to be to be a porter?" asked Crump. "Twenty-one," was the reply. "Then," said Crump, "that's how old I am." He got the job.

Even though it reinforced an ethnic occupational stereotype, taking the railway porter's job did bring Crump the advantages of steady employment and a decent wage. With a basic salary of about $85 a month, and tips of up to $30 for every transcontinental run between Vancouver and Montreal, Crump lived reasonably well by the standards of the day. Between train trips he pursued an interest in music by drumming for dance bands in Edmonton, first with one led by Ollie Wagner—the musician who taught him how to play drums—and then with a band led by Crump's cousin, saxophonist Les Bailey. Like many of his generation, Crump found that doors did open for black people who wanted to make their mark in entertainment or sports. They might not make enough money to give up their day jobs, but they could still find a measure of respect and acceptance in those spheres that was not otherwise attainable within white society.

Finding acceptance was not easy for Alberta black people during the 1920s and 1930s. They were always made to feel—as Crump's friend and fellow musician Big Miller would say in later years—like "the flies in the buttermilk." While never officially sanctioned by law, as in parts of the United States, racial discrimination existed nonetheless. Some landlords refused to rent to black people, many businesses refused to hire them, and some dance halls, bars, and even skating rinks refused them admission. Crump first felt the sting of racism while in elementary school. Though small in stature, he confronted a schoolyard bully and threatened to draw blood if he ever again heard the bully uttering what Crump called "the N-word." One of Crump's mottos became, "Never start a fight, but if a fight begins, finish it."

The porter's job brought Crump a taste of what racial discrimination was like in the United States when he and five black colleagues worked on a train bringing a group of Canadian Shriners to a convention in Helena, Montana. They had been travelling overnight so the porters adjourned to a Helena restaurant for breakfast. When they hadn't been served after waiting for more than half an hour, Crump asked the waitress what was going on. "We don't serve coloured people in here," she said.

"Why didn't you tell us that in the first place?" asked Crump.

"I thought you'd get the message," she replied.

Crump led his party out of the restaurant and returned a few minutes later with the potentate of the local Shrine club. The potentate had a few words with the waitress and the porters were served. "That was one experience in my life that really set me back on my heels," Crump said afterward. "I felt some part of the feeling of what blacks go through in the South. I had never received this type of treatment in Canada." He did not return to Helena for a second visit, nor did he work any more on trains travelling to the southern United States, where the passengers addressed him as "boy" and treated him like a slave. Crump offered to "turn in my uniform and all the rest" when he got back to Calgary after his first and only trip to Georgia, but a supportive supervisor politely rejected his resignation and told him that his future trips would go no farther south than St. Paul, Minnesota, the divisional point for trains heading to Georgia and Mississippi. As a result of the abuse he had received in the United States, Crump subsequently became active in Canadian branch of the Brotherhood of Sleeping Car Porters, whose motto was "Service not Servitude." While the Canadian porters didn't have to face the kinds of racial taunts and threats prevalent in the southern U.S., they did have other problems to contend with, including long working days without rest periods and vacations without pay.

During the Second World War, Crump left his porter's job temporarily to work on a civilian construction crew, building a hangar for the Royal Canadian Air Force at Penhold, Alberta, 20 kilometres south of Red Deer. He then tried to join the air force with a view to becoming a fighter pilot. "I wanted to bomb bridges and blow up the enemy," he said afterward. "I wanted to take dangerous chances. But the major said to me that nobody was allowed to do that unless they were lily-white." Crump then asked for and received a letter from the air force major saying, "I had volunteered my life for my country and was refused on account of the pigment of my skin." Instead, he served his country by going back to his porter's job and working on troop trains transporting American soldiers and construction workers north from Seattle to Dawson Creek, British Columbia, from where they were building the Alaska Highway.

In 1942, at age twenty-six, Crump married Beatrice Crosland, a twenty-six-year-old chambermaid at Calgary's Victoria Hotel. They raised a son and daughter and settled in Calgary where, after the war, Crump became active in the local music scene. He drummed for many years with the Proctor Swingsters, a family band led by guitarist Bert Proctor, which played commercial dance gigs in Calgary hotels and jammed after hours at the Utopia Club. This was a popular jazz venue, later known as Foggy Manor, located in a cellar across the road from the St. Louis Hotel. Oscar Peterson was one of the many Canadian jazz stars who played at Foggy Manor whenever he had a concert date in Calgary. Future senator Tommy Banks was one of the Alberta musicians who launched his jazz career at Foggy Manor.

As well as serving as recording secretary for the Calgary division of the Brotherhood of Sleeping Car Porters, Crump was active with the Alberta Association for the Advancement of Coloured People, working to rid Calgary of such derogatory depictions of black people as the woolly-headed children pictured in the schoolchildren's storybook, *Little Black Sambo*; the blackface minstrel carrying a tray of fried chicken on a sign outside Kensington Road's Chicken on the Way; and the fat washerwoman in the red, polka-dot bloomers on the animated neon sign of the Snowflake Laundry. "It was insulting," said Crump. "It was not acceptable to coloured people." He brought his complaints to school principals, business owners, and to city hall, and he invariably received a sympathetic hearing. "Usually, it was just a matter of making people aware that these things hurt."

Crump worked for the CPR until 1960, when a chance meeting with philanthropist Eric Harvie resulted in him getting a job as Harvie's personal chauffeur. He drove Harvie for about three years and then transferred to the Glenbow Museum—which Harvie had founded—as a mail clerk and courier. At the same time, Crump continued to work part-time as a musician. One of his proudest moments occurred in 1972 when the Proctor Swingsters broke the colour barrier at the ritzy Palliser Hotel to play for the wedding reception of future premier Ralph Klein and his bride, Colleen. "The hotel had told us they didn't hire coloured bands," said Crump. But Klein convinced the hotel management to change its discriminatory policy. After leaving the Swingsters, Crump teamed up with pianist Kashmir Akim Bey in a group called Kashmir's Jazz Men, and he played with him on a CFAC television show, *Kashmir's Jazz Jam*.

Even at the Glenbow, Crump encountered racial discrimination. One of his supervisors made the mistake of referring to him publicly as "Sunshine" and Crump vowed to "straighten him out, *right now*." "My name is Melvin Crump; I do not appreciate the word 'Sunshine' when referring to me," he told the supervisor. The supervisor promptly apologized.

Beatrice Crump died in 1976 at age fifty-nine, and for decades afterward Melvin could not mention her name without weeping. His long absences from home as a railway porter had been tough on their marriage for eighteen years, but they put up with the separations and the relationship endured. "There was never any question of fooling around," said Crump. "I kept my nose clean. I was one of the few entertainers who never paid any attention to the beautiful girls. These other musicians had girlfriend after girlfriend. I had only one girlfriend, and I married her."

In 1981 Crump retired from the Glenbow Museum at age sixty-four and landed a regular gig at Mazzini's Restaurant with pianist Bobby Van. They played together until the early 1990s, when Crump rejoined the Proctor Swingsters—then led by Bert Proctor's son Larry—to play at seniors' clubs and residences. "If you feel it, you can do it," said Crump in his eighties, when his doctor suggested he give up playing drums because of a heart condition. When he did eventually put away his big Pearl drum kit, Crump continued to keep the beat by shaking his maracas and tapping his sticks on tabletops and other flat surfaces within easy reach. In his early nineties, he was regularly entertaining neighbours at his Calgary seniors' apartment and playing at local church services with Calgary gospel troubadour Denis Grady. Crump never cared which religious denomination they were playing for. "As long as they are doing the Father's work, that's all I care about," he said. "When I'm playing and singing, I'm in my glory."

Melvin Crump died in November 2009 at age ninety-three. Some months beforehand, he had told a *Calgary Herald* reporter he felt he had made a difference through his work with the Alberta Association for the Advancement of Coloured People. "Look at the various coloured people who are getting so much attention that they didn't get before. Look at the kids that don't ever come home crying. That is the way things should go." Crump is one of forty-eight Albertans honoured for their contributions to the province in a permanent exhibit, *Mavericks*, at the Glenbow Museum.

JACK WEBSTER
Talk-Show Host
1918-1999

J ack Webster was an aggressively enterprising newspaper reporter from Scotland who immigrated to Canada in 1947 and went into radio six years later, after quitting his job at the *Vancouver Sun*. His name subsequently became synonymous with the kind of hard-hitting, politically oriented style of talk radio later popularized in western Canada by the likes of Charles Adler in Winnipeg and Dave Rutherford in Calgary.

Webster always placed career before family. In his later years he questioned the wisdom of this decision, especially when his wife, the former Margaret Macdonald, died in 1985 after a long struggle with mental illness. Webster believed that immersing himself in his work was the only way to leave behind the cares of the day. Was he right, he wondered? He expressed his doubts in an autobiography published in 1990 when he was seventy-one:

> *Now when I think about my life, my career and my relationship with Margaret, I'm not so sure. Looking back, I am overwhelmed—countless television programs, thousands of radio interviews, numerous news stories, columns and editorials. And what is any of it worth? What have I learned? What truths can I impart after five decades of fulminating, muckraking, gossiping, hanging out and carrying on? I'm*

Jack Webster. (Courtesy of the Jack Webster Foundation)

not sure any of it means anything. I do know Margaret was
disappointed that the nice young man she met in Glasgow
grew into such a hustler.

They met when he was sixteen and she was fifteen. He was a
shipyard worker's son who, with his mother's encouragement,
became a trainee newspaper reporter instead of following his
father onto the Clydeside dockyards. She was a chartered
accountant's daughter from the same southside Glasgow neighbourhood—"the pretty, proverbial girl next door"—who waited
outside the Glasgow *Evening Times* office while Webster finished
his afternoon shift typing up the racing results. Teenagers in love,
they went for coffee after his shift and travelled home together
on the streetcar.

Margaret became pregnant two years after they met. Webster's
mother, Daisy, would not hear of them getting married at that
young age, and so the baby, a girl named Joan, was given up
for adoption. The loss of her first-born child would torment

Margaret for the rest of her life. When an eventual reunion with her daughter took place thirty-six years later, it was too late for her grief to be assuaged. By then Margaret could express little emotion because surgeons had cut into the prefrontal lobe of her brain as treatment for agoraphobia—an anxiety disorder involving fear of public places from which escape might be difficult.

Webster and Margaret married in July 1939 after he had learned shorthand at night school and graduated from cub reporter to crime correspondent at the *Evening Times*. They honeymooned in Belgium and three months later Webster was back in Europe serving as an army sergeant in the Second World War. He returned to Glasgow in July 1946 after finishing the war as a lieutenant colonel with the Sudan Defence Force in Khartoum.

Webster was restless in Glasgow after his war experience. "It had fed my appetite for broader horizons. I wanted more out of life." He followed a *Times* colleague to London's Fleet Street where Webster became night city editor of the *Daily Graphic*. Margaret stayed in Glasgow with their second daughter, Linda, and moved to London just before their third daughter, Jennifer, was born in 1947.

Margaret did not like London, and Webster did not want to go back to Glasgow so they compromised by moving to Canada. Webster had a letter of introduction to the publisher at the *Vancouver Sun*, and he started working there as a reporter in September 1947. He was hired as a replacement for Pierre Berton, who had moved to Toronto to seek his fortune. Webster and Margaret bought a small house in Burnaby, where she was even less happy than she had been in London. The house had a septic tank that backed up into the basement, an icebox that had to be refilled with ice every few days, ditches out front, no sidewalks, no streetlights, and no stores nearby. "Talk about culture shock!" wrote Webster. "But we muddled through."

He worked the crime beat at the *Sun* just as he had in Glasgow and found it a comfortable fit because he had no problem intruding on the private grief of victims. "I had developed the brass-neck approach to reporting," he explained. "I'd ask anyone anything for a story and be unmoved by their immediate, personal tragedy." Among the events he covered was the 1950 hanging of a mentally challenged murderer and sex offender named Fred Ducharme, who suffered so much during his botched execution at Oakalla Prison that Webster became a lifelong opponent of capital punishment.

He quit the *Sun* in 1953 because of an overtime dispute with his editor, Hal Straight. Webster had returned early from vacation after receiving a tip that a condemned murderer, Walter Pavlicoff, had committed suicide while awaiting execution for the killing of a Vancouver bank manager. Webster broke the story of the suicide, and when he filed for overtime, Straight refused it. "Webster is paid over scale," he scribbled on the invoice. Webster responded by resigning on the spot.

He found a job with CJOR Radio as the host of a daily current-affairs program. He didn't know anything about radio and thought it was a dying medium, but he needed the $125 a week. By that time he and Margaret had a third child at home, son Jack, and Webster was the only breadwinner. He worked at CJOR for four years, moved back to Scotland temporarily when Margaret began to experience symptoms of agoraphobia, and returned in 1959 to work as a crime reporter with New Westminster's CKNW Radio. Four years later he made national and international headlines when three inmates at the BC Penitentiary took a prison guard hostage at knifepoint and refused to go back to their cells until they could speak with Prime Minister Pearson or Webster. "We can't get Lester Pearson," the warden told Webster on the phone, "so we're calling you."

Webster took his tape recorder to the prison, spent several hours talking to the three prisoners about their grievances, and filed regular reports to the radio station by telephone. One of the captors wanted to be given credit for the six months he had spent in jail while awaiting trial on a charge of armed robbery. The second claimed to be dying of throat cancer and wanted immediate medical attention. The third, from Quebec, wanted to be transferred to a prison where the guards and inmates spoke French. After the prisoners' demands had been relayed to the commissioner of penitentiaries in Ottawa, Webster went on the air to say he had agreed to act as personal escort for the convicts while they awaited transfers to other prisons.

The hostage crisis ended thirteen hours after it started when the commissioner approved the prisoner transfers. In the meantime, prisoners in other parts of the penitentiary had rioted, smashing toilets and television sets and washbasins until the RCMP came in with hoses and tear gas to restore order. When Webster left the prison, he found himself in the midst of a media scrum fielding questions. He went back to the station and spent two hours on air, broadcasting the tapes he had made during his time inside.

Webster's widely publicized involvement in the prison incident led to several job offers from big Toronto media companies, but he had no interest in moving east. He didn't like Toronto and felt a move there would aggravate Margaret's steadily worsening mental condition. She had undergone insulin therapy and electroshock treatment to no avail. A lobotomy made for a temporary improvement, but then she relapsed. She could not cry or laugh, and she worried incessantly.

A couple of months after the prison incident, in the fall of 1963, Webster was asked to host a new open-line show on CKNW that the station was introducing as a reaction to the popularity of CJOR's Pat Burns, the pioneer of talk radio in Canada. Webster had no interest in being "the someone who chatted up little old ladies in running shoes about the change in life." But the CKNW bosses convinced him to take the job by doubling his salary to $3,000 a month and providing him with a company car.

For two years Webster went head-to-head with Burns in a battle for ratings. Then Burns was fired because politicians stopped taking his calls and the CJOR brass thought he was getting too controversial. That left Webster as the dominant personality in Vancouver radio. His bluntness became legendary. "Get on the topic or off the air," he would growl at callers in his rasping Scots burr. If they did not comply, he would cut them off. He kept politicians honest, and he championed the underdog. *Time* magazine called him "a paladin of the poor, the powerless and the oppressed."

Talk radio gave Webster a larger-than-life persona. "It forced those of us who considered ourselves reporters to be actors," he wrote. "You had to be an antagonist against all governments, stir the pot, go on crusades and broadcast your arguments with ordinary people." He did the show at CKNW for nine years and then jumped to CJOR for a raise that brought his yearly salary up to $110,000. By that time he had earned a national profile as a correspondent for CBC Television's weekly newsmagazine program, *This Hour Has Seven Days*, and as a regular guest panellist on the quiz show, *Front Page Challenge*. He didn't have to hustle as much as he did in the days when he was earning less money, and Webster began to think he should stay home more for his family's sake. To this end he bought a thirty-eight-hectare farm on Saltspring Island with the idea of using it as a weekend getaway. But old habits die hard. Webster could never let go of the notion that if there was something important happening in the world of politics or crime, he had to be in the thick of things.

Because he spent so much time working, Webster was completely unaware that Margaret had made it her mission during the early 1970s to track down their daughter, Joan, who had been given up for adoption in 1936. In 1972 Margaret struck gold. She received a letter from an Edinburgh insurance investigator saying that Joan was living in a rural village in Essex with her husband and three children. The subsequent reunion, wrote Webster, "was the most exciting personal thing that ever happened in my life." He and Margaret visited with Joan and her family in Essex, and he noticed immediately that Margaret, while emotionally flattened because of her brain surgery, seemed happier than at any time during their marriage. "I think that was the first time I understood how Margaret felt for those 36 years." When he and Margaret celebrated their forty-fifth wedding anniversary on Saltspring in 1984, Joan flew over from London to make a surprise appearance.

In 1978, when he turned sixty, Webster left talk radio behind. He briefly considered retiring to the Saltspring farm, but instead he went into television as the host of an interview show on BCTV simply called *Webster!* He sparred with Pierre Trudeau, flirted with Shirley MacLaine, and sang an impromptu duet with Anne Murray. He did the show for eight years and then decided he had nothing left to prove as a broadcaster. He had won most of the major broadcasting awards in Canada, been inducted into the Canadian News Hall of Fame, and received honorary law degrees from the University of British Columbia and Simon Fraser University.

He retired in 1987, two years after Margaret died. Her illness had been the source of both his sorrow and his strength. She had kept him rooted when he might have been inclined to roam. He recalled that she once told a reporter she still had one unanswered question after more than four decades of marriage: "Webster, where have you been all these years?"

"Margaret, I was just making the rounds," he replied in his autobiography. "I still am."

Jack Webster died in March 1999 at age eighty of congestive heart failure and Alzheimer's. *The Globe and Mail* noted approvingly in an editorial that his style of broadcasting had added a valuable element of accountability, openness, and immediacy to democracy:

> *When important personages came to Vancouver, they would be summoned to the Webster studio. Those that refused were excoriated for refusing to subject their character and their views to a public probing by the host and by callers. Those who went knew that the questions could come from anyone with a telephone, and that phoniness or disingenuousness would be fatal.*

After Webster left broadcasting, the *Globe* added, talk radio often deteriorated into trash radio. "Sometimes there is crudity and demagoguery but, on balance, the effect on our society has been positive."

"Don't touch that dial," concluded the *Globe* editorial. "Thanks, Jack."

STANLEY CHARLES WATERS

Soldier and Elected Senator
1920–1991

He was the first person in history to gatecrash the Senate without a prime ministerial invitation. Stan Waters was a rookie politician who, at age sixty-nine, brought a semblance of democracy to an institution previously defined by patronage. He claimed his seat in the upper chamber after a 1989 Alberta provincial senatorial race that the prime minister of the day, Brian Mulroney, could well have ignored. But Waters finally got to take his seat nine months after the election, when Mulroney risked losing a crucial constitutional amendment vote that required the support of all the provinces.

Waters's late chance for a political appointment came after a distinguished career in the military and in business. Born in Winnipeg in 1920, he attended a private high school in Calgary and the University of Alberta in Edmonton before joining the 14th Army Tank Battalion (Calgary regiment) as a private in 1940. After serving in England, he returned to Canada to be commissioned. He then volunteered for parachute training and was posted to the First Special Service Force, a unique u.s.-Canadian assault unit secretly formed in Montana to face the enemy overseas.

The parachute unit was the first dual-nation fighting force to serve as a combat unit with the Allied armies. It became popularly known as the Devil's Brigade after Hollywood made a

Lieutenant Colonel Stan Waters, 1953. (Glenbow Archives, PA-2807-3984)

movie about it in 1968. The name "devil" referred to the fact that members blackened their faces for night raids. Waters served with the unit in the Aleutians and in Italy. He earned a United States Silver Star for a 1944 mission during the Italian campaign, when he was serving as a major temporarily in charge of a casualty-stricken battalion. Waters walked under direct fire to coordinate his infantry unit with a supporting tanks regiment for a successful attack on an enemy-held mountain village.

After the war, Waters remained in the military and became chief instructor at the Joint Air Training Centre in Rivers, Manitoba. He then held staff appointments in Ottawa. In 1953 he commanded the Second Battalion of the Princess Patricia's Canadian Light Infantry in Germany, later returning to Canada to convert the battalion into a parachute company, part of the Canadian Airborne Regiment.

Waters served in a variety of liaison and military-observer postings with the United States Marine Corps, the United Nations, and NATO, and then he became commander, Mobile Command, at St. Hubert, Quebec—in effect the commander-in-chief of Canada's land forces. He retired from the army in 1975, at the compulsory retirement age of fifty-five, with the rank of lieutenant general. Then he began his career as a captain of industry, working for Calgary billionaire Fred C. Mannix, and heading companies involved in various commercial construction projects.

Waters retired from the Mannix empire in 1989, at age sixty-nine, and immediately embraced what seemed to be a futile cause. He became the western-based Reform Party's candidate in an Alberta senatorial election that offered no guarantee of a subsequent Senate appointment. The provincial premier, Don Getty, had grown tired of waiting for Prime Minister Mulroney to fill a vacant Senate seat and called a vote to determine whom Albertans would like to see in the position.

Waters had been a Reform Party member for just two years when he threw his hat into the ring as a Senate contender. "I was a federal Conservative and a provincial Tory and the parties left me," he told the *Edmonton Journal.* "They abandoned me."

He said that when the federal Conservatives took power, most of the party members were elated with the apparent strong view they took on trying to restore fiscal responsibility to the federal government. "But we've added, since they came into power, $150 billion to $170 billion of additional debt, which, to most of us, indicated continued financial irresponsibility."

He added that the provincial Tories were equally in trouble, financially. "Here we have one of the richest provinces in Canada and, my God, we've got the highest per capita debt of all the 10 provinces."

Although he had no previous political experience, Waters proved to be an accomplished campaigner. "So you don't trust politicians," he would say in a typical speech. "Well, neither do I. So let's change the system." A practiced and entertaining speaker, given to quoting Winston Churchill, Waters even made political hay of his age. If appointed senator, he could only serve six years before compulsory retirement at age seventy-five, and that period exactly coincided with the Reform Party's timetable for Senate reform. Against all odds, Waters scored an election victory with 265,000 votes—more than twice that of his nearest rival, Liberal lawyer Bill Code.

Waters wasn't the preferred candidate of Premier Getty, a Conservative, but Getty was gracious. He swallowed his Tory pride and undertook to support the Reformer. The prime minister vacillated for eight months. He finally agreed to make Waters's Senate appointment official when Getty threatened to withdraw Alberta's support for the Meech Lake constitutional accord, a national unity initiative that subsequently foundered when some of the provinces balked at giving special status to Quebec. Mulroney declared that Waters's appointment would be strictly a "one-shot deal."

He was a bundle of contradictions, this war hero turned politician. Publicly, Waters sang the songs of the Reform Party, yet if you listened closely you could hear him singing different lyrics in private. He publicly opposed what he called "enforced bilingualism," yet he had learned French through immersion programs while serving as operational commander in St. Hubert. Waters insisted he had no intention of brushing up on his French when he became senator, but he did admit to listening occasionally to the French news broadcasts on Radio Canada.

He railed against the "tyranny of the minorities" that led to government grants for "black lesbians from Dartmouth" and "groups working on banana horticulture." He also preached tolerance for the racist regime in South Africa. Yet he founded the Calgary Native Opportunities Committee and advocated sharing of commercial wealth and prosperity among First Nations communities.

He promoted industrial growth and declared categorically that environmental dangers were exaggerated. He recommended spending Alberta Heritage Fund money on diversion of northern waters into southern Alberta river basins. Yet he fished those northern waters for salmon and was an organizing member of the International Wildlife Association.

Waters spent his time as a senator focussing more on the way he had arrived than on the job itself. He was criticized for having one of the lowest attendance records in the upper house, but he did oppose the goods and services tax and said he always participated in major votes.

He had little more than one year to enjoy what he called "the place where longevity was created." In July 1991, Waters was diagnosed with brain cancer. Three months later, he was dead at age seventy-one. Seven years after that, in October 1998, Alberta renewed its push for Senate reform by holding an election for two so-called "senators-in-waiting." One of the candidates was to have been Waters's widow, seventy-one-year-old Barbara Waters, a grandmother of eleven. "We just have to have elected senators," she told *Alberta Report* magazine three months before the election. "The business of appointing your hairdresser or your high school buddy is ridiculous. We're the only Western democracy that tolerates this nonsense." She later withdrew her candidacy for health reasons.

The winners of the 1998 Senate race were Reform Party nominees Bert Brown and Ted Morton. But this time around, the prime minister of the day, Liberal Jean Chrétien, showed no inclination to appoint the winners to the upper house. It wasn't until June 2007, when Conservative Stephen Harper was prime minister, that one of the senators-in-waiting, nominee Brown, finally became the second elected representative to take a seat in the Senate. Since that time, three more elected nominees have been appointed, but Senate reform continues to proceed at glacial pace.

ROY ALEXANDER FARRAN

Decorated War Veteran and Politician
1921–2006

R oy Farran was a much-honoured British war hero who immigrated to Alberta in 1951. He had but one dark stain on an otherwise spotless military record. Four years earlier, while serving in British-ruled Palestine, Farran had been charged with murder in the abduction and alleged killing of a sixteen-year-old Jewish insurgent named Alexander Rubowitz. Though the charge was dismissed for lack of evidence, questions were raised for years afterward about what role Farran might have played in the unsolved crime. Rubowitz's body was never found, and nobody else was ever charged.

At the time of the 1947 abduction, Farran was working with the Palestine police, setting up paramilitary hit squads to strike at Jewish militants who wanted to drive the British out of Palestine and establish their own national homeland. Just twenty-six, Farran had distinguished himself during the Second World War as a tough and fearless fighter who conducted a series of daring commando raids behind enemy lines in various parts of Europe and North Africa. The son of an RAF warrant officer, Farran grew up in India, trained as an officer at the Royal Military Academy in Sandhurst, and first saw action at age nineteen in 1940–41 when British and Commonwealth forces defeated the Italians in Libya. He received numerous decorations for wartime gallantry, including the Distinguished Service Order, three Military Crosses, the Croix de Guerre, and the American Legion of Merit.

The transition from war to peace was difficult for Farran. After spending all of his adult years in combat situations, he was unprepared for a life without fighting and guns. By 1946 he was back in the military, seeking action wherever he could find it. He eagerly welcomed the opportunity to put his specialist knowledge of guerrilla warfare at the disposal of the Palestine police. He organized counter-terrorist squads to spearhead an offensive against the militant Jewish underground and bring a measure of security and stability to Palestine.

These special squads had limited success in their efforts to infiltrate the underground and curtail the increasing levels of violence in Palestine. Though well trained in army combat skills, the squad members could not speak Hebrew and had no intelligence-gathering expertise. Farran claimed, however, that they were on the brink of a major victory when the abduction of the Jewish teenager effectively put an end to his mission in Palestine.

The abduction took place in Jerusalem on May 6, 1947. Some of Farran's men were in an unmarked car cruising the city when they saw Rubowitz putting up posters calling on Britain to get out of Palestine. Witnesses said they saw a man in an "army-type of shirt" chase after Rubowitz, order him into the car at gunpoint, and then lose his hat in the resulting scuffle. Rubowitz was driven away and never seen again.

Farran was implicated in the abduction when bystanders found a felt hat near the scene with the letters "FAR-AN" inked into the sweatband. After this was reported in the English-language *Palestine Post*, the British government ordered Farran to submit to questioning by the police and military. Instead he fled to Syria, suggesting he had something to hide. Farran claimed, however, that the government was trying to make him a scapegoat and that he had an "unshakeable" alibi for his movements during the time of the alleged kidnapping.

Farran eventually agreed to return to Jerusalem for questioning when his superior officer, Colonel Bernard Fergusson, met with him in Syria. Fergusson appealed to Farran's sense of patriotism, saying that Britain's prestige in the Middle East would take a severe battering if one of its citizens were allowed to evade justice. When Farran got back to Jerusalem, however, he discovered that the *Palestine Post* had already pronounced him guilty of murder. Fearing he would never get a fair trial, Farran fled again, this time in the direction of Saudi Arabia. He only agreed to give himself up the second time when he heard that Jewish militants had shot and killed three British soldiers in retaliation for the Rubowitz abduction. Because one of the murdered officers was a friend of Farran, he decided he should give himself up. "It just wasn't worth it," he said afterward. After returning to Jerusalem, Farran was demoted from major to captain for twice going AWOL during the investigation into Rubowitz's disappearance.

Farran was brought to trial before a British court-martial in a heavily guarded Jerusalem courtroom on October 1, 1947. The following day, he was freed. The prosecutor had conceded there was "no case to answer." Rubowitz's body had not been found, it could not be definitively proven that the hat with the ink-smudged sweatband belonged to Farran, and two witnesses had failed to identify him in a police lineup. The prosecutor, Maxwell Turner, did say that Farran had talked to his superior officer, Fergusson, on the day after the abduction, but Fergusson refused to testify about this conversation "because it might possibly incriminate me." Turner also alleged that Farran had left behind a notebook containing an unsigned, potentially incriminating statement before he fled custody. But the judge, Melford Stevenson, ruled that the contents of the notebook were privileged because they had been written at the request of Farran's regimental commander, Lieutenant Colonel P. H. Labouchere, and he—according to army protocol—was Farran's legal adviser.

After the trial, Farran's lawyer, William Fearnley-Whittingstall, petitioned the court to have all documents relating to the case—including any written statements attributed to Fergusson or Farran—destroyed for national security reasons. This was duly done but copies of some documents had already made their way to the Colonial Office in London, where they remained under lock and key for the next sixty years.

Farran returned to England eleven days after being acquitted. Nine days after that, on October 22, 1947, a Jerusalem magistrate issued a warrant for his arrest. The magistrate said Rubowitz's brother had given him "reasonable cause" to assume Farran had something to do with the teenager's disappearance. The arrest warrant was voided, however, when the Palestine Attorney General ruled there was no new evidence to link Farran with the abduction. On November 22, 1947, Farran resigned his army commission and announced he was writing a book about his wartime and postwar experiences.

The book, *Winged Dagger*, was published in 1948. In it, Farran claimed that at the time of Rubowitz's disappearance he was "disguised as an Arab, having dinner with Arabs in another part of Jerusalem." This, he claimed, was his alibi. He fled to Syria, he said, only because he felt he was being "thrown to the wolves" for political reasons, at a time when Britain was trying to decrease its costly military presence in the Middle East. He wanted to be in a neutral country where he could challenge what he saw as the British government's attempt to frame him, and seek political asylum if necessary. In its effort to show "British impartiality to the world," he said, the government had taken a course of action that could have resulted in him being wrongfully convicted and hanged.

Farran spoke little about the Rubowitz affair after writing his book. Nor would he talk about a deadly incident that occurred in England in May 1948, one year after Rubowitz's disappearance. A parcel bomb mailed to an R. Farran in Wolverhampton was opened by his younger brother, Rex, who died in the ensuing blast. Farran, away in Scotland at the time, blamed Jewish militants for the bombing. While obviously a marked man, he refused to disappear from public view. In 1950 he ran, unsuccessfully, for the Conservatives in the British general election. The following year, he moved to Alberta with his Calgary-born wife, the former Ruth Ardern, whom he had met while running a construction company in Rhodesia in 1949. They settled west of

Calgary in Springbank, where Farran started a dairy farm and freelanced for the *Calgary Herald*.

After three years of farming and freelancing, Farran decided to become a newspaper proprietor. In 1954, at age thirty-three, he founded the *North Hill News*, a tabloid community weekly with the masthead motto, "Without Fear or Favour." The paper attracted a sizeable readership by printing the names of Calgarians charged with the kinds of relatively minor offences—mainly shoplifting and impaired driving—that the larger Calgary dailies tended to ignore. Farran also delighted in passing along gossipy tidbits from city hall. One of his more talked-about items was a cryptic question he posed in 1958 that precipitated a local political scandal: "What city father had his basement poured with city cement?" The mayor, Don Mackay, admitted to council that he had "borrowed" thirty-five bags of cement for his holiday home in Banff, and then "forgot" about it. A judge ruled that Mackay had derived an improper advantage through his position as mayor, and Mackay lost the mayoralty race in the following municipal election.

After seven years of using his column to keep city politicians on the straight and narrow, Farran decided to run for politics himself. He was elected alderman for Calgary's Ward 2 in 1961, and he remained on council for ten years. During that time, he campaigned successfully for the preservation of Nose Hill and Fish Creek as municipal parks, and he also campaigned successfully to keep sodium fluoride out of the municipal water supply. During one civic election campaign, he was asked about the murder charge in Palestine, but Farran gave the questioner short shrift. "I was accused of murder though no body was ever produced," he said. "I was tried and honorably acquitted. I feel no shame."

In 1971, with the rise to power of Peter Lougheed's Conservatives, Farran moved into provincial politics. After two years on the backbenches, he was appointed minister of telephones and utilities, and he improved telephone service in rural Alberta by eliminating unpopular party lines. At the same time, he sold the *North Hill News* and its associated printing-press operations, which he had promoted with the motto, "We print everything but money." "I'm finding this a very time-consuming and demanding job," Farran said of his ministerial position. "I will not meet my government deadlines unless I sell."

After being re-elected in 1975, Farran was promoted to Solicitor General, where he established a reputation as a hard-line advocate of tough treatment for lawbreakers. Instead of receiving long prison sentences, he said, hardcore criminals should receive shorter, but more severe, sentences. "If I was allowed to, I would have inmates running around a drill square with packs on their backs until they drip with sweat," he said. "I would institute things like six strokes on the backside." For hardened criminals who refused to be rehabilitated in prisons, he suggested a Canadian version of Devil's Island. "Put them on an island in the Arctic wastes and leave them to their own devices. You could drop food into them by aircraft."

For juvenile offenders, Farran advocated the establishment of Borstal-style reform schools based on a strict regimen of discipline. Canings, cold showers—"whatever it takes to build character"—would be the order of the day. "The only hope for these young offenders is work," he said. "Permissiveness has been the root of a lot of problems of these young kids. They were never told the right way and never held accountable until it was too late." He dismissed "woolly-headed liberals" who saw criminals as victims, and lamented their growing influence in the crime-punishment debate. Farran never found any political support for his hard-line approach, but he believed—based on calls to his office—that his views were shared by a majority of Albertans.

He left provincial politics in 1979, chaired the Alberta Racing Commission for 16 years, raised cattle on his acreage near Millarville, south of Calgary, and received the French Legion of Honour in 1994 for his role in a post–D-Day battle with retreating German soldiers. Often photographed with a pipe in his mouth, Farran lost his larynx to cancer in 1999, but he did so well talking through an artificial voice box installed in his throat that he was able to return to public speaking.

He died of throat cancer at age eighty-five on June 2, 2006, and was given a hero's funeral amid solemn pageantry. A ten-block procession was followed by an artillery salute. But there was one blot on Farran's otherwise impeccable escutcheon that would never be erased. In March 2009, a New York private investigator named Steve Rambam announced in London that an Israeli citizen living in the United States had hired him to reopen the sixty-two-year-old Rubowitz case. Documents recently declassified by the Public Record Office in London had appeared to again point the finger of guilt at Farran. Among them was a statement given in June 1947 to a Palestine police detective by Farran's superior officer, Bernard Fergusson. The officer told the detective that Farran had confessed to killing the Jewish teenager by "bashing his head in with a rock" after squad members grew frustrated interrogating Rubowitz at a remote location outside Jerusalem. However, there was nothing in the records to independently corroborate Fergusson's statement, aside from what Farran might have written in his notebook at the request of his regimental commander, and this notebook had been destroyed after the trial. One of Farran's former military colleagues dismissed Fergusson's statement as a fabrication, a deliberate attempt to frame an innocent man. "The whole thing is a put-up stunt," said Gerald Green, who served with Farran in Palestine. "Someone tried to pin something on him to provoke trouble out there."

One former admirer of Farran became convinced of his guilt when he learned about the declassified Public Record Office documents. Maurice Yacowar, who had worked as Farran's editorial assistant at the *North Hill News* in the late 1950s, put it bluntly in an article he wrote for *Alberta Views* magazine in June 2009. "Apparently, I have idolized a sadistic war criminal," he wrote. "How do I deal with that?"

Others felt, however, that sleeping dogs are best left to lie. "He's dead and gone now, what can be gained?" asked Ron Ghitter, Farran's former MLA colleague in the Lougheed government, in an April 18, 2010, interview with the *Calgary Herald* following publication of a book by British author David Cesarani about Britain's war against Jewish terrorism in the late 1940s. In the book, *Major Farran's Hat: Murder, Scandal and Britain's War Against Jewish Terrorism, 1945–1948,* Cesarani alleged that

Farran was guilty of murder and had been wrongly acquitted. But Ghitter suggested that such speculation was now pointless. "It's better to keep him in fond memory," he said. "I prefer to remember him in a very positive light. He contributed considerably during his public life in Alberta. He had a remarkable life."

HAL SISSON
Lawyer, Author, Comedian, and Marbles Player
1921-2009

Hal Sisson was a small-town lawyer who delighted in telling naughty jokes to "preserve my sanity while dealing with other people's problems." In between court appearances, he performed his comedy on stage, and then he weaved it into his novels, all the time expressing his conviction that if you want to do something in life, "you should just get your arse in the saddle and do it."

Sisson did so many different things during his lifetime that when a Victoria newspaper reporter wrote a profile of him in 2006, she was at a loss to know where to begin. By that time, Sisson had published several books, played marbles competitively, and established himself as one of Canada's top croquet players. He was then eighty-four, still performing occasionally at Victoria and Vancouver comedy clubs, and promoting an anthology of revue skits drawn from his twenty years as an amateur burlesque comedian in Peace River, Alberta. "You can't beat a mixture of comedy, dancing girls, and booze to produce a winning theatrical combination," he said. In characteristically roguish, Sisson style, he launched the book at a Victoria strip club before doing twenty minutes of what he called "sit-down" comedy (made necessary by a heart condition) and then introducing the stripper.

The anthology, *Sorry 'bout That: A Tribute to Burlesque*, was one of eleven books that Sisson published after he retired from

Hal Sisson, performing at the Vancouver International Children's Festival, circa 1990s. (Courtesy of Lindy Sisson and Clare Thorbes)

practicing law in 1990 at age sixty-nine. The other titles ranged from Leacock-inspired depictions of small-town life to murder mysteries and adventure novels. Additionally, he wrote what he called a "factional" novel that purported to tell "what really happened" to the World Trade Center towers on September 11, 2001. Although it dealt with a serious topic, Sisson described the novel, *Modus Operandi 9/11*, as a "comedy-driven drama." Fellow author Jim Marrs said, "It's a bit like having 9/11 explained to you by Benny Hill."

Sisson developed his flair for comedy while growing up in Moose Jaw, the son of two schoolteachers, during the 1920s and 1930s. His abiding memory of those years was of being kicked out of his local Presbyterian Church for trying to organize dances in the church basement. By the time he got to law school in Saskatoon in the late 1940s, Sisson had also developed a flair for practical joking. One of his most celebrated stunts involved borrowing a friend's horse and taking it up several floors in a hotel elevator so the animal could be his guest at a law-school function.

Before bringing his hijinks to law school, Sisson was involved in the more serious business of serving his country in the Second World War, as an RCAF weapons mechanic based in Alaska, Ireland, and Wales. He later described the wartime experience in language that showed another, angrier side of Hal Sisson:

> *It is not until you get a lot older that you learn the utter futility of war, and who the SOBS are who cause and run these immoral and illegal wars in their own self-interest. I'm talking about the military-industrial-banking complex and the corporate fascist police state that has gradually taken over society. This is a planet we live on, not an American empire.*

Sisson also revealed his anger when he joined a group called Lawyers for 9/11 Truth, an organization of American and Canadian attorneys, judges, and legal scholars who criticized the report of the 9/11 Commission as inadequate and called for a new, independent investigation into the September 2001 attacks on the World Trade Center and Pentagon. "It's the lie that launched, not a thousand ships, but countless conveyances of war," Sisson said. "The charade first floated by the Bush administration to explain the infamy of that day persists, yet few dare to question the absurdity of the Emperor's squirrelly tale."

His anger, however, was always leavened by humour. When he was invited in October 2007 to appear as the "oldest active 9/11 'Truther' in the world" at a University of Victoria presentation on the 9/11 Commission report, the eighty-six-year-old Sisson filled his talk with lawyer jokes, doctor gags, allegorical stories, and Jack Ross's classic 1962 retelling of the Cinderella story ("Prinderella and the Cince"), replete with spoonerisms. "There's a moral to this story because Cinderella never gave up," Sisson told the audience. "If Christopher Columbus had given up, you wouldn't be sitting here tonight listening to me. John Diefenbaker, he never gave up, either. And then there is the 9/11 Truth Movement. We don't give up. We don't quit. We're never going to give up until

9/11 is properly investigated and the real culprits brought to justice. All the 9/11 Truth Movement asks you to do is look at the facts, look at the evidence, and make judgments for yourself."

Sisson spent a lot of time looking at evidence and making judgments during his thirty-seven years as a lawyer in Peace River. He went into law because he figured it would give him an opportunity to exercise his talent for theatrics. More important, he figured it would give him an opportunity to help the dispossessed, the needy, and the voiceless. He earned his law degree after a short stint as a reporter with *The Star Phoenix* in Saskatoon, articled in Edmonton, and then settled in Peace River. He spent most of his time after that "trying my damnedest to instill a sense of justice into the RCMP." Lawyers need to ask a lot of questions, Sisson said, and the police need to do the same. "They should be taking nothing on faith or at face value. They should be taking a good hard look at the evidence of any case, deciding what the facts are, and what are the probable causes." Sisson also felt the police had a tendency to come down particularly hard on the kinds of poor and underprivileged defendants he was representing.

When not hectoring the RCMP about their need to gather reliable evidence before laying charges, Sisson was having fun at his law practice, injecting humour into his court arguments, and collecting anecdotes for the books he would eventually write with his law partner, Dwayne Rowe, about rural life as it used to be. Not all of his cases were laughing matters, however. In 1953 he defended a trapper who was convicted of murder and, despite Sisson's best efforts, sentenced to hang. "And I worked my guts out for two months on that case," Sisson said. The accused, however, told him not to worry. He said he'd rather be executed than spend a lifetime in prison.

After that early reverse, Sisson decided that, whenever appropriate, he would play to the gallery for laughs, even when defending murderers or thieves. Like Paddy Nolan, the legendary, turn-of-the-century, Calgary defence lawyer and wit, Sisson believed that laughter in court could often relieve tension and boost the morale of the accused. "Even if the guy was guilty, you might get him a year less." Occasionally, Sisson would try to set up a funny courtroom scene that he could talk or write about afterward. He once asked two of his clients to sue one another because he thought the combination of their last names, Eek and Ek, would make the judge laugh. The clients, however, declined to play along. They were not amused, it seems.

After developing an interest in English vaudeville humour, Sisson joined the London-based British Music Hall Society, acquired comedy material from other members, reworked the routines for a Canadian audience, and produced a series of burlesque revues for his hometown Peace Players that ran for twenty years. Sisson starred as the featured funny man. His accountant wife Doreen, whom he had met in university, played his comic foil and managed the box office. Their jazz dancer daughter Lindy choreographed the dance numbers and performed in the chorus, starting when she was sixteen. As well as playing in Peace River, the revue also toured to other parts of northern Alberta and played in Edmonton during Klondike Days. *Edmonton Journal* reviewer Keith Ashwell described the show as a "raunchy romp through the best of the sexy skits in showbiz."

Sisson also made comedy a part of his platform when he went into provincial politics in the late 1950s. Like a dispenser of fortune cookies, he handed out empty drug capsules containing the message, "If you don't vote for Hal Sisson, you're a real dope." He ran unsuccessfully three times for the Progressive Conservatives during a period when Ernest Manning's Social Credit Party was sweeping the province in every election. Because teetotaller Manning seemed in no rush to reform Alberta's archaic drinking laws, Sisson arranged for the governor of Jamaica to phone the premier and propose tongue-in-cheek that the island nation keep Alberta continually supplied with cheap rum in return for a share of the province's tax revenues. Manning laughed and declined the offer. He also laughed upon hearing that Sisson met with British Columbia's premier, W. A. C. Bennett, to propose that the Peace River district be annexed by the neighbouring province. Sisson wanted the district's gravel roads to be paved, but Alberta had other spending priorities.

British Columbia became Sisson's home after he gave up his law practice. He and Doreen moved to a condominium in Victoria, and he rekindled his boyhood love of marbles after writing a story about losing his favourite "shooter" in a schoolyard game. The story appeared in his first book, *Coots, Codgers and Curmudgeons*, co-written with former law partner Rowe and published in 1994 when Sisson was competing in—and winning—marbles championships in the United States. He also was ranked among the top fifty competitive croquet players in Canada. "I like to play a sport I can win," he said. "And I don't skate or ski."

Sisson kept playing and winning, telling jokes, writing and publishing, until he died while awaiting a heart valve replacement at age eighty-eight on December 26, 2009. His aim, he said, was to keep writing as much as possible before "kicking off through the goalposts of life." His last piece of published writing was his own obituary, written with the encouragement of "my comely, long-suffering wife, Doreen." He wasn't about to go peacefully or quickly, Sisson said, because "I am a dead atheist, and they are persona non grata anywhere." He left his collection of 40,000 marbles to son Ted in Peace River, and bequeathed his file of jokes and skits to daughter Lindy, who runs a community arts centre in Maple Ridge, British Columbia. "When all is said and done, more is said than done," wrote Sisson. "But just keep hoping for the best and expecting the worst, because life is a play and we're all unrehearsed!" A self-promoter to the last, he concluded his obituary with information on where people could buy his books.

MILT HARRADENCE
Gun-Toting Lawyer and Judge
1922–2008

Milt Harradence began his legal career as a combative criminal defence lawyer who packed a gun for protection and excelled at undermining the testimony of prosecution witnesses. He ended it as a judge, still carrying weapons for protection, who felt that being on the bench was like "going to heaven, but not yet." "What I miss most about leaving the practice," he said, "is the fact that you are no longer a competitor but rather a referee—and the transition isn't easy."

His role model was John Diefenbaker, the jowly, growly, small-town lawyer who rose to become prime minister of Canada. Harradence spent his early years in Prince Albert, Saskatchewan, where Diefenbaker practiced law, and he often skipped classes at Prince Albert Collegiate to watch Diefenbaker in action in the courtroom. "He's the reason I got into law," Harradence would say in later years. "In my opinion, he was the finest trial lawyer that Canada ever produced. The moment he walked into a courtroom, he owned it."

Harradence became a lawyer after serving in the Second World War as an army corporal based in Alaska. He had hoped to see action overseas as a fighter pilot, but his daredevil behaviour as a nineteen-year-old flight sergeant in the Royal Canadian Air Force put paid to his chances. When posted to a bomber reconnaissance squadron in Vancouver, Harradence buzzed a

The Honourable A. Milton Harradence, Q.C., photographed in his Calgary law office in 1979. (Courtesy of the Legal Archives Society of Alberta, 115-G-11)

farmer's hayrack and struck a tree. He was court-martialled for "unauthorized low flying," fined $50, and denied promotion for six months. Instead of being promoted, however, he was discharged when he angered his commanding officer in Lethbridge by performing aerobatic stunts in an RCAF training aircraft, and then he lobbied too aggressively for transfer to a combat unit. At that point, he was told, "my services were no longer required." A firm believer in military service, Harradence then re-enlisted in the infantry and was dispatched to Alaska, "where I rose to the dizzying height of corporal."

When the war was over, Harradence took advantage of a veteran's education allowance to study law at the University of Saskatchewan in Saskatoon. Active in sports, he played with the university tennis team and won an intervarsity middleweight boxing title. He graduated with a law degree in 1949 and returned for an additional year to earn the B.A. that would allow him to be called to the bar in Alberta. He then moved to Calgary to article with the firm of Bennett, Nolan, Chambers, Might and Saucier (now, Bennett Jones).

In 1950 Harradence married Catherine Richardson of Calgary. He had met her five years earlier at a dance in Calgary's Glencoe Club put on as a fundraiser for young servicemen. A formal introduction was arranged between the twenty-three-year-old soldier and the seventeen-year-old doctor's daughter, and they married as soon as he finished university. They raised two sons and a daughter.

Harradence reignited his passion for flying after he settled in Calgary. He joined the 403 Fighter-Bomber Squadron (Auxiliary) at RCAF Station Calgary and did formation flying with the unit for five years before retiring as deputy flight commander. One of his stunts during that time was to have two RCAF Mustangs buzz a civil-defence caravan passing through Calgary when his commanding officer asked the squadron to provide some "entertainment" for the watching crowd. "There were a few people with some ruffled feathers because of that," he said. After retiring from the squadron, Harradence teamed up with a fellow 403 Squadron pilot, Lynn Garrison, to fly decommissioned RCAF Mustangs to new owners in New York. As part of their compensation, he and Garrison each received a Mustang, the first of three retired fighter aircraft that Harradence would acquire for his own use.

His career in criminal law began after Harradence had practiced commercial law for three years as a junior with Bennett, Nolan, and company. He started his own criminal law practice in partnership with a Calgary lawyer named Robert D. Freeze, and he soon became a familiar figure in the Calgary courts with his impeccably tailored suits and a style of courtroom performance that owed much to his childhood hero, Diefenbaker. Harradence's bag of actor's tricks included the furrowed brow, the jabbing accusatory finger, the piercing gaze, and a wicked smile that might have foreshadowed the poster image of Jack Nicholson for *The Shining*. Harradence even combed his hair much like Diefenbaker, straight back in a wavy, modified pompadour.

In 1957, with his fellow pilot Garrison as his campaign manager, Harradence took a break from the law to run for Calgary city council. Though elected, he quit after one term, bored with the mundane routine at city hall. In 1962 he was elected leader of the provincial Conservatives, but he never won a seat in the Legislature. The electorate, it seems, was not impressed by the fact that Harradence campaigned throughout the province in his fighter plane. The incumbent Social Credit premier, Ernest Manning, wasn't impressed either. "That Harradence and that Mustang have a lot in common," said Manning. "They're both noisy, expensive, and obsolete." Harradence stepped down as Conservative leader after the election and was replaced by fellow lawyer Peter Lougheed, who did considerably better. In 1971 Lougheed led the party to victory over the Socreds, establishing a dynasty that continued for the next 44 years.

Though wooed by the federal Liberals, Harradence left politics behind after his defeat in the 1963 provincial election. "The defeat convinced me I had little or no future in political life," he said. He went back to practicing law and flying for pleasure. He joined the Confederate Air Force, a playfully named, Texas-based group of former fighter pilots, and in 1966 became the first Canadian to fly in one of the group's annual air shows. Piloting a Mustang, Harradence took part in a demonstration of military aircraft that had flown during the Second World War. "There is no one in the world who can fly the Mustang the way he does," said the air show organizer.

He practiced criminal law for more than twenty years, often acting as counsel for the RCMP and for municipal police officers charged with serious crimes. In one notable instance, he represented a fellow lawyer, Webster Macdonald, who had been charged with forgery and uttering false documents in a land deal. To prepare for the trial, Harradence closeted himself in the Palliser Hotel for a week and committed to memory the contents of all the documents the Crown had produced to make its case. In characteristic Harradence style, he then conducted his defence without referring to notes or even taking notes. "Who needs notes," he said afterward. "Guys are so busy writing, they don't get the courtroom atmosphere. There's a lot they miss by not looking around." Through skillful and thorough cross-examination, Harradence systematically shredded the testimony of the Crown witnesses, leaving the judge to rule there was "not a tittle of evidence" to warrant a guilty verdict. Macdonald was, as he put it himself, "resoundingly acquitted."

Aside from representing lawyers and police officers, Harradence acted for some of the toughest criminals to appear in the Calgary courts during the 1960s and 1970s. In a city with a relatively low crime rate, he said he couldn't afford to be too choosy about his clients. One was an American with a long list of convictions for violent crimes, arrested in Calgary and held without bail pending extradition. Harradence tried unsuccessfully to get bail for the fugitive, who retaliated by issuing death threats from the prison in Montana where he was incarcerated after extradition. Taking the threats seriously, Harradence applied for and received a police permit to carry concealed, restricted weapons. He packed a pistol in a leg holster, kept one loaded shotgun under his desk and a second shotgun under the dashboard of his Cadillac. For additional protection, he replaced all the windows in his house with bulletproof glass. Harradence was asked about this in a television interview with Toronto broadcaster Patrick Watson. "Why do you have bulletproof glass in your house, and why do you carry a firearm? Is it the telephone calls that you get?" asked Watson. "No, Mr. Watson, it's the telephone calls I *don't* get," replied Harradence ominously. He never actually had to fire the weapons but insisted he always needed to have them close at hand because he continued to receive death threats from other angry clients.

In July 1975 *The Canadian*, a Toronto magazine, named Harradence one of Canada's ten best trial lawyers. "At 53, he's a tall, handsome, commanding presence who can often win a case simply on the force of his overpowering personality," said the magazine's writer. The writer complimented Harradence on his cross-examination skills, especially when dealing with doctors. "Very fragile egos," Harradence said. "They're used to asking questions, not answering them." The writer then went on to claim, paradoxically and without elaboration, that "law is not his strong point." This assessment was clearly not shared by federal Justice Minister Marc Lalonde who—four years after publication of the *Canadian* article—appointed Harradence to the Alberta Court of Appeal.

Going directly from private practice to the Court of Appeal, without first serving as a provincial court judge and then as a justice in the Court of Queen's Bench, was a rare occurrence in Alberta. The fact that it happened to Harradence was a testament to his exceptional legal skills. Over the next eighteen years, Harradence became the appellate court's most frequent dissenter, almost always in favour of criminal defendants. Six of his nine dissenting opinions were ultimately upheld by the Supreme Court of Canada, and thus became the law of the land.

One of the Alberta Court of Appeal decisions that was struck down by the Supreme Court involved the 1994 appeal of Holocaust denier Jim Keegstra against a 1992 conviction—his second—of willfully inciting hatred against Jews. As a high-school teacher in Eckville, Alberta, Keegstra had taught that the story of six million Jews being killed in the Holocaust was a hoax perpetrated by an international Jewish conspiracy. First convicted of hate mongering in 1985, Keegstra was tried a second time in 1992 after the original case went to the Supreme Court for a decision on whether Canada's so-called anti-hate law was constitutional. The Supreme Court upheld the law's constitutionality and sent the case back to the Alberta Court of Appeal, which ordered a new trial.

Keegstra was convicted a second time in 1992, and the Alberta Court of Appeal overturned this conviction on a technicality. Writing for the three-member appeal panel, Harradence said the trial judge, Arthur Lutz, had given inappropriate direction to the jury. He had failed to respond to the jury's request for a transcript and for help in understanding the Criminal Code. But Harradence also argued against granting Keegstra a third trial, on grounds that it would "only serve to exacerbate the harm and injury already done to both the target group and society in general." This set the stage for another appeal to the Supreme Court, which in 1994 overturned the Alberta Court of Appeal decision by Harradence and his colleagues, and upheld the original conviction, which brought Keegstra a $3,000 fine. Harradence was not at all unhappy about this Supreme Court reversal. In his mind, justice had finally been served.

Harradence suffered a terrible loss during the years he served on the Court of Appeal. On June 6, 1986, his eldest son, Rod Harradence, was killed when the single-engine Cessna in which he was a passenger crashed into the side of Mount Lougheed in Kananaskis Country while searching for victims of another plane crash. Seventeen years later, on July 3, 2003, tragedy struck the Harradence family again when son Bruce Harradence was killed in a traffic accident in Mesa, Arizona, where he was living at the time. Bruce was riding his motorcycle and making a left turn when an oncoming vehicle T-boned him. Harradence grieved the loss of his two sons for the rest of his life. He found it difficult to accept that they had been killed while he had survived any number of daredevil stunts as a barnstorming pilot.

Harradence's final stunt as a pilot occurred in 1997, when he stepped down from the bench at the mandatory retirement age of seventy-five. He became an honorary colonel with the 416 Tactical Fighter Squadron at Cold Lake, Alberta, and was invited to take the controls of a CF-18 Hornet when it was on its way to breaking the sound barrier. Ever the daredevil, Harradence added some moves to the exercise and thus became, as he said afterward, "the oldest pilot to slow-roll an F-18 at Mach 3 plus." His appointment as honorary colonel with the squadron more than compensated for his banishment from the RCAF during the Second World War. Harradence said he "felt as good as the bellhop who was fired and later returned to buy the hotel."

In 1998, at age seventy-six, Harradence was diagnosed with prostate cancer. The disease went into remission after treatment and the prognosis seemed positive. In fact, his doctor assured him he was more likely to die *with* the disease than *from* it. Nine years later, however, the cancer returned and spread. The medication made Harradence drowsy, but it didn't dull his mental faculties. When a close friend asked if he had been flying an F-16 or an F-18 when he broke the sound barrier, Harradence immediately replied, "F-18." Then he added with a wry smile, "I suppose you need to know that for the eulogy." He died on February 28, 2008, at age eighty-five.

DONALD CORMIE
Disgraced Financier
1922–2010

Albertans always loathed the big banks. Their antipathy dated back to the Great Depression when the Social Credit government blamed "eastern bankers" for Canada's economic woes. That's why Donald Cormie was welcomed like a knight in shining armour when he came on the scene during the 1950s. Albertans viewed his Edmonton-based financial services corporation as a safe and appealing western alternative to the big institutions with head offices in Toronto and Montreal.

"All your money is kept in a vault, like a bag with your name on it," said a typical sales pitch for what came to be known as the Principal Group of Companies. For those who invested, however, the vault eventually turned out to be an empty coffer. More than 67,000 investors were out a total of $554 million when the company finally declared bankruptcy in 1987. It was one of the biggest financial failures in Alberta history.

Cormie had no experience in the financial services industry when he first became involved with Principal. He was a thirty-two-year-old Edmonton lawyer who specialized in real-estate, commercial, and securities law. Educated at the University of Alberta and at Harvard, he spent his university years serving as secretary-treasurer for his father's feed mill. After graduation he did the legal work for the mill as a lawyer with the firm of Smith, Clement, Parlee and Whittaker.

In 1954 Cormie struck out on his own. He founded the law firm Cormie Kennedy with a twenty-eight-year-old litigator named Jack Kennedy. By that time, however, Cormie no longer saw a fulfilling future for himself as a corporate lawyer. He had been working at it for seven years, and he wanted out. "It was frustrating to act for clients and lay out careful business plans for them which they wouldn't follow," he said. "I was dying to try out my ideas."

To promote his ideas, Cormie became a major shareholder with First Investors Corporation (FIC), an investment firm founded by an Edmonton realtor named Stan Melton. FIC sold what it called "investment contracts" to people who purchased them on an installment plan at the rate of $10 to $30 monthly and held them for up to twenty years. The contracts functioned like savings bonds with a cash surrender value. At the end of the specified savings period, the contract holder would receive the total saved plus interest. The contract holder had no direct stake in any of the company's investments. Each contract was, in effect, an IOU payable by the company at maturity.

From 1954 to 1958 Cormie played no direct role in the day-to-day operations of FIC. Then came a palace coup, followed by a changing of the guard. Founding president Melton was pushed out for reasons never made public. Cormie took control of the firm. By that time, the company was starting to expand rapidly. It had branch offices in Calgary, Red Deer, Regina, and Moose Jaw. With Cormie at the helm and an enterprising salesman named Ken Marlin in charge of the Edmonton headquarters, FIC flourished.

In the fall of 1959, FIC expanded into the United States. It couldn't use the name First Investors because there already was an American company operating under that name, so it adopted the name Principal for its U.S. operations. It started with an office in Seattle and then opened offices in Oregon, Colorado, and other parts of Washington State. At the same time, FIC opened offices in Nova Scotia, New Brunswick, and Newfoundland.

Through all this growth, Cormie remained decidedly low-key. He rarely granted media interviews and came across in public as cool and aloof. "You like to stay a little quiet until you get to a certain size," he said. "Once you get over a billion dollars, the environment changes. We've always avoided publicity. Your competitors leave you alone when you're small. But when you get big, they start shooting at you."

In December 1959 Cormie and his FIC partners transferred all their shares to a holding company they owned called Collective Securities. It was a deal that an Alberta government regulator would call later a "well-watered" stock transaction. This referred to the habit—common among unscrupulous bartenders—of topping up partially filled wine carafes with water. The partners valued their FIC shares at six times the original cost. In the process, they grossly inflated the book value of Collective Securities. This was the first of many dubious transactions that brought the operations of Cormie's companies to the attention of regulators.

One of those regulators was a thirty-year-old chartered accountant named Jim Darwish. He worked as an auditor for the Alberta Securities Commission. When he first checked the FIC file in 1959, he noticed that something seemed out of whack. Under the province's Investment Contracts Act the company was supposed to maintain up to $500,000 in "qualified assets" (for example, cash, secured mortgages, bonds, or debentures) in its bank account to cover its liability to contract holders. These assets only existed on paper, however. Apparent increases in FIC share capital had been achieved through a series of book-keeping transactions involving associated companies owned or controlled by Cormie. These companies included an 8,900-hectare cattle-ranch business at Tomahawk, seventy-five kilometres west of Edmonton. In most instances no money actually changed hands. Author Wendy Smith illustrated the strategy in her book, *Pay Yourself First: Donald Cormie and the Collapse of the Principal Group of Companies*:

> If I buy a mongrel puppy for a dollar and sell it to you in exchange for an IOU of $1,000, and you sell the puppy to your uncle for an IOU of $1,000, and he sells the puppy back to me for an IOU of $1,000—is there $1,000 anywhere?

Certainly not. There's just a mongrel puppy, a dollar bill, and a lot of damp paper.

The inflated increases in share capital were just one irregularity that Darwish detected. He also noticed that Cormie and his fellow company officers paid themselves high salaries and withdrew large sums of company money to pay off personal bank loans. In a 1961 memo to his supervisors, Darwish complained about excessive management fees paid to companies owned or controlled by Cormie. Darwish said more capital would have to be put into FIC to meet the financial requirements of the Investment Contracts Act. Many of the company's holdings were not legally qualified assets under the act. Cormie didn't like such regulatory interference in his affairs, but he did undertake to comply with the legal requirements. It was a meaningless undertaking. The requirements were so vague they could have been interpreted in any number of ways.

Cormie and his associates created the beginnings of an impenetrable corporate system when they transferred their FIC shares to their holding company, Collective Securities. In 1962 Collective acquired Associated Investors of Canada (AIC), an investment contract company similar to FIC. AIC soon began to cause headaches for Darwish and his fellow regulators. In 1965 Darwish reported on a number of irregularities he detected in AIC's audited financial statements. An independent accounting firm, Peat, Marwick, and Mitchell, identified these as over-valuation of assets, improper intercompany transfers, and excessive dividends and management fees.

FIC and AIC operated as relatively independent entities, with their own sales forces and executives, until 1966. Then they were consolidated under the umbrella of Principal Group, a holding and management company Cormie created as a vehicle to provide complete, one-stop, personal financial services to customers. Principal billed itself as "The Department Store of Finance." Its holdings included its flagship company, Principal Savings and Trust, as well as a Canadian insurance company and a number of Canadian and American mutual fund companies.

The creation of Principal allowed Cormie and his partners to streamline their operations by keeping all their administrative activities under one roof. But it posed difficulties for the regulators trying to assess the actual financial state of the individual companies within the system.

The regulators achieved a victory of sorts in 1966 when they threatened to suspend the operating licences of FIC and AIC because of "totally improper conduct in operating these companies." The alleged conduct included paying millions of dollars in dividends to shareholders out of paper profits and paying "exorbitant" management fees to related companies in which Cormie had a direct or indirect interest. The regulators forced Cormie and his associates to return $300,000 in management fees taken from AIC, and extracted a promise from Cormie that the payment of excessive management fees and dividends, and improper intercompany transfers, would cease. But the victory was short-lived. A pattern soon resumed whereby FIC and AIC borrowed money to pay off maturing investment contracts while simultaneously loaning money and paying dividends and management fees to related companies.

During the early 1970s, FIC and AIC switched from selling installment plans to "single pay" certificates similar to the guaranteed investment certificates sold by banks or trust companies. However, unlike the larger financial institutions, which were required by law to have a debt-to-equity ratio of fifteen to one (meaning that the institutions could borrow up to a maximum of $15 for every dollar invested), FIC and AIC had no debt-to-equity restrictions. Under the provisions of the toothless Investment Contracts Act, they were required only to hold $500,000 in liquid assets for the protection of the investing public.

Between 1973 and 1975, regulator Darwish sent a series of reports to provincial cabinet ministers expressing concern about the financial standing of FIC and AIC. In one of them, he urged that the Attorney General be called in to investigate whether or not "there has been a breach of trust or other Criminal Code violations." A report by an external auditor had led Darwish to conclude the assets of the Principal companies were over-valued by millions of dollars and that the companies were hard pressed to cover their liabilities to certificate holders. The Attorney General never did become involved. But Darwish's reports did result in strict new guidelines being established for the Principal companies and a timetable being set for compliance.

Darwish continued to worry that investors' money might be at risk. He had reached what he thought was a "gentleman's agreement" with Cormie and other Principal officers that the companies would operate with a debt-to-equity radio of twenty-five to one. However, the agreement was—as Alberta Ombudsman Alex Trawick noted later—"continually violated and ignored." In 1984 one of Darwish's fellow regulators, Allan Hutchison, reported that the two Principal Group units were "virtually insolvent" and had a "staggering" debt-to-equity ratio of 560 to one. The companies held a total of $18.8 million in foreclosed mortgages following the collapse of the Alberta real-estate market in the early 1980s; 71 per cent of their entire mortgage portfolio was in arrears and 42 per cent was in foreclosure.

There were no outward signs that the Principal companies were in trouble, however. The corporate headquarters, Principal Plaza, dominated the downtown Edmonton skyline. From the top of the thirty-storey tower, the letters spelling out the Principal name shone like a beacon, visible from several kilometres away. (Investors believed Principal actually owned the building, but the company was, in fact, just leasing the ground floor and three upper floors.) The company's holdings included one subsidiary, County Investments, which became known as Cormie's "little bank," as well as an actual bank in the Cayman Islands. The fruits of success for Cormie included homes in Edmonton, Stony Plain, Arizona, and Victoria, as well as a ranch, and a forty-one-foot yacht.

Regulator Hutchison estimated that if FIC was liquidated, its debts would exceed its assets by more than $73 million. He recommended appraisals on all mortgages that were six months or more in arrears and urged that the companies be made to comply with the Investment Contracts Act's capital requirements. Darwish sought a meeting with Alberta's consumer and corporate affairs minister, Connie Osterman, to explain the urgency of the situation. When she didn't reply, he sent her a long memo listing conditions with which the companies should immediately comply or have their licences pulled. Among them was a demand that the companies reverse a transaction in which FIC and AIC paid $23 million to Principal Savings and Trust for nineteen mortgages and four properties of dubious value.

Osterman reacted furiously. In a telephone conversation on April 30, 1984, she told Darwish that she didn't want any more advice from him. "If you keep making these recommendations, you're going to have to make a career decision," she said. "You're on the outside looking in. There have been discussions with company officials, and you don't have a clue about the other side of this." This was an apparent reference to a luncheon meeting Osterman had a couple of months previously with Cormie and some of his vice-presidents.

Cormie and his associates had always enjoyed a friendly relationship with Alberta politicians. Over the years, they had often sought relief from what they perceived as unreasonable demands on the part of hostile regulators. They had repeatedly warned that the province's entire financial services industry would be endangered if the Principal companies were hurt. This struck a sympathetic chord with the politicians because Alberta had a long history of favouring homegrown savings companies and credit unions over eastern financial institutions. Rather than rewrite and strengthen what the regulators regarded as an inadequate Investment Contracts Act, the politicians entrusted their civil servants with the task of making "gentlemen's agreements" that invariably turned out to be worthless.

Darwish interpreted Osterman's telephone remarks as a threat to get rid of him. Six months later, he took early retirement at age fifty-five. There was no retirement party to honour his thirty-five years of government service. Only his wife and a few of his colleagues knew he had left involuntarily.

The Principal companies limped along for another two years after Darwish's departure. Regulators asked for an independent accounting firm to look at the companies' books but were told that Osterman would not authorize this "because it would cause a run on the companies." The companies lost $13.6 million in the first nine months of 1985. Finally, in January 1987, the provincial Treasury department decided to act. It called in an accounting firm, Price Waterhouse, to determine whether or not the companies could survive.

Price Waterhouse reported that the Principal companies would need at least $150 million to stay afloat. Cormie tried to negotiate a government bailout but to no avail. On June 30, 1987, Provincial Treasurer Dick Johnston cancelled the operating licences of FIC and AIC. Six weeks later Principal Group declared bankruptcy.

A court-ordered inquiry was conducted by Calgary litigation lawyer Bill Code. A separate investigation was done by Ombudsman Trawick. Darwish was a key witness in both. He struggled to hold back tears when he testified about his April 1984 phone conversation with Osterman. "She was agitated. As a matter of fact she was yelling at me," said Darwish. "I feel that I was fired or forced out." Osterman said that her reaction to Darwish's memo was "reasonably negative" because she felt he was interfering in areas that were not his concern.

The Code investigation, which took two years to complete, found "evidence tending to show" that Cormie and his partners had defrauded investors with misleading sales pitches, and had evaded taxes and manipulated stock markets. "Principal Group ran a funny business," said Code. But the RCMP couldn't find any evidence of criminal conduct and decided not to lay charges. The Code report also accused Osterman of being "neglectful and misguided" when she refused to act on the recommendations of her subordinates.

Trawick's report praised Darwish and his fellow auditors for reporting "thoroughly and tenaciously" in the face of a "clear failure" by their department superiors to "heed or in some instances to understand" their warnings. Darwish was jubilant. "It was one of the best things that ever happened to me," he said. "I was able to stick by what I thought was right and, in the end, I was vindicated."

Premier Don Getty dismissed Osterman from his cabinet one week after the Code report came out in July 1989. At the same time, he announced a partial compensation to Alberta investors of 15 to 18 cents on every dollar invested. Cormie pleaded guilty under the Investors Act to misleading investors and was fined $500,000. The Tax Court of Canada ordered him to pay $4 million in back taxes on a $7.2 million loan he took from Principal just before it collapsed. A Court of Queen's Bench judge ruled that he made improper payouts totalling $500,000 to creditors who were family members or company employees. The judge ordered these creditors to give back the money.

While the bankruptcy diminished Cormie's personal fortune, it hardly reduced him to penury. *The Globe and Mail* reported that he still owned multi-million-dollar residential properties in Edmonton, Victoria, and Arizona, as well as that forty-one-foot yacht valued at $1.25 million.

It took fourteen years for investors to receive their final payments. Most of them were elderly people who had entrusted their retirement savings to Principal. Seventy-five per cent of them lived in Alberta. The rest were in British Columbia, Saskatchewan, and the Maritimes. At the end of the day, the Albertans obtained about 90 cents for every dollar invested, with no compensation for any interest that might have accumulated. Investors in other provinces received less because their provincial governments put in a smaller amount of money to reimburse them. The final payments came from the sale of Cormie's cattle ranch in Tomahawk. Purchased in 1962 for $77,000, the ranch was worth an estimated $20 million when sold.

Darwish sued the province for $7,678 in back holiday pay and won. The severance package he negotiated with the Alberta government included about a year's salary and full government pension, allowing him to ease comfortably into retirement.

Cormie was banned from trading on the Alberta Stock Exchange for ten years. He moved to Arizona and lived there, with occasional trips back to Edmonton, for the rest of his life. He had no opportunity to start another business after the Principal Group debacle. He spent all his time with lawyers and accountants, sorting through the company's ruins. He had some regrets about that. "He missed the biggest boom in Alberta history," one of his sons, Bruce, told *The Globe and Mail*. Cormie's legal battles eventually cost him an estimated $10 million. They dragged on until 2005, when the Canada Revenue Agency finally signed off on a transfer of money that had been tied up in a trust. Cormie spent his remaining years travelling with his wife, Eivor, and pursuing an interest in photography, until Parkinson's disease slowed his movements.

He died in Scottsdale, Arizona, on February 20, 2010, at age eighty-seven. His eldest son, John, told the *Edmonton Journal* that the RCMP investigation into the Principal Group collapse had amounted to a "concerted effort to criminalize his activities that greatly damaged his reputation, in our minds unfairly." The demise of Principal radically changed the course of Cormie's life, said John, "and yet my father was never one to spend time looking backward. We just sort of had to get on and deal with the hand that was dealt us."

CLAIRE HEDWIG CHELL

Co-Inventor of the Bloody Caesar
1924–2003

Claire Chell's long and varied career trajectory took her from a Second World War posting as a signals officer in the German air force to a stint as a 911 dispatcher with the Toronto Metropolitan Police when she was in her sixties and seventies. Along the way, she spent eight years with the United States Army in postwar Germany, worked in the jewellery business in Canada and South Africa, and earned a footnote in the annals of the Canadian hospitality industry when she helped her husband Walter Chell create the Bloody Caesar, the clam-and-tomato infused vodka drink that is now the most popular cocktail in the country. If Claire had one regret, it was that she and Walter never trademarked the Bloody Caesar. Just one cent from each cocktail, she calculated, would have brought them an estimated $350,000 annually.

Claire was all set to make a career for herself in either fashion design or interior decorating in Mannheim, Germany, when the Second World War took her life in another direction. The youngest daughter of a Mannheim carpenter, Karl August Thomas, and his wife Anna, a hotel chef, Claire joined the Luftwaffe in 1943 when the war called her to patriotic service. She was not a Nazi supporter, nor a fan of Hitler, but she felt obliged to do her duty.

A single-minded firebrand who stood just four-foot-eleven, Claire inherited a strong independent streak from her mother

Claire Hedwig Chell at the U.S. Army base in Mannheim, Germany, where Chell worked as a civilian translator and switchboard operator after the Second World War. (Courtesy of Rose and Sheena Jay Parker)

who, according to family lore, once sought and obtained a judicial order from the German courts to have her husband do more housework, be more devoted to her, and spend more time with their children. Claire learned from her mother that she had to be "emotionally, intellectually, and financially independent from your spouse in the event that some day you might be left alone."

Claire did find herself left alone in 1950 when her first husband, an alcoholic United States Army corporal named Robert Meyering, was sent home in disgrace after punching out a military policeman on the base in Mannheim where the two were stationed. The policeman had rebuked Meyering for borrowing an army jeep without permission to take Claire's ailing father to hospital for heart treatment. Claire, who was fluent in English as well as German, French, and Italian, had met and married Meyering after the war when she was hired by the U.S. Army as a civilian translator and switchboard operator. She was happy to work for the Americans, she said, because her parents had been forced to forfeit property during the war, and Claire felt that her country had betrayed them.

Meyering wanted Claire to accompany him when he was sent back to the States. However, she didn't think that she, as a German national, would be particularly welcome in postwar America. Besides, with her father close to death, she didn't want to abandon her mother. So she opted to remain in Germany with her daughter Rose, who was then two years old.

Claire kept in touch with her husband by correspondence for the next several years, but she eventually lost contact with him. A year after he left for the States, she moved with her daughter to the Bavarian resort town of Garmisch-Partenkirchen, where she completed her service with the u.s. Army and then worked as a switchboard operator in a hotel. There she met Walter Chell, a handsome Italian front-desk manager with a Clark Gable moustache, who became her second husband. Raised in a Trieste orphanage after his parents died, Walter had trained in the hotel industry in Switzerland and worked in the kitchen of the Aga Khan in Geneva before moving to Germany. With the German tourism industry in decline, Walter immigrated to Canada in 1958 in search of better opportunities. When he found a job, he sent for Claire and Rose. The couple shared a love of cooking, dancing, and opera. Walter sang arias from *The Marriage of Figaro* in the shower, and Claire mimed the role of a conductor directing the orchestra in her favourite Puccini recordings whenever friends came to visit. She and Walter were married in Vancouver in June 1959. Daughter Joan was born the following year.

Although Walter had worked for fifteen years in the hotel industry in Switzerland and Germany, he had to start over—as a dishwasher at the Hotel Georgia—when he moved to Vancouver. He didn't mind. Canada was the land of opportunity, and things would soon work out for the better. Claire took a job across the street at Birks because she wanted to learn about the jewellery business.

Walter worked his way up to maître d' at the Hotel Georgia and was transferred as food and beverage services manager to the new Calgary Inn when it opened in 1964. Claire, rekindling an early career interest, worked for a Calgary interior-decorating firm.

In 1969 the Calgary Inn opened Marco's, an Italian restaurant, across the street from the hotel, and Walter was asked to create an Italian-style cocktail for the occasion. Walter, who preferred a good red wine to hard liquor, enlisted Claire to assist him as taster, and together they concocted a vodka, mashed-clams, and tomato-juice drink to go with the linguine alle vongole. They figured that if tomato-and-clam sauce was good for pasta, it should also be good for a drink. They named the drink the Caesar, and the story goes that the cocktail acquired the other part of its name when an English-born bar customer sampled it and exclaimed, "Walter, that's a damn good bloody Caesar."

The Bloody Caesar was an immediate success at the new restaurant and, when an American company named Duffy-Mott later patented a mix called Clamato, the drink became a favourite across Canada. The Chells never received a penny for their creation. But daughter Rose hoped that somewhere in her parents' papers she would eventually find a document showing they were entitled to royalties.

The Chells lived in Calgary until 1972, during which time the Calgary Inn became part of the Westin hotel chain. Walter was transferred to South Africa to help open the Westin's Carlton Hotel in Johannesburg. He also worked as the chain's chief North American restaurant troubleshooter, making flying visits to Westin hotels across the continent and fixing any problems they had with food and beverage services. Claire worked for Stern Jewellers in Johannesburg and also did some interior decorating work.

In 1975 the Chells returned to Canada. Walter worked at Hotel Toronto and Claire worked as switchboard operator at a Sheraton hotel for a number of years until she decided, at age sixty-five, that she wanted to work for the police department. "She's going to drive me crazy," said Walter, throwing up his hands and shaking his head. "She should be retired, and now she wants to work for the police." But Claire said she had always dreamed of working with people who caught bad guys, and she was not about to be deterred. She told the Canada Pension Plan people she was not ready to start collecting her benefits yet, joined the Toronto Metropolitan Police as a 911 dispatcher, and went to work every night on the subway.

She was mugged not once but twice while travelling home from work, yet she stubbornly refused to quit her job. After the second mugging, her boss had a police officer drive her home in a squad car after her shifts ended. Walter, at that point, was retired from the Westin chain and working part-time as a consultant for Duffy-Mott, the American company that reformulated and patented the clam-and-tomato mix he and Claire originally concocted for the Bloody Caesar.

Claire worked until she was seventy-two, when she finally retired from the police service to look after Walter, a heavy smoker, who had lost a lung to cancer. He died in March 1997 at age seventy-one. He told Claire he wanted to be buried in Calgary, where they had made many friends, a new life, and their famous drink. Claire bought one condominium in Calgary, where she could be close to her two granddaughters, and a second condominium in Kelowna, British Columbia, which became her summer vacation home. She also had her condominium in Toronto, which she began to renovate by herself at age seventy-seven, despite the onset of bladder cancer and macular degeneration.

As her cancer progressed, Claire began to empathize with fellow sufferers. A devout Catholic, she tried phoning Pope John Paul II to express condolences about his illness, but she had to settle for leaving a message with a cardinal in the Vatican. She told the cardinal she would always remember the pope in her prayers.

Claire died on December 29, 2003, at age seventy-nine at her Calgary home, surrounded by family. She said she wanted to go out in style, in a mahogany casket similar to the one built for President John F. Kennedy in November 1963. The family had to scramble to find one, but they did manage to track one down in Syracuse, New York—the only such casket available in North America, apparently—and got it to Calgary just in time for the funeral on January 2, 2004. The beverage of choice at the reception afterward was, of course, the Bloody Caesar. In May 2009, on the fortieth anniversary of the drink's invention, an online petition was launched to have it designated Canada's national cocktail. The petition was successful. Canada's first National Caesar Day was celebrated on May 14, 2015.

ROBERT KROETSCH
Author
1927–2011

Robert Kroetsch was an original, an experimenter who did more than any writer to find new ways of telling western Canada's story. "We haven't got any identity until somebody tells our story," he was famously quoted as saying. "The fiction makes us real." Often described as a literary "trickster" (i.e., a rogue), Kroetsch was both hailed for his achievements as an artistic trailblazer and criticized as a self-consciously academic practitioner of post-structuralist writing. Or as his friend Rudy Wiebe once put it, "Bob, you're always horsing around with language."

Kroetsch first became aware of the absence of a distinctive western Canadian literary style when he was a young teenager living in rural Alberta during the early 1940s. Raised on a farm in the grassy Battle River country near Heisler, southeast of Edmonton, he was an avid reader who gravitated toward writing because he wanted to make up for what he was missing as a reader. "The stories I read were not about us and I wanted to tell our stories," he said. "And I wanted to use our language." In other words, he wanted to use the colloquial speech of the West, not the elevated diction of British, high-society drawing rooms.

He also wanted in some manner to emulate his father, who was well-known throughout the Battle River region as a raconteur. Whenever his father told a story that young Kroetsch found particularly engaging, he would retreat to his bedroom and try

Robert Kroetsch. (Courtesy of Nicholas Mather)

to recapture it on paper. "I tried to write it down because I didn't have my father's talent," he said. "I guess a lot of writers are failed storytellers, in a paradoxical way."

The act of writing things down helped clarify his thinking but also made Kroetsch wonder how much of what he saw and heard was objectively true. He traced this skepticism to an event from his childhood when he saw the local priest blessing ordinary water with the intent that it should be transformed into something sacred. The holy water was then placed in a font outside the church. It was the middle of winter. The young Kroetsch dipped his hand in the font to make the Sign of the Cross after Mass and was shocked to discover the water had frozen solid. "I had a crisis of faith right there," he jokingly said afterward. "If holy water can freeze, can I believe anything else? I came to profound doubt in my own way."

With the encouragement of his high-school English teacher in Red Deer, Kroetsch earned an English degree at the University of Alberta, and then set out—at age twenty—to gain the kind of experience that would make it possible for him to write a novel. "Hemingway was the model," he said afterward. "I went up North to have the necessary experience and then the novel would take care of itself. It was an old-fashioned notion in a way." Never interested in taking over the family farm ("my father always figured I'd eventually come to my senses"), Kroetsch decided to work and save money for a few years and then devote the rest of his life to writing.

After three years as a purser on Mackenzie River riverboats and four more working for the U.S. Air Force as an information specialist in Goose Bay, Labrador, Kroetsch moved to Montreal in 1954 to "live in a garret," as he put it, and become a writer. He took a course from novelist Hugh MacLennan, tried unsuccessfully to learn French, and then went to Middlebury College, Vermont, to complete an M.A. in English. He married a fellow student, Mary Jane Lewis from North Carolina, had two daughters and later divorced. His second marriage, to Greek poet and academic Smaro Kamboureli, also ended in divorce though they remained friends and colleagues.

After spending the better part of a decade bouncing around American universities—first as a post-graduate student and then as a teacher—Kroetsch finally published his first novel, *But We Are Exiles*, at age thirty-eight. In it he endeavoured to write in a narrative style, with plenty of western Canadian vernacular, a story that somehow reflected his upbringing. "I wanted to tell the story in a way that spoke in our language, out of our climate, out of our geography, out of our emotional context," he said.

Based on his experiences working on the riverboats, *But We Are Exiles* was written primarily in a conventionally realistic mode while alluding to elements of Greek myth (specifically, Ovid's version of the Narcissus story) and Joseph Conrad's *Heart of Darkness*, the most important of Kroetsch's early literary influences. Published in 1965, the book launched Kroetsch on a writing career that produced close to five decades' worth of novels, poetry, essays, nonfiction books, and literary criticism.

In the novels that followed *But We Are Exiles*, Kroetsch moved away from the traditional prairie realism of Sinclair Ross toward what he called "tall tales" and the literary critics called magic realism or surrealism. *The Words of My Roaring* (1966) is a comic fable about a small-town undertaker named Johnnie Backstrom who, inspired by a blustering politician modelled on Social Credit evangelist William Aberhart, runs for office in the 1935 Alberta election on the whimsical promise of bringing rain to the drought-stricken countryside. *The Studhorse Man* (1969) is a ribald tale about a lecherous horse breeder named Hazard Lepage who wanders Alberta in search of the perfect mare for his rare blue stallion. It won the 1969 Governor General's Literary Award and gave rise to one of Kroetsch's favourite stories about himself. In the story Kroetsch told about a New York editor who took him to lunch in 1970 to celebrate the success of *The Studhorse Man*. After a few drinks, the editor leaned across the table and asked, "Say, does this place called Alberta really exist, or did you make it up?" Kroetsch's answer, he jokingly said afterward, was not the right one. "I should have said it doesn't."

The third of what Kroetsch called his "Out West" novels, *Gone Indian* (1973), is about a New York creative-writing student named Jeremy Sadness who, inspired by the British impostor who reinvented himself as Grey Owl, comes to the Canadian West in search of the last frontier. In between these three novels, Kroetsch published a nonfiction travel book, *Alberta* (1968), commissioned by a Toronto publisher, Macmillan, as part of a ten-volume, province-by-province project marking Canada's centennial. "I'm intrigued by travel writing as a genre," Kroetsch said. "It's an interesting form, based on motion through the world." The difference here was that he wasn't travelling to some exotic place. "I was looking at home. Do something like that and you find out how much you know."

Alberta was always home for Kroetsch. Though he spent enough time teaching at the University of Manitoba—seventeen years—to qualify as what CBC broadcaster Eleanor Wachtel called an "almost native son" of Winnipeg, and also spent fifteen years in Victoria, Kroetsch felt more at home in Alberta than anywhere else. It was his magic kingdom. "I think it's partly imprinted in childhood," he said in an interview with fellow novelist Aritha van Herk for a June 2011 story in *Alberta Views* magazine. "The landscape that I feel at home in is our landscape. A lot of my attraction to Alberta is nature, but it's also city and town, a distinctive flavour here."

Perhaps the most memorable description of how Alberta shaped Kroetsch's writing comes from author Michael Ondaatje who wrote in an email to *The Globe and Mail* that Kroetsch was a "great force out of the west…a bolt of energy for the Canadian novel at a time when it really needed it. He took the novel right out of the parlour, kidnapped it, and repositioned it in a prairie bar or in open country." In the beer taverns and horse barns of Alberta, Kroetsch found his voice and the settings for his novels.

All told, Kroetsch published ten novels over a period of thirty years. He also published poetry, something he started to do relatively late in his career. "Ordinarily, you begin with poetry when you're young, and then you graduate to other stuff," he said. Whenever he wrote poetry, he stopped writing novels. "It's like being a split personality," he said. "I do one or the other. I can't do both at once."

Recognition for his poetry came in the form of a shortlisting for the Governor General's Award in 2004. That same year he also was made an Officer of the Order of Canada. A few years later he received a Writers Guild of Alberta Golden Pen Award for lifetime achievement. But he regarded such recognition as little more than a "pat on the back that says, 'Keep at it.'" True success, he maintained, lay in the act of writing. "I would hate to think that at the end of my life I should have done some writing, but I didn't." He regretted the fact that while he had wanted to see at least three of his novels turned into movies, none ever got made.

When he turned eighty in 2007, Kroetsch was hailed by novelist W. P. Kinsella as "Canada's most neglected novelist." "His novels have never had the huge audience they deserve," Kinsella wrote in an article for the *Edmonton Journal.* "Yet he has left a literary legacy of a half dozen unforgettable prairie novels. Novels that are meant to be read for the sheer joy of his story-telling, and his ribald humour." Kroetsch had the remarkable power, said Kinsella, to make readers "hear the wind whining through the coulees, the rumble of thunder, the jagged zap of lightning across a black sky. You can smell the fields after rain, and feel the warmth of the soil as crocuses hatch from the earth like chicks from an egg." Author Rudy Wiebe acknowledged in a letter to the paper's editor that readers did not know much about Kroetsch's "marvellous stories and incisive poems" and that it was "high time that such ignorance was corrected. Robert Kroetsch deserves a full-page interview in the *Journal*." The *Journal* never acted on the suggestion.

The end came suddenly and without warning. One minute, Kroetsch was receiving a standing ovation for his poetry reading at an arts festival in Canmore, Alberta. The next, he was killed in a two-car collision while being driven to his home at an assisted-living facility in Leduc. In the early stages of Parkinson's disease, he had come back to the province of his birth in 2009 after fifteen years of semi-retirement on the west coast. "I never really thought I'd end up being a retired guy in Victoria," he said with a smile. He was just a few days short of his eighty-fourth birthday when he died.

His friends said Kroetsch's loss leaves a hole that can never be filled. "He was a mentor, he was an encourager, he was a reader, he was just the best of all possible literary leaders," said fellow Alberta novelist Aritha van Herk. "Nobody can walk into that space."

SHAY DUFFIN
Entertainer
1931–2010

Shay Duffin had much in common with Brendan Behan, the boozy Irish playwright he portrayed thousands of times in a one-man stage play that toured North America for more than thirty years starting in the early 1970s. Both were born in Dublin into Catholic, working-class families. Both left school as young teenagers to serve apprenticeships in trades designed to bring them future prosperity. And both eventually found their mark in the theatre, where critics for *The New York Times* and other major newspapers hailed their achievements.

They both lived for a time in the southside Dublin neighbourhood of Crumlin, but they rarely crossed paths. Behan, who trained as a house painter and learned about revolutionary activities as a junior member of the Irish Republican Army, found himself in Liverpool at age sixteen, facing a sentence of three years in a reform school for his role in the IRA bombing of a British battleship. Duffin, eight years younger, was confined at that time to the Dublin Orthopedic Hospital where he underwent two years of inpatient treatment for a congenital deformity affecting both feet.

Behan returned to Dublin in 1942 at age nineteen and immediately found himself in trouble with the law again. He was sentenced to fourteen years, later commuted to four, for the attempted murder of two detectives. He served part of his term

Shay Duffin (left) and the author performing as the Dublin Rogues in Kitimat, BC, 1967. (Photo by Kitimat Photo Supply, from the collection of the author)

in Dublin's Mountjoy Jail, next door to a furniture factory where Duffin—recently liberated from leg braces—was training as an upholsterer.

Behan began to write while in prison, and his first produced play, *The Quare Fellow*, drew extensively from his jail experiences. Duffin completed his six-year apprenticeship in 1951 and began to look for work abroad because employment prospects had grown dismal for tradespeople in Ireland. First he went to London, where one of his jobs—he delighted in recounting afterward—was to install leather padding on a toilet seat in Princess Margaret's Kensington Palace apartment. "We all start at the bottom," he joked. In 1963, when Duffin was thirty-two, he and two brothers immigrated to Toronto where the employment situation turned out to be as dismal as in Ireland. "We were promised the moon and we didn't even get a drop of rain," he recalled. "We got snow and sleet and cold."

Behan by 1963 had seen his plays produced successfully in London, Paris, and New York, and he had gained notoriety as a rowdy who frequently went to jail for public drunkenness, had fights with police and bartenders, and was barred from a St. Patrick's Day parade in New York for being a "disorderly person." Behan offered a feeble excuse for his unruly behaviour: "In Dublin, during the Depression when I was growing up, drunkenness was not regarded as a social disgrace. To get enough to eat was regarded as an achievement. To get drunk was a victory."

Duffin, meanwhile, had moved to Vancouver where he married, became a father, found steady work as an upholsterer, and moonlighted as an actor and ballad singer. A naturally gifted performer who had never taken acting or singing lessons, Duffin appeared in dramas and musicals staged by the amateur Emerald Players, and did bit parts in such CBC Television shows as *The Littlest Hobo* and *Cariboo Country*.

Behan died in March 1964 at age forty-one. He had suffered from diabetes, jaundice, and kidney and liver complaints, aggravated by his frequent bouts with alcohol. "Too young to die. Too drunk to live," famously commented René MacColl in the *Daily Express*. Word has it that Behan awakened briefly from a coma before he died, looked at the nun who was watching over him, and whispered: "Thank you, Sister—may you be the mother of a bishop." Duffin made a note of that quip, widely reported in the newspapers at the time, and vowed to use it in a one-man stage play about Behan that he planned to develop in the future.

While researching the Behan show, Duffin satisfied his desire to perform professionally by singing at weddings, banquets, and golf-club dinners. He wasn't ready to give up his day job yet. With a wife and four daughters to support, Duffin needed the regular paycheque from the upholstery business until he could hope to earn a comparable living from performing.

In the spring of 1967, Duffin heard the siren call of full-time show business. He and I had been performing part time as a singing duo called the Dublin Rogues since I immigrated to Canada in November 1966. We had recorded an album of Irish ballads, *Off to Dublin in the Green*, which had been picked up by RCA Records for distribution on its Camden label, and now we were being hired to spend the summer performing in the *Gay Nineties Gaslight Follies* show at the Palace Grand Theatre in Dawson City. At the end of the summer we returned briefly to our jobs in Vancouver—I had been working there as a customs broker—but the lure of the limelight was strong. In September 1967 we moved to Toronto, where we hoped there would be more performing opportunities for us.

With an agent booking gigs for us, we worked out of Toronto for about ten months, touring Ontario and Atlantic Canada, playing bars, nightclubs, and the occasional concert engagement. The work was steady and the money was good. Each of us earned an average of $300 weekly, which meant that Duffin could take care of his family in Vancouver and I could treat myself regularly to a plate of filet mignon and a glass of Johnnie Walker Red Label.

We recorded a second album for RCA, *Roamin' and Wanderin'*, and a couple of singles that we hoped would take us to the same heights as those achieved by the Irish Rovers with their hit recording of "The Unicorn." When that failed to happen and we didn't get the hits that would have brought us national exposure and perhaps a television show, Duffin and I parted company. He continued to tour with two other musicians while I went back to Vancouver to attend journalism school.

By the beginning of 1970, Duffin had completed a draft of a one-man play entitled *Shay Duffin is Brendan Behan*. He showed it to Denis Hayes, theatre department head at St. Francis Xavier University in Antigonish, Nova Scotia, who workshopped it at St. Michael's College, Toronto. About a year later, in December 1971, Duffin and Hayes did a commercial production of the show at Toronto's Theatre in the Dell. *The Globe and Mail's* theatre critic, Herbert Whittaker, observed that Duffin bore a passing physical resemblance to Behan and that the show, while charming, "needs some whittling down and spacing out." Duffin by then had disbanded the Dublin Rogues to focus on his acting career. He had also gotten divorced. The long separations from his family in Vancouver had taken their toll on the marriage.

Duffin took the Behan show to Vancouver, Edmonton, Calgary, Victoria, Ottawa, and Montreal before returning to Toronto in August 1972. *Globe* critic Whittaker still had reservations about the performance. "He can be quite engrossing, this Behan out of Duffin," he wrote. "But at times he drags it out a bit too much."

With a second director, New York's Marvin Gordon, at the helm in January 1973, Duffin took the show to off-Broadway's appropriately named Abbey Theater. (Dublin's more famous Abbey Theatre had twice turned down Behan's plays before the playwright found acceptance in London and New York.) *The New York Times* critic, Mel Gussow, wrote that Duffin's performance reminded him of Behan's "boisterous gift for dramatic elaboration." "For two hours this mock Behan is amiable company."

Duffin's New York performance led to other stage appearances in the United States, including a 1974 standing-room only performance at Chicago's Goodman Theatre and a series of performances in California that won him best actor awards from both the Los Angeles and San Francisco theatre critics. These led in turn to television offers. By the mid-1970s Duffin was appearing regularly in U.S. TV movies, playing stereotypically Irish bartenders, cops, and priests. He made his big-screen debut in 1977 playing a bartender in *The White Buffalo*, a western starring Charles Bronson and Jack Warden. Three years later he played a ring announcer in Martin Scorsese's *Raging Bull*. By that time Duffin had moved from Vancouver to an apartment in California's Redondo Beach.

Like Hal Holbrook with his acclaimed *Mark Twain Tonight* show and Emlyn Williams with his famous Charles Dickens impersonation, Duffin dusted off the Behan show whenever there was a lull between screen jobs. In 1981 he took it back to New York, to the Astor Place Theater, where *The New York Times* critic John Corry was generous with his praise: "Mr. Duffin, if not Behan, has given us a memorable evening." In Toronto *Globe* critic Ray Conlogue, Whittaker's successor, also used the word "memorable" in his review. *Time* magazine called the show "a one-man cultural invasion." In Ireland, however, the critics were not so complimentary. "His American twang is very distracting," wrote Brian Brennan (not me) in Dublin's *Sunday Independent*. "He's been out in Hollywood too long."

The hometown critics in Vancouver always gave a warm welcome to the Behan show, which Duffin retitled *Confessions of an Irish Rebel* after a posthumously published Behan autobiography of the same name. In August 1989, after seeing a revival at North Vancouver's Centennial Theatre, the *Vancouver Province*'s Max Wyman reported that Duffin was "still as adroit as ever with Behan's material; still as roguish with the bawdy and the blasphemy." Duffin was then fifty-eight years old—seventeen years older than Behan had been when he died in 1964.

After a succession of one-off appearances in various U.S. television series, Duffin landed a recurring role as a newsstand manager in a 1989–90 CBS sitcom called *City*. It was created as a starring vehicle for Valerie Harper, who had first risen to fame as Rhoda in *The Mary Tyler Moore Show*. *City* ran, however, for only one season before cancellation and Duffin returned to doing the Behan show and the one-off television appearances. His next recurring role was, in what could have been an irresistible casting decision, as a priest named Father Behan in the 1994–99 Canadian comedy crime series *Due South*.

Duffin achieved his greatest on-screen prominence as the bartender in the early scenes of the Oscar-winning movie *Titanic*, and as the racehorse trainer, Sunny Jim Fitzsimmons, in *Seabiscuit*. The latter role brought him particular satisfaction because his father, the late George Duffin, had been a horse trainer for the Irish National Stud. Shay, the third youngest of George's children, recalled that his father used to say jokingly to his pub friends, "Even though I have eleven kids, I'm not the National Stud."

Duffin continued to do the Behan show as he aged into his sixties and seventies. In 2009, when he was seventy-eight, he told a Los Angeles radio interviewer, Lorraine Chambers, that he had played the role 6,894 times. "And I'm going to do it until I get it right." He had completed a draft screenplay based on the show, which attracted some interest from Sean Penn, Robin Williams, and other actors but never got made into a film. Duffin said he hoped to play Behan's father if the movie ever made it to the big screen.

He died at age seventy-nine on April 23, 2010, at his home in Redondo Beach after undergoing heart surgery. His daughters and friends put together a "Shay Duffin Remembered" Facebook page that attracted comments from around the world and was still active in 2015. In April 2012, when *Titanic* was re-released in 3D, a fan recalled Duffin's quip about Celine Dion's hit song from the movie: "She sang 'My Heart Will Go On.' I sing 'My Residuals Will Go On.'"

RICK McNAIR
Theatrical Free Spirit
1942–2007

Rick McNair was the Peter Pan of Canadian theatre, an eternal child who never seemed entirely at home in the world of adults and was clearly in his element when making theatre for children. Yet this red-haired maverick made an important contribution to adult theatre in this country by defying the odds and proving that new Canadian plays could do just as well on the big stages of Calgary and Winnipeg as the hits of Broadway or the West End.

Like many Canadian theatre professionals of his generation, McNair trained for another career—teaching—before deciding in his early thirties to make theatre his vocation. He taught high-school English in Sarnia, Ontario, and then moved to Cambridge, Ontario, where he indulged his love of sports by teaching physical education and coaching basketball. At the same time, he indulged his love of theatre by starting a drama program at the Cambridge school, Galt Collegiate, and by directing community theatre productions in his spare time. Additionally, he wrote educational plays for children that took their storylines from some of the world's greatest myths and legends.

His opportunity to make the leap into full-time theatre came in 1977, when McNair was appointed director of Calgary's Stage Coach Players, a touring troupe that performed in schools and community halls throughout Alberta. He wrote and produced

Rick McNair. (Courtesy of Theatre Calgary)

several plays for this company, including *Napi, the First Man, Beowulf!* and *Merlin and Arthur*. A year later, McNair was appointed artistic director of the troupe's parent company, Theatre Calgary, when the former director, Harold Baldridge, quit and moved to New York City. By that time, local entertainment reporters were viewing McNair with some bemusement because he liked to talk about sports as much as he did about Shakespeare. He relished his image as a jock. He would tell friends years later that his favourite *Calgary Herald* article was one documenting his achievements as a relief pitcher in the "A" division of the Calgary Softball Association league. If the English playwrights Tom Stoppard and Harold Pinter could play cricket in their spare time and still retain their credibility as theatre professionals, McNair figured he could spend his off hours throwing balls from the mound.

McNair made it clear from the outset that he wouldn't be relying entirely on certified crowd-pleasers from Britain or the United States when it came to choosing plays for presentation by Theatre Calgary. He would stage some of these imports for financial reasons, because the company was carrying a $150,000 deficit when he took over, and there was no guarantee that untried Canadian plays would be box-office winners. But gradually McNair planned to convince his audience that theatre rooted firmly in its own community could be just as successful—if not more so—than theatre that drew its inspiration from non-Canadian sources. "Second-hand plays from other places make for second-rate theatre," he said. "I believe the way to change things is to start doing our own plays."

His first Canadian hit was a stage adaptation of W. O. Mitchell's *The Black Bonspiel of Wullie MacCrimmon*, a show that had begun life in 1950 as a script for CBC Radio. The 1979 stage version of this Faustian comic fantasy, about a shoemaker gambling his soul on a curling match against the Devil, was so successful that McNair mounted it for a second time at Theatre Calgary in 1980. At the same time, he commissioned Mitchell to adapt for the stage two of his other works: a comic novel, *The Kite*, and a television drama, *For Those in Peril on the Sea*.

The success of *Black Bonspiel* at Theatre Calgary convinced McNair that the show should be seen elsewhere. The committee organizing the 1980 celebrations for Alberta's seventy-fifth birthday agreed and gave him money to tour the show around the province. By then convinced that Canadian playwrights had earned the right to have their work featured on the main stage at Theatre Calgary—the city's largest professional theatre—McNair began to do what no other artistic director had ever dared do before him. In every six-play season, he included at least one play, sometimes two, written by a Canadian. And these were not low-budget, two-handed chamber pieces. Nor were they necessarily Canadian plays that had already made the grade elsewhere. McNair managed to convince a skeptical board of Theatre Calgary directors that they should give him the green light to commission large-cast plays from such promising Canadian playwrights as Sharon Pollock and John Murrell, as well as new adaptations from the veteran Mitchell.

The gamble generally paid off. Sharon Pollock's *Whiskey Six*, about a Prohibition-era rum-runner, was the hit play of one

McNair season. Her next play, *Doc*, about her physician father, sold more seats than any of the Broadway hits staged in Calgary that year. John Murrell's *Farther West*, about a frontier prostitute's attempt to escape from the social and sexual constraints imposed by male lovers, was also a big success. McNair clearly was doing something right.

Not all of his Canadian choices were box office triumphs, of course. McNair's adaptation of *The Words of my Roaring*, Robert Kroetsch's surrealistic novel about the early Social Credit years in Alberta, was a brave failure. So was Mary Humphrey Baldridge's Frankenstein drama, *The Mary Shelley Play*. But for every flop there was a new Canadian stage hit. Mitchell's *The Kite*, about an irrepressible old maverick whose lifetime spans the "white" history of the West, was one. Pollock's Lizzie Borden drama, *Blood Relations*, was another. By the time McNair left Theatre Calgary in 1984, Calgary audiences had witnessed a flowering of made-in-Canada theatre on the local stage, the likes of which had never been seen before at a large regional theatre in this country.

His departure from Theatre Calgary came as a surprise to many. McNair had taken the company out of debt and proven that a regional theatre could do just as well with a new play by W. O. Mitchell as it could with a warmed-over comedy by Neil Simon or Alan Ayckbourn. But McNair was anxious to get back to his own playwriting, which he had largely put on hold after accepting the Theatre Calgary job. He also had some concerns about the company's pending move from a converted tractor warehouse called the QR Centre into what is now called the Arts Commons. As the "establishment" theatre in the new centre—with Alberta Theatre Projects providing the edgy alternative—Theatre Calgary would be expected to have a strong focus on theatrical classics and musicals. The days of workshopping new Canadian plays on the main stage would be no more. Wullie MacCrimmon had taken his final curtain call. Uncle Vanya and Pal Joey would soon be in the wings, waiting to take his place. McNair viewed this as a disturbing prospect. "If we don't think Canadian plays can fill that theatre, we're selling ourselves short," he said. "If we think that only the American and British plays can do it, then we have failed as a community."

McNair had another reason for wanting to leave Theatre Calgary. After six years of being a responsible adult, dealing with such grown-up concerns as production budgets, subscription sales, and box-office figures, he wanted to start feeding his inner child again. He wanted to get back to producing theatre for the amusement of ten-year-olds. "With children's work you're far freer," he said. "You can do things that you can't do with adult theatre." As an example, he cited the ability of children's theatre to deal in an entertaining way with such social issues as poverty and racial discrimination. When adult theatre tackled the same subjects, it turned into a propaganda vehicle.

His opportunity to get back into children's theatre came within a month of his leaving Theatre Calgary. The Stage Coach Players had folded, and McNair was on hand to fill the gap with another touring troupe. With Stage Coach alumnus Duval Lang he co-founded Quest Theatre, an independent, fully professional theatre for young people. McNair and Lang shared the administrative duties of artistic director and general manager while simultaneously satisfying their creative inclinations—McNair as resident playwright and stage director, and Lang as an actor and director. McNair was in his element again. A charming story from that period tells how an actor came to audition for one of his plays and found McNair rolling around on the floor of his office, wrestling with a colleague and giggling like a teenager. "People tell me I've never grown up," said McNair. "I've still shown no signs of maturity. I hope I never do."

Two years after co-founding Quest, McNair answered the call of adult theatre for the second time, this time to become artistic director of the Manitoba Theatre Centre in Winnipeg. Fifty-two candidates applied for the job at Canada's oldest regional theatre, including fifteen Americans and two from England. After a three-month search, the board of directors rated McNair as the best choice because he had led a theatre of similar size in Calgary and had the magic touch when it came to picking box-office winners.

An appealing aspect of the Winnipeg job for McNair was the fact that, once again, he could put new Canadian plays on the same stage as confections from New York and London. One of these was *Royalty is Royalty*, yet another neglected gem from the archives of W. O. Mitchell, about Queen Elizabeth II visiting a small Saskatchewan town in the 1950s. Another was Allan Stratton's *The 101 Miracles of Hope Chance*, a comedy about television evangelism. Winnipeg also afforded McNair an opportunity to launch an off-the-wall theatre festival, the Winnipeg Fringe, which has since grown to become the second-largest event of its kind in North America after the Edmonton Fringe.

McNair's magic touch deserted him in Winnipeg, however. Manitoba Theatre Centre incurred a $431,000 deficit during his third season, 1988–89, and the board of directors fired him at the season's end. A board spokesman said the abrupt termination was in response to complaints and cancellations from irate subscribers. The subscribers were particularly upset by the content and language of *Brass Rubbings*, a new play by actor Gordon Pinsent about an affluent Toronto family with inherited wealth, living in a downtown mansion, trying to come to grips with the encroaching street crime that threatened the family members' genteel existence. There was a recurring pattern here. The board of directors had also fired McNair's predecessor, James Roy, for allegedly losing money on shows that Manitoba Theatre Centre subscribers didn't want to see.

McNair never took the opportunity to discuss his firing publicly. Nor did he sue the board for wrongful dismissal, as his predecessor had done. Like the coach of a losing hockey team, McNair simply accepted the consequences and got on with his life. He did say, however, that the firing was "probably the best thing that could have happened to me." He had been plagued by health problems during his three years in Winnipeg and was spending more time attending board meetings than being in the rehearsal hall where he felt he truly belonged.

With his adult troubles behind him, McNair turned again to children's theatre for inspiration and sustenance. He kept Winnipeg as his home base, wrote and staged more plays for

Quest Theatre in Calgary, freelanced as a director and film actor, and found a new calling as a professional storyteller. He travelled to schools and libraries across Canada, telling stories to children of all ages, and said he could relate to any age group. "I've maintained all the ages within me since I was a child," he said. "I can be five, 10 or 20 years old." By the time he was in his early sixties, McNair estimated he had told stories to more than 100,000 children. He published a popular illustrated children's book, *The Last Unicorn on the Prairies*, about a group of farm animals looking for a unicorn to save their struggling farm. And he demonstrated his artistic versatility by writing the libretto for an Allan Bell opera about the Frank Slide, *Turtle Wakes*, which toured Alberta under the auspices of the Calgary Opera.

McNair died of a heart attack on January 31, 2007, at age sixty-four. One wake was held in Winnipeg, another in Calgary. Excerpts from his children's plays were performed, and a slideshow reading of his *Unicorn* book was presented. A friend commented that the fun-loving McNair would have enjoyed knowing that his Winnipeg pals had left empty beer glasses on his casket.

RALPH KLEIN
Journalist Turned Politician
1942–2013

Much has been written about Ralph Klein the politician—the ambitious, hard-drinking, chain-smoking, street-smart political fighter who rose to become mayor of Calgary and premier of Alberta. As a fellow journalist, however, I prefer to remember him as a reporter driven by a passion for social justice. That's how he made his mark before entering politics.

I met him in April 1974. He was a thirty-one-year-old civic affairs reporter for CFCN TV in Calgary. I was a thirty-year-old police reporter for the *Calgary Herald*. As a newly arrived staffer at the so-called "newspaper of record" for southern Alberta, I was led to understand that television reporters were a lower form of journalistic life. They did little more than parrot on the six o'clock news the stories the *Herald* had broken earlier that day. "We have a saying about Ralph Klein," one of my newsroom colleagues told me. "There are eight million stories in the *Naked City* and Ralph doesn't have any of them."

As it turned out, Ralph had lots of them. But they weren't necessarily the kinds of stories *Herald* reporters were encouraged to pursue. We interviewed business leaders, sports heroes, and politicians. Because of the unashamedly pro-establishment bias of our editorial bosses, we referred to ourselves, ironically, as the "fearless champions of the overdog." Klein talked to bikers and hookers, and saw himself as a voice for the outcasts and the

Ralph Klein, 1966. (Glenbow Archives, PA-2807-2148)

dispossessed. He offered the view from the street, focussing on those marginalized by society.

He had been working as a reporter for six years when I met him at a Calgary police commission meeting held to discuss progress on construction of a new remand centre for the city. A high-school dropout raised mostly by his maternal grandparents in Calgary after his parents divorced, Klein had been principal of a business college and worked in public relations before deciding, at age twenty-six, that journalism was his true calling.

He started in radio with Calgary's CFCN, rewriting wire stories and press releases, and reading them on the air. After two years of that, he switched to television, first as a CFCN weatherman, chalking temperatures backward on a glass weather map, and then as a general assignment reporter. He began by following the standard television reporter's routine of interviewing cops and firefighters after crimes, traffic accidents, and house fires, getting reactions from witnesses, and filing his reports from the scene. Then he branched out and started doing enterprise stories on the homeless and the disenfranchised, often contrasting the predicament of the many with the privilege of the few. He reported sympathetically on the plight of city Natives, motorcycle gangs, and the Chinese community. In the process, he abandoned all semblance of journalistic objectivity.

He used unorthodox methods to get his stories. While other reporters waited for press releases, pre-arranged interviews, or phone calls from trusted sources, Klein rooted through city-hall garbage cans or eavesdropped on in-camera meetings to find evidence of municipal wrongdoing. On one occasion he astonished a fellow reporter by showing him the unlocked mechanical room behind city-council chambers, from where Klein could surreptitiously monitor private meetings. Away from city hall, his vast network of contacts, whom he usually met in downtown bars, included detectives, bikers, gamblers, madams, drug dealers, gangsters, social workers, priests, and pimps. "There are no stories in the newsroom," he liked to say, echoing a line first attributed to New York newspaper columnist Pete Hamill.

Klein told me about his loss of journalistic objectivity after he'd been mayor for a few years. He said he eventually had to get out of television news because he'd reached a point where he wasn't reporting fairly. "It bothered me when I realized I was writing one-sided stories instead of getting all the facts."

Case in point was a story he did in 1977 on the hundredth anniversary of the signing of Treaty Seven. Organizers envisaged the commemoration ceremony as a splendid photo op for the visiting Prince Charles, with costumed Natives dancing, drumming, and singing in the background. Klein, however, saw it as an opportunity to show how residents of the Blackfoot (now, Siksika) reserve near Gleichen had suffered since their forefathers surrendered their ancestral hunting territories to Queen Victoria's representatives. Klein spent three weeks on the reserve, gained the confidence of the people he met, noted their dreadful living conditions, and learned a bit about their language and culture. The resulting documentary was far from an exercise in journalistic objectivity, but it did endear him to the people he was reporting on. In 1993 Klein became one of the few white persons in history to be adopted into the Siksika Blackfoot Nation. "Can you believe that in 1977 it had only been a couple of decades since Natives were able to do the kinds of things the rest of us take for granted?" said Klein. "Before that, they weren't able to vote, conduct cultural ceremonies, or possess and drink alcohol off the reserve."

Another example of Klein's advocacy journalism was a year-long crusade he launched, starting in 1978, against a grandiose city-council plan to spend $234 million on a civic centre complex to house an ever-expanding city-hall administration. Klein never tried to hide his feeling that this monument to civic bureaucracy would be a colossal waste of taxpayers' dollars. "I really couldn't present a balanced report because I thought everything that was happening was so wrong."

Calgary voters who shared Klein's concerns about the exorbitant cost of the civic centre rejected the proposed expenditure in a 1979 plebiscite. When the mayor of the day, Ross Alger, announced he would try to get the project approved when he ran for re-election the following year, Klein saw red. He decided to do something about it and run for mayor himself. "Nobody suggested I do this. Everyone thought I was absolutely crazy."

But Klein didn't think he was crazy. He felt Alger had lost touch with the voters and that a television reporter who knew the inner workings of city hall could be a viable alternative. With a twenty-seven-year-old political science student named Rod Love orchestrating his campaign, Klein ran on a platform of keeping the lines of communication open at city hall. He soundly defeated the incumbent by more than 15,000 votes.

I never thought he was going to win. Neither did my *Herald* colleagues. We thought that if Alger lost, it would be to an ambitious former alderman named Peter Petrasuk, not to a thirty-seven-year-old television reporter named Ralph Klein. So in a spirit of journalistic solidarity we gave Ralph our sympathy vote. But in the end he hardly needed it. Most of his support came not from the suits who frequented the Petroleum Club and occupied the executive boxes at the Calgary Stampede, but from the ordinary folks who went to the beer parlours and the curling bonspiels. In his first speech to the Chamber of Commerce Club after his victory, Klein quipped: "I'd like to thank all the people who voted for me in the recent civic election. I understand they're all working in the kitchen."

After having asked the tough questions as a reporter for eleven years, Klein was more than ready to mix it up with other reporters when he found himself on the opposite side of the microphones. When a CFCN newsman, Murray Cunningham, criticized the mayor's office for refusing to act on a sexual harassment complaint from a Handi-Bus passenger, Klein—in the presence of other journalists, with cameras and tapes rolling—accused Cunningham of "torquing" the story—i.e., giving it a harder edge for the sake of urgency. Replied Cunningham, "Well, you should know about torquing. You did enough of it in your time." Retorted Klein, "That's how I can tell when a story is being torqued. I've been in the media long enough to know all the tricks."

Afterward Klein conceded that had he been in Cunningham's shoes, he likely would have played the story the same way. "But maybe being mayor has taught me a little bit more about getting both sides of the story."

There was nobody on stage to talk about Klein's journalistic achievements during his Calgary memorial service in April 2013, after he died at age seventy due to complications from pulmonary disease and dementia. All the eulogies were given by politicians, present and former, who talked about his political contributions and his drinking escapades. That left a big part of his story untold. Klein was a reporter before he was a politician. Though he often wore his heart on his sleeve, he did so because he cared. Even if he only told one side of the story, he could never be accused of having willfully distorted the truth for the sake of being sensational. He carried that passion for truth-telling with him through twenty-six years of often turbulent political life to the end of his days.

HEATHER ROBERTSON
Author and Journalist Rights Advocate
1942–2014

On April 5, 2009, thousands of freelance writers across Canada opened their morning newspapers to find good news. A class action lawsuit against *The Globe and Mail* newspaper that had been before the courts for thirteen years had finally resulted in a big settlement. The newspaper's owners—while admitting no wrongdoing—had agreed to pay $11 million dollars to the freelancers for unauthorized electronic reproduction of their work.

The suit had been launched in 1996 by Heather Robertson, a self-styled "leftist anarchist maverick," after she discovered that two of her freelance articles for the *Globe*—for which she retained the copyright—had been stored in the newspaper's electronic database and offered for sale without her permission. Many of her freelancer colleagues were in the same boat. After trying unsuccessfully to get compensation from the *Globe*, they joined together to sue.

Robertson, with several books to her credit, willingly agreed to attach her name to the lawsuit. She figured she had the least to lose. "I wasn't dependent on journalism for my income so I could offend these people," she told the *Ryerson Review of Journalism*. Besides, "it was in my blood to stick it to the corporation."

She traced the roots of her anti-establishment leanings back to her childhood in Winnipeg, where her Scottish-born

Heather Robertson. (Courtesy of the Writer's Union of Canada)

grandfather had worked as a toolmaker for the Canadian National Railway and had taken part in the 1919 general strike. "He was a proud labour man," she told the *Ryerson Review*. "I still have his copy of *Das Kapital* by Karl Marx on my bookshelf." Her father was a high-school principal who worked with troubled kids, and her mother was an early feminist who encouraged her daughter to think progressively. Heather recalled many conversations around the family dinner table about unions, the CCF, and medicare.

Winnipeg, with its small-town feel, was a comfortable, secure, and safe place in which to grow up. By the time she was in her teens, however, Robertson was ready to move on. "It was as if the city's purpose was simply to give us life and shape, and then send us out into the world," she wrote in a *Globe and Mail* column in 1974.

She earned a B.A. in English from the University of Manitoba and received her first taste of newspapering when at age nineteen she served as editor of the student newspaper, *The Manitoban*.

She delighted in recalling how the college's football supporters burned her in effigy when she wrote an opinion piece saying that money spent on the college's cash-strapped football program would be better spent elsewhere. "Again this year they are peddling football, an easy, instant remedy for all the ills that affect Manitoba," she wrote. "Are three expensive games per season in a makeshift stadium in foul weather against teams from places most of us wouldn't particularly care to visit going to suddenly make us full of college spirit?"

The football fans were up in arms. "She wasn't objective," they said, and called for her head. "It was an editorial," she retorted, and kept her job. When she finished her undergraduate degree, she went to Columbia University on a fellowship and completed a master's degree in English literature. Columbia offered her a scholarship to complete her Ph.D. but at that point Robertson realized she wasn't cut out to be an academic. "I wanted to write books, not teach them."

She returned to Winnipeg at age twenty-two in 1964 and spent a summer at the *Winnipeg Free Press*. She then went to work for the competing *Winnipeg Tribune* where, she vowed, she would never be confined to the traditional newspaper ghetto known as the "women's pages." Previous generations of female reporters were hired to write about cooking, fashion, and beauty tips. Robertson got herself assigned to the police beat where she worked alongside male reporters who thrived on cutting through the guff of anodyne press releases to find the real stories. "They taught me a great deal about being courageous to tell the story you found, not the story that somebody thought you should be telling." In an essay for *Saturday Night* magazine, she described how her generation of female reporters differed from their predecessors. "We had no tits," she wrote. "It had been customary to measure the talent of female staff members at the *Tribune* by the size of their bra cups; the women's editor was a statuesque 38D, columnist Ann Henry a stunning 36 triple C. We were all As."

In 1966 Robertson won a $3,000 prize from Imperial Tobacco to write a book about Canada's Natives. She quit the *Tribune*, borrowed her father's 1958 Nash Rambler, and spent eight months travelling across Manitoba and Saskatchewan visiting reserves, conducting interviews, and taking notes. When she got back to Winnipeg, she landed a job at CBC Radio as a news producer and started working on her manuscript. The resulting book, *Reservations are for Indians*, was published in 1970 by James Lewis & Samuel, a Toronto press.

Reservations was praised as a revelation and denounced as racist. It was the first book by a white writer to confront Native drunkenness, dependency, violence, suicide, and prostitution. "I am told that a group of Indians from Alberta travelled to The Pas, Manitoba, to denounce my portrayal of Indian prostitution," Robertson wrote in an introduction for a new edition of the book released in 1991. "Only to discover the same pitiful crowd of teenage girls in the bars that I had seen."

The book sold more than 10,000 copies in the first few months and caught the eye of *Maclean's* magazine editor Peter C. Newman, who commissioned Robertson to write a monthly column about television. "Nobody in the country is writing as well as she," he said. He encouraged her to write about TV-related issues, as opposed to writing about the merits or otherwise of such programs as *Get Smart* and *All in the Family*. She duly complied. In one column Robertson wrote about television's tendency to exploit the people it marginalized. "Ethnic groups, hard hats, rural people, religious sects make it onto TV only as part of a news item or as subjects of a documentary," she wrote. "They are categorized, observed, manipulated, photographed, edited, scripted and packaged." She suggested television could improve by putting more "real people" on the air.

An editor at *Maclean's*, Erna Paris, said she was "bowled over" by Robertson's "direct fearless writing. She was a Canadian nationalist; a *western* Canadian nationalist." Paris, who later collaborated with Robertson on a book, *Her Own Woman*, about significant Canadian women, said Robertson might have been writing about herself when she wrote about politician Judy LaMarsh: "Why should a woman not be proud, ambitious, aggressive, angry in the face of deceit, contemptuous of stupidity, intolerant of corruption? Why should she suffer fools and bores meekly?"

Robertson wasn't afraid to make hackles rise. She infuriated American readers and the higher-ups at *Maclean's* with an anti-American column expressing her distaste for "our good friend and neighbour to the south" who "treats us with contempt and robs us blind." She confessed tongue-in-cheek to a desire to "toss a hand grenade into every American camper I pass on the highway." Her *Maclean's* bosses wanted her fired for this column, but somehow Newman managed to convince them she should stay.

In 1973 Robertson published her second book, a study of rural Manitoba and Saskatchewan entitled *Grass Roots*. Focussing on a farm family living west of Saskatoon, and on the general living conditions in such prairie towns as Miami, Winkler, Bienfait, Biggar, and Moose Jaw, it attracted both praise and condemnation for its conclusion that Western rural society was generally in decline. Some reviewers hailed it as an extraordinary book, rich in detail and darkly mythic. Others denounced Robertson for her lack of real understanding of the people and towns of western Canada. But like her first book, it sold well.

Robertson was still living in Winnipeg when *Grass Roots* was published, but that was about to change. In the summer of 1973, at a broadcasting conference in Ottawa, she met Andrew Marshall, a freelance broadcaster and record producer from Toronto. After they had one dinner together, he wrote afterward, "we both knew we would spend the rest of our lives together." They settled first in Toronto and later in rural King City, north of Toronto, where Robertson freelanced extensively for newspapers and magazines across Canada.

Robertson continued to generate books on prairie topics after she moved to Toronto. *Salt of the Earth* was a portrait of the settlement of the West drawn from the letters, diaries, and photographs Robertson had collected while researching *Grass Roots*. *The Flying Bandit* chronicled the life of a Winnipeg bank robber, Ken Leishman. She also wrote the introduction and some of the descriptive text for *A Terrible Beauty*, a picture book featuring reproductions of paintings done by Canadian war artists during the First and Second World Wars.

After five books of nonfiction, Robertson switched gears in 1983 when she published a novel, *Willie: A Romance*, a fictional recreation of the life and times of Prime Minister Mackenzie King. She viewed King as a "satanic minotaur at the centre of the Canadian labyrinth" and thought she could do a better job on his biography by giving him the fictional treatment. Explaining her choice of genre in an interview with *Books in Canada* magazine, Robertson said that those who wrote nonfiction were not taken seriously. "In this country, if you write a novel—any novel—you are considered to be a real writer." Expanding on this theme later, she wrote that nonfiction, while enormously popular and influential, was "shunned by the literary and academic establishments as uncreative or unscholarly: a bastard defined by what it is not."

Willie was the first of three novels loosely based on King's life. The second, *Lily: A Rhapsody in Red*, took as its point of departure a claim by a Guelph woman that she had been King's secret wife. The third, *Igor: A Novel of Intrigue*, focussed on the 1945 defection of cipher clerk Igor Gouzenko from the Soviet embassy in Ottawa. The first book was widely praised. The second was panned for playing fast and loose with the historical facts. But that negative criticism only boosted sales, Robertson said. The third book was deemed a failure, mainly because it turned King into a minor character and took place thirty years after his death. "Robertson thus deprives herself of the rich opportunities his eccentricities offer," wrote William French in *The Globe and Mail*.

Robertson abandoned fiction after completing her King trilogy. Journalism had always been her forte, and she wanted to get back to it. During the early 1990s she published a book about the wives of Canada's prime ministers, an alphabetical guide to Canada's Parliament, and a history of the founders of General Motors Canada. She also continued to freelance extensively. Then came the big lawsuit against *The Globe and Mail*.

Robertson said she thought of her Scottish grandfather as she girded herself for battle against the media giant. "Here I was, this middle-aged Canadian woman [then fifty-four], suddenly being robbed of my creative work by a laird. I saw it as this tremendous challenge. I reached for my dirk and off I went."

As well as suing the *Globe*, Robertson also sued the *Toronto Star*, Canwest newspapers, and other news organizations in a case she called "Robertson vs. Everybody Else." The argument in each instance was that publishers could not simply repurpose a writer's work electronically without credit or payment.

Her first victory, a partial one, occurred in 2006 when the Supreme Court ruled that newspapers could not reproduce free-lance work electronically without the agreement of the writers. However, the *Globe* argued there was an "implied" agreement between the newspaper and the writers, so the case dragged on for another three years until a settlement was reached. Robertson said the settlement was "fair and reasonable" and was glad she had pursued the case for all those years.

After the *Globe* settled, the other newspaper defendants resolved their disputes with her in short order. The freelancers received amounts ranging from $1 to $55,000. Robertson received just $5,000, which seemed like a poor return for the hundreds of hours she had put in each year toward the lawsuits. But she didn't mind. "It wasn't that onerous," she said. "It was just a matter of keeping people up to date with what was going on. It was a collective effort."

Robertson wasn't in the best of health when the lawsuits were under way. She suffered successive breast, colon, and brain cancers from the 1990s onward. She kept a journal to record her dreams and hallucinations while being treated for brain cancer. And all the time she kept writing books.

In 2000 she published *Meeting Death: In Hospital, Hospice and at Home*. It was prompted primarily by her anger over the poor hospital care her father received when he died of cancer. It also stemmed from her own feelings of mortality. "I will search silk and string in my cultural rubble," she wrote. "And I will go to the dying and find out how they do it." She took a course in caregiving and visited hospices in Canada, London, and Uganda. While she could hardly contain her rage at the system for providing nothing but compassionless and empty care during the last days of her father's life, she still managed to inject occasional touches of wry humour into her writing. "Never die in Winnipeg in July," she advised. "Everybody goes to the lake."

Writing *Meeting Death* seemed to prepare Robertson for her own death, which occurred on her seventy-second birthday, March 19, 2014. She died at home in her sleep after she and husband Andrew had enjoyed a dinner of pork chops, their favourite. "She had explored what death entailed, disentangled from religion and emotional mumbo jumbo," Andrew told *The Globe and Mail.* "She died peacefully."

BILLY COWSILL
Singer
1948–2006

Billy Cowsill was known across North America as the lead singer of a wholesome, 1960s family band that inspired *The Partridge Family* television series. In western Canada—where he lived for the last twenty-seven years of his life—he was also remembered as a self-destructive boozer and drug addict who eventually found redemption and a cult following as a rockabilly singer. First in Vancouver and then in Calgary, Cowsill left his mark as a performer with a "voice from heaven" who conjured up the musical ghosts of the past with his pitch-perfect renditions of country and pop classics by Hank Williams, Buddy Holly, Elvis Presley, Roy Orbison, and other greats from the 1950s.

He compared himself to a bird that was born to sing. The oldest child of an American naval officer who served on bases in Virginia, California, and New England, Cowsill taught himself guitar as a youngster in Rhode Island and performed with his brother Bob at family gatherings when both were in their early teens. They were later joined by two other brothers, Barry and John, singing Beatles songs at parties and church socials around Newport. Their father took charge of their musical career when he retired from the Navy in 1965. Billy, at that point, was seventeen, and had been performing semi-professionally for three years. Believing they were destined for better things than parish functions and weddings, the father added their mother

Promotional photograph of Billy Cowsill at the Crystal Ballroom, Palliser Hotel, Calgary, July 1985. (Courtesy of Neil MacGonigill. Photo by Alexander W. Thomas, Black Rose Images)

and sister to the group and began promoting the Cowsills as "America's first family of music."

Billy resented the addition of other family members to his four-piece "guy band." "You don't want your mom in a rock 'n' roll band," he said years later. "How can you get to screw girls when you're up on stage with your *mom*, and you have to go to your room afterwards because you've got a 12 o'clock curfew?"

The father, William (Bud) Cowsill Senior, borrowed $100,000 to spend on musical instruments, transport, and promotion for his talented family. It took a while, though, for the gamble to pay off. The family lived in virtual poverty, chopping up furniture for firewood when unable to buy heating oil on credit, and neglecting to shovel snow off the driveway to keep the bill collectors away. When they were on the verge of having their home repossessed, they were spotted by a writer for television's *Today* show who arranged for the Cowsills to appear as musical guests on the program. That led to a recording contract and to a hit single,

"The Rain, the Park and Other Things," which was released in 1967 and sold one million copies. A second million-seller followed in 1969 when the Cowsills released their bubblegum version of the title song from the rock musical, *Hair*. By that time they had become a target for critics of synthetic pop music, primarily because of their cutesy image coupled with their participation in an advertising campaign for milk.

Billy Cowsill enjoyed the pop music success while it lasted. The high point for him was the group's appearance on the *Ed Sullivan Show* in 1968, when he got to stand in the same place where Paul McCartney had stood in 1964. Asked how he knew it was the same spot, Cowsill replied, "I just knew." After that appearance, there was talk of having the Cowsills star in their own weekly television series, based on their lives. However, the family refused to have anything to do with it when the producers said they were hiring an actress, Shirley Jones, to play the mother. The show subsequently aired on ABC as *The Partridge Family*, with Jones as the mother and David Cassidy playing the role that would have been performed by Billy.

Cowsill's association with his family's band ended abruptly in 1969 when he got into a violent argument with his father, who promptly kicked him out of the group. In one version of the story, reported by *People* magazine, Cowsill was fired when his father caught him smoking marijuana after a gig in Las Vegas. However, Cowsill insisted this never happened. The two had been drinking heavily, he said, and got into a fistfight after his father started criticizing his friends. "My father was a real good guy, a guy who would give you the shirt off his back," he said. "But if he'd got a gut full of liquor, he'd beat your head into the wall." Cowsill, too, had a serious drinking problem at that point—when he was twenty-one, "I didn't know it yet, but I was an alcoholic." He was also married to a "wonderful woman who was an artist," and was soon to become a father. The booze, however, wrecked the marriage. His wife had left him by the time son Travis was born. Cowsill later joked that he considered writing a song for his son titled, "How Can I Look up to Daddy When He's Passed Out on the Floor."

Cowsill had no regrets about leaving the group. He felt the same way the critics did about the "schmaltzy" music the record producers had forced the Cowsills to play. "I felt like a Clydesdale hooked up to a Budweiser wagon." He wanted to try his hand at another kind of music, combining elements of rock 'n' roll with the traditional country songs his mother had sung to him as a child. "We lived in Virginia for a while, and she just loved that hillbilly music. I'm sure I was hearing country music in the womb because she played it all the time. It was all around me growing up, and I never lost my love for it."

After leaving the family group, Cowsill said, "I left the middle of the road and headed for the ditch." He recorded a solo album that went nowhere because Cowsill didn't have a clear idea yet what kind of sound he wanted to produce. He drifted back and forth across the United States, drinking heavily, popping pills, playing in roadhouses, "getting my butt kicked left and right, spitting in the devil's eye, and watching it sizzle." He stopped in Los Angeles to learn studio production techniques from Harry Nilsson, best known as the singer who recorded "Everybody's Talkin'" for the *Midnight Cowboy* soundtrack. Cowsill also learned more about the roots of rock 'n' roll by touring with such genre-crossing singers as Joe Ely and J. J. Cale. Then Cowsill moved to the Northwest Territories. Why?

"Why not?" he told a newspaper interviewer. "I had never been there, right? I left Los Angeles, took a wrong turn, and just woke up there. At night, I was playing in bars. In the day, I was working for United Van Lines, taking furniture across the Great Slave Lake ice bridge from Hay River to Yellowknife." He lived in motels and continued with the heavy drinking and drug-taking. In 1977 Cowsill took what was left of his family band savings and bought a bar in Austin, Texas. "I drank it dry. I drank a quart a day at least."

In 1979 a friend suggested Cowsill move to Vancouver. He stopped drinking for a while, joined a country-rock band named Blue Northern, and cut a few records. He liked Vancouver and had decided to stay there when the band broke up in 1982. He put together another band that included future guitar hero

Colin James, and played a few concert gigs opening for k.d. lang. During the early 1990s, Cowsill disbanded that group and joined forces with a Winnipeg-born rockabilly singer named Jeff Hatcher. It turned out that Hatcher, like Cowsill, was interested in reviving the classic rock sounds of the 1950s and 1960s, not trying to be trendy with hip-hop, rap, grunge, or Europop. They formed a group called the Blue Shadows and wowed audiences with their accurately rendered recreations of Roy Orbison's quasi-operatic falsetto, the gospel-inflected sound of early Presley ("I only do skinny Elvis," said Cowsill), and the high harmonies of the Everly Brothers and the Beatles. Their aim was to pay homage, not reinvent the form. "You have to get the arrangements right," Cowsill said. "These guys are like Mozart. You get them right or you don't do them." For the first time in years, Cowsill was making music he truly enjoyed. "How happy am I?" he said to a reporter. "I'm happy as a junkyard dog in hillbilly heaven, and you can quote me on that." He described the band as "three vegetarians and a junkie."

He performed what he called his "dead guys' set" with great respect and reverence. "Honour, don't imitate," Cowsill told younger musicians. It wasn't about impersonating; it was about saluting. "When Billy sang that music, Roy Orbison was in the room," said a fellow musician. "Elvis was in the room. It wasn't covering, it was channelling."

As well as paying tribute to the rock 'n' roll legends of the past, Cowsill and Hatcher composed and recorded an album of country-rock songs, *On the Floor of Heaven*, that brought them a recording contract with Sony Music in Canada, and the hope of a similar deal in Nashville. While critically acclaimed, the album did not lead to bigger things. A second album also failed to connect with the Nashville music establishment. The music proved too rock-oriented for country radio and too country for rock radio. The Blue Shadows broke up in 1995, and Cowsill hit the bottle and the pills again.

Friends in Calgary rescued him from substance abuse when he reached rock bottom. By that time Cowsill was filling his body with prescription drugs because of a bad back and other health problems. He underwent back surgery in Calgary, suffered a collapsed lung, gave up the booze again, came out of rehab, and resumed performing, with a group known as the Co-Dependents. "He may not be the Cowsill of old, but he can still sing better with one lung than most can with two," observed *Calgary Herald* columnist Bob Remington. Then aged fifty-six, Cowsill told a radio interviewer his aim was to "keep on rockin'" for as long as he was able. "You stop rockin', you die," he said. "That's the moral of my story." When he was on stage, Cowsill said, "I have the ability to give and receive love. Off-stage, life is more difficult." He recorded two CDs with the Co-Dependents and released a live recording that was captured on cassette tape when he played at Calgary's Palliser Hotel, opening for k.d. lang in 1985.

His health continued to decline. Osteoporosis fractured his bones; he underwent two more back surgeries, and also had hip-replacement surgery. Then he fell and broke his shoulder. Broke, no longer able to play, and depressed by the drowning death of his brother, Barry, in New Orleans during Hurricane Katrina, Billy Cowsill died in Calgary in February 2006 at age fifty-eight. His long-time friend and sometime manager, Neil MacGonigill, told reporters Cowsill had suffered from emphysema and Cushing's syndrome—a hormone disorder—as well as osteoporosis.

The *Calgary Herald*'s *Swerve* magazine devoted the better part of an entire issue to the story of the troubled troubadour who had made Calgary his home for the last decade of his life. "If Cowsill channelled Orbison, and the Everlys, and skinny Elvis, the world lost a true musical clairvoyant," wrote columnist Remington. Cowsill's son, Travis, thanked the father he knew mainly at a distance for giving this "sometimes very dark world something so pure and filled with light: your voice, your craftsmanship, and your contribution to the betterment of humankind through your music." Freelance writer Mary-Lynn Wardle characterized him as a "true original, the real deal, the gunfighter, the Voice."

Three years after Cowsill's death, the old inner-city Calgary rooming house where he had lived was declared a municipal historic resource. Its heritage designation came primarily because the ninety-eight-year-old building was considered a good example of colonial-style design in the early twentieth century. However, a city heritage planner was quick to add, "The fact that he lived there definitely adds to the heritage value of the site." The grizzled country-rock legend was still in the room.

Sources

I am grateful to the following authors for writing the books and articles that supported my storytelling in *Rogues and Rebels*.

Anthony Amaral for *Will James: The Last Cowboy Legend*. Reno: University of Nevada Press, 1980.

Gladys Arnold for *One Woman's War: A Canadian Reporter with the Free French*. Toronto: James Lorimer & Company, 1987.

William Gardner Bell for *Will James: The Life and Works of a Lone Cowboy*. Flagstaff, AZ: Northland Press, 1987.

Diana Birchall for *Onoto Watanna: The Story of Winnifred Eaton*. Chicago: University of Illinois Press, 2001.

Jim Bramblett for *Ride for the High Points: The Real Story of Will James*. Missoula, MT: Mountain Press, 1999.

Tony Cashman for *The Best Edmonton Stories*. Edmonton: Hurtig, 1976; and *The Edmonton Story: The Life and Times of Edmonton, Alberta*. Edmonton: Institute of Applied Art, 1956.

David Cesarani for *Major Farran's Hat: Murder, Scandal and Britain's War Against Jewish Terrorism, 1945–48*. London: William Heinemann, 2009.

John Robert Colombo for *Mysterious Canada*. Toronto: Doubleday Canada, 1988; 1998.

Frank Dabbs for *Ralph Klein: A Maverick Life*. Vancouver: Greystone Books, 1995.

Hugh Dempsey for *Jerry Potts: Plainsman*. Calgary: Glenbow Museum, 1989.

L. James Dempsey for *Warriors of the King: Prairie Indians in World War I*. Regina: Canadians Plains Research Center, 1999.

Winnifred Eaton for *Me: A Book of Remembrance*. New York: The
Century Company, 1915, and Jackson, MS: University Press of
Mississippi, 1997.

Marsha Erb for *Stu Hart, Lord of the Ring: An Inside Look at
Wrestling's First Family*. Toronto: ECW Press, 2002.

C. D. Evans for *Milt Harradence: The Western Flair*. Calgary: Durance
Vile Publications, 2001.

Roy Farran for *Winged Dagger: Adventures on Special Service*. London:
Collins, 1948.

Don Gillmor, Achille Michaud and Pierre Turgeon for *Canada: A
People's History, Volume Two*. Toronto: McClelland & Stewart,
2001.

Ruth Gorman and Frits Pannekoek for *Behind the Man: John Laurie,
Ruth Gorman and the Indian Vote in Canada*. Calgary: University
of Calgary Press, 2007.

Charlotte Gray for *Nellie McClung*. Toronto: Penguin Canada, 2008.

James H. Gray for *Talk to My Lawyer: Great Stories of Southern
Alberta's Bar and Bench*. Edmonton: Hurtig, 1987; *Red Lights on
the Prairies*. Toronto: Macmillan of Canada, 1971; and *The Boy
from Winnipeg*. Toronto: Macmillan of Canada, 1977.

Paul Grescoe and David Cruise for *The Money Rustlers: Self-made
Millionaires of the New West*. Markham, ON: Viking, 1985.

Bret Hart for *Hitman: My Real Life in the Cartoon World of Wrestling*.
Toronto: Random House, 2007.

Diana Hart and Kirstie McLellan for *Under the Mat: Inside Wrestling's
Greatest Family*. Bolton, ON: Fenn Publishing, 2001.

Harold Adams Innis for *Peter Pond: Fur Trader and Adventurer*.
Toronto: Irwin and Gordon, 1930.

Georgina Keddell for *The Newspapering Murrays*. Toronto:
McClelland and Stewart, 1967.

Vincent Lam for *Extraordinary Canadians: Tommy Douglas*. Toronto:
Penguin Canada, 2011.

Daniel S. Levy for *Two-Gun Cohen: A Biography*. New York: St.
Martin's Press, 1997.

Charles Lillard, Ron MacIsaac, and Don Clark for *The Devil of
DeCourcy Island: The Brother XII*. Victoria: Porcepic Books, 1989.

James G. MacGregor for *Edmonton: A History*. Edmonton: Hurtig,
1975.

Alexander Mackenzie for *The Journals and Letters of Sir Alexander
Mackenzie*. Edited by W. Kaye Lamb. Toronto: Macmillan, 1970.

Margaret MacPherson for *Nellie McClung: Voice for the Voiceless.*
Montreal: xyz Publishing, 2003.

Dave Margoshes for *Tommy Douglas: Building the New Society.*
Montreal: xyz Publishing, 1999.

Mike Mountain Horse for *My People, the Bloods.* Calgary: Glenbow-
Alberta Institute, Blood Tribal Council, 1979.

Marjorie Norris for *A Leaven of Ladies: A History of the Calgary Local
Council of Women.* Calgary: Detselig Enterprises, 1995.

John Oliphant for *Brother xii: The Strange Odyssey of a 20th-Century
Prophet and his Quest for a New World.* Halifax: Twelfth House
Press, 2006.

Howard Palmer and Tamara Palmer for *Alberta: A New History.*
Edmonton: Hurtig Publishers, 1990.

Frits Pannekoek for "Ruth Gorman: A Strong-Minded Woman." In
Remembering Chinook Country. Calgary: Detselig Enterprises,
2005.

Kay Sanderson for *One Hundred Years of Alberta Women.* Calgary:
Alberta Historical Resources Foundation, 1982.

Stan Sauerwein for *Ma Murray: The Story of Canada's Crusty Queen of
Publishing.* Canmore, AB: Altitude Publishing, 2003.

Hal Sisson for *Sorry 'bout That: A Tribute to Burlesque.* Coral Springs,
FL: Llumina Press, 2005.

Donald B. Smith for "John Laurie: A Good Samaritan."In *Citymakers:
Calgarians After the Frontier.* Calgary: Historical Society of
Alberta, Chinook Country Chapter, 1987.

Wendy Smith for *Pay Yourself First: Donald Cormie and the Collapse
of the Principal Group of Companies.* Toronto: Bruce Press, 1993.

Rodger D. Touchie for *Bear Child: The Life and Times of Jerry Potts.*
Surrey, BC: Heritage House Publishing, 2005.

Aritha van Herk for *Mavericks: An Incorrigible History of Alberta.*
Toronto: Penguin Viking, 2001; and *Audacious and Adamant: The
Story of Maverick Alberta.* Toronto: Key Porter Books, 2007.

Bill Waiser for *Canadians: Tommy Douglas.* Markham, ON: Fitzhenry
& Whiteside, 2006.

Jack Webster for *Webster: An Autobiography.* Vancouver: Douglas &
McIntyre, 1990.

Index